# Theory and the Disappe

Paul de Man is often associated with an era of 'high theory', an era which, it is argued, may now be coming to a close. This book, written by three leading contemporary scholars, includes both a transcript and facsimile print of a previously unpublished text by de Man of his handwritten notes for a lecture on Walter Benjamin. Challenging and relevant, this volume presents de Man's work as a critical resource for dealing with the most important questions of the twenty-first century and argues for the place of theory within it.

The humanities are flooded with crises of globalism, capitalism and terrorism, contemporary narratives of financial collapse, viral annihilation, species extinction, environmental disaster and terrorist destruction. Cohen, Colebrook and Miller draw out the implications of these crises and their narratives and, reflecting on this work by de Man, explore the limits of political thinking, of historical retrieval and the ethics of archives and cultural memory.

**Tom Cohen** is Professor of Literary, Cultural and Media Studies, University at Albany, SUNY, USA.

**Claire Colebrook** was Professor of Modern Literary Theory at the University of Edinburgh from 2000–2008 and is now a professor of English at Penn State University, USA.

**J. Hillis Miller** is Distinguished Research Professor of English and Comparative Literature at University of California, Irvine, USA. He holds honorary degrees as Doctor of Letters from the University of Florida, Doctor of Humane Letters at Bucknell University, and Doctor Honoris Causa at the University of Zaragoza. He is also Honorary Professor of Peking University and past president of the Modern Language Association.

# Theory and the Disappearing Future

On de Man, On Benjamin

**Tom Cohen, Claire Colebrook and J. Hillis Miller**

**With a manuscript by Paul de Man**

Routledge
Taylor & Francis Group

LONDON AND NEW YORK

First published 2012
by Routledge
2 Park Square, Milton Park, Abingdon, Oxon OX14 4RN

Simultaneously published in the USA and Canada
by Routledge
711 Third Avenue, New York, NY 10017

*Routledge is an imprint of the Taylor & Francis Group, an informa business*

*British Library Cataloguing in Publication Data*
A catalogue record for this book is available from the British Library

*Library of Congress Cataloging in Publication Data*
Cohen, Tom, 1953–
    Theory and the disappearing future : on de Man on Benjamin / Tom Cohen,
Claire Colebrook and J. Hillis Miller.
        p. cm.
    Includes bibliographical references and index.
    1. de Man, Paul–Criticism and interpretation. 2. Criticism. I. Colebrook,
Claire. II. Miller, J. Hillis (Joseph Hillis), 1928- III. Title.
    PN75.D45C64 2011
    801'.95092–dc23
                    2011019279

ISBN: 978-0-415-60452-9 (hbk)
ISBN: 978-0-415-60453-6 (pbk)
ISBN: 978-0-203-80672-2 (ebk)

Typeset in Bembo
by Taylor & Francis Books

Printed and bound in Great Britain by
TJ International Ltd, Padstow, Cornwall

# Contents

# Acknowledgements

We would like to thank Martin McQuillan and Erin Obodiac for hosting the symposium on de Man that inspired this volume. We are also grateful to Patsy de Man for extending her support to this project.

# Part I
# De Man on Benjamin

# Introduction

*Claire Colebrook*

Anecdotes aren't very de Manian, but I will begin with one anyway. (De Man focused on texts as objects torn from anything like 'life', praxis, humanity, ecology or unity. Texts, like 'life' and unlike anecdotes, tend to destroy relations and connectedness, tend to annihilate what have come to be known as 'aha' moments. That said, de Man's textual objects were never sacred and self-enclosed works but possessed a destructive power that could – *if read* – allow for a radical disturbance of the present).

My anecdote is this: I began writing on de Man while living in Manhattan. I was surrounded by educated, well-read, thoughtful, highly literate but not necessarily academic types. When I mentioned that I was writing on de Man they all *either* knew about de Man almost solely via the 'de Man affair' or had de Man introduced to them there and then (by me) through an account of the de Man affair. It seemed that if I were to explain who de Man was then the first significant detail would be his notoriety. I would like that not to be case. I would like a world in which other aspects of de Man's existence were more significant, but that world does not exist, both because of the scandal that came to mark de Man's work but more because of de Man's unreadability, which made any canonization of his work outside scandal and journalism *almost* impossible. To use the term unreadable here is not to signal a particular difficulty or obscurantism of de Man's work. On the contrary, de Man often said the most important things quite directly, including his statement – explored by Miller in this volume – that one should not take the impossibility of reading too lightly. That is a clear enough statement, and yet de Man was often read as though he took the impossibility of reading very lightly indeed – so much so that he supposedly said anything at all about the texts he was reading. De Man also, in his talk on Benjamin (transcribed in this volume), was very clear that one could neither return all texts to some original intention, nor read a text without some orientation to what the text *really says*. Yet despite the clarity of some of his most important claims he was both deemed to be unreadable (in the sense of being willfully misleading) or, worse, he was simply not read. What he was saying about reading would have required the sort of thinking and intellectual labour that many seemed simply unwilling to undertake. As a result de Man emerged from the 1980s as a 'black box': many critics held very strong opinions of the effect of de Man's work, and where one ought to go in order to overcome the damage he had caused, even if what de Man actually wrote was not examined with the sort of rigor de Man expended on the texts he analysed, nor with the sort of scholarly standards that many accused de Man of destroying.

The aim of this volume is to create what Gilles Deleuze and Felix Guattari (1994, 76) referred to as a conceptual persona, which is quite different from, though not unrelated to, biography. (A biography includes all possible concrete facts that one might list about an individual, but a conceptual persona is that same biography as narrated in the understanding of a concept: how could we understand 'the unconscious' without a certain story about Freud?).

At present de Man is a figure in a conceptual landscape. If we want to know what deconstruction *as a concept* is then we also encounter the persona of Jacques Derrida (and to a lesser extent, de Man). Derrida has a biography, including his birth-date, his Algerian origin, and so on. But his *persona* is crucial for the concept: just as we think of Descartes as the philosopher who came and doubted, and need to do so if we want to understand the concept of the *cogito,* so we need to have some notion of Derrida the French philosopher who harangued literature departments in order to understand 'deconstruction.' Part of the concept of 'deconstruction' today includes the figure or persona of de Man on the horizon: deconstruction can now be deemed to be ethically responsible and properly philosophical because of a certain story. Deconstruction once threatened to be playful, literary and irresponsible but avoided this fate by creating a relation between an ethical Derrida and scandalous de Man (O'Rourke 1997).

If a thinker creates concepts then he or she does so also by co-creating a dramatic figure; in de Man's case this persona – as so many of the denunciations and apologies suggest – is tied to a melee regarding responsibility. De Man's created concepts – of irony, allegory, materiality, history and modernity – were all written in such a way as to shift the terrain or plane upon which discussion took place. Concepts not only require assumed personae, they also occur in complex connections and establish a plane of problems: we cannot think about irony without thinking about texts, reading, meaning and (after de Man) temporality. De Man used these concepts in ways that rendered the traditional terrain of literary criticism – or the *interpretation of texts for the sake of meaning* – null and void. Irony would not signal an original intent that has been concealed or deferred, but a capacity of a text to be detached from any grounding sense. De Man used concepts that were once tied to projects of meaning and interpretation (concepts such as 'history') to signal a certain machine-like or inert and dead quality of textual objects. In doing so he created a new 'plane' of responsibility where a text could be interrogated *not* in order to disclose its original animating intent, but to examine its force or the ways in which it operated outside anything like our usual understanding of human communication. So there would be two ways (at least) of approaching de Man: one would be to restore his quite alienating and inhuman work *back* into what we usually understand as responsible human history. Responsibility would refer to who owns or who can answer to a text's force, and history would refer to the narratives through which we make sense of, and contain, a text's operations. Another mode – one which is pursued in this volume – is to take de Man's dislocation of literary concepts seriously, and this in two senses.

First, what de Man took to be the *literary* was – quite literally – a text's tendency to exist as something like a dead mark or trace, something that had left the author's hand but would nevertheless survive and require reading, even if every reading would always have to project some imaginary sense that would never be the text itself. Second, this would then require something like literary history, but only if history could be understood *not* as the narrative that restores texts to contexts and authors with social biographies but as something like a non-chronological (or non-linear, non-clock) time – something that would always be outside the order and sense 'we' make of the world. It would be counter de Manian, then, to read words like 'text', 'irony,' 'rhetoric' or 'aesthetic' as though they referred to human practices of making meaning of the world. Yet the persona we have of de Man today, including the scandalous de Man of the 'de Man affair' goes something like this: de Man was a literary critic, and he therefore saw all events and history in terms of stories or texts, and therefore lacked all moral judgement and all sense of history.

The future, though, calls for another de Man, not only a different persona but a different approach to personae. At present – and this is an increasing tendency – concepts are domesticated by personal narratives. This is evidenced both at a 'high' theoretical level, where concepts such as deconstruction are accompanied by celebrity narratives. (There is more than one feature-length movie of Jacques Derrida, including one where he quotes Martin Heidegger saying that one should narrate a philosopher's biography by saying that he 'lived, wrote philosophy and died.'[1] And there are also several pocket guides to famous philosophers.) And it is also a prevalent tendency in popular culture where broader inhuman threats and promises, such as terror and hope, are accompanied by personalities (Bin Laden or Obama). Another, inhuman, plane is possible whereby a text's author is not akin to a celebrity narrative but something closer to an alien or monster, someone we cannot read, or whose time and desires are necessarily always blocked from us (despite projections). De Man read literary history *as literary history*: literary, because it consisted of nothing more than marks or traces (what he referred to as materiality), and history, because it had a temporality *and future*. The future would be historical, not because it would play out human expectation, nor because we might have an ethics of the future where we would save the earth for our children or our own memories. On the contrary, for de Man history was inhuman. *Literary* or *rhetorical* reading would, if you like, treat the past not as our own (as though within our narrative) but as though it arrived from a time without us. In this sense it is perhaps the monstrous de Man, the de Man who lacked all morality, responsibility and humanity, who needs to be read today. This would not be so we could look wisely upon the error of his ways and be more mindful of our humanity and ethics, but because he would confront us as a force from outside. De Man could not be, then, someone whom we could consign to the dust-bin of high theory because he was too literary (and unethical) *nor* someone who we might save, forgive or ameliorate because we too might have acted badly had we been in his position. Rather, we might read de Man as though his text arrived for us without persona, as though it came from an inhuman future.

Gilles Deleuze (2004, 167) argued that all philosophy and criticism had been accompanied by an 'image of thought'; this is distinct from the specific persona (a doubting Descartes, a meditative Heidegger, a revolutionary Marx), but is more general: thinking presupposes someone who wants to know, understand, be understood, and be oriented to truth and wisdom. What, Deleuze asks, if we could imagine thought without an image? What if thinking could occur as though, let us imagine, humans did not exist, as though this world of ours with our future were not a self-evident value? This may seem insanely abstract but nothing could be more pertinent for the present. 'We' are, after all, living in a present that is at once intensely self-destructive (terrorism, climate change, resource depletion, economic pillage) and intensely self-loving (for our over-whelming question appears to be how 'we' might survive or adapt, as though 'we' need not question who 'we' are and our worth). This may then be the time to create this persona of de Man as anti-persona: the man who came and practiced literary criticism in highly literary terms, and yet who destroyed what 'we' felt literature (and especially literary ethics) to be.

So let us return to de Man as the figure or persona he is today, and back to the mode of the anecdote even if that is precisely the mode that a reading of de Man might annihilate. I began university study (not in an English department) in 1984 and I (like so many others) therefore heard of de Man first by way of journalism and commentary. If you google de Man today, 'de Man affair' is promptly suggested. What one learns in a nutshell is this: de Man can be accounted for *either* by saying that he was a value-destroying, apolitical, de-historicising literary critic who was discovered to have written anti-Semitic journalism in Belgium during the war (thus proving that nihilistic textual criticism has very disturbing origins, affiliations and causes). *Or* one can reverse the explanatory sequence: it's not that being a literary aesthete follows from being amoral and anti-Semitic, but if you have a certain formalist bent then you are more inclined to end up advocating disastrous causes such as Nazism. In the first case literary theory is a sign of moral penury; in the second it is a cause.

That is the de Man affair and problem in a nutshell, but like so many things it exceeds its nutshell. These concerns seem to be extrinsic to a close reading of de Man – and they are if they are composed as questions of biography – but there is also a way in which they strike at the heart of problems that de Man refigured. How is it that something like speaking historical life is captured in language? When we read a text how do we attribute sense, meaning, life or intentionality to what we are actually given? In the lecture on Benjamin, and particularly in the manuscript that is included in this volume, one can see the ways in which de Man posed this question through a series of oppositions – between poetic naming and translation, between experience or perception and critical philosophy, or between literature and theory. The second term would always seem to be secondary and dependent, but would also operate as a certain style or mode of questioning – a belated and distanced mode that would open up questions regarding the very possibility of language's relation to what is not, or what is prior to, language. That is: from the present in which we are given a text that arrives *without sense or life* we can either imagine some original poetic or sacred act of which this text would be a fragment – so that reading would be restoration – *or,* we might confront the annihilating and discomforting possibility that reading is a form of translation (not the retrieval of a life from which the text has been severed but the generation of more text, but this time in 'our' own terms).

For de Man there are two ways of approaching these questions: one is poetic or sacred, in which we imagine that there is some possible act of authentic naming, some mode of language that would be a proper grasp of a lived present. If this were so then we could see de Man's wartime journalism as the truth or origin of de Man, as though all his later obfuscatory literary criticism talking about rhetoric, irony, disfiguration, tropes and unreadability were really just a way of covering over a rather nasty intentionality or hatred, an original and originating immoral contempt for others. Further, and continuing in this mode, we could regard de Man's anti-Semitism and wartime journalism as a fallen mode of inauthentic, journalistic or parasitic language. He ought to have considered history, others, context and the real life of suffering. If we pursue this path we make a commitment to stepping outside texts, relations and the non-linearity of time and posit, possibly pragmatically or politically, some guiding foundation. The problem with such a decision – some commitment to a *proper* language grounded in something other than itself – is not simply its critical naïveté, but its infantilizing narcissism. There is a received idea of de Man today (insofar as anyone still receives de Man) as being literary, playful or textual. But this type of opposition whereby *either* we are really in history *or* we are trapped within language is just what de Man sought to deconstruct. We are never simply within language; there is always the 'relapse' or imagination of some sacred dimension that we would see as the ground or genesis of text, and this would be so especially if we reduced all the world to 'text' or language in a simple sense. For de Man text, language, history or rhetoric are not entities or single systems so much as a condition: a condition of splitting. We exist within text, always belated and always negotiating registers of signs and differences; however, we never live that system as dispersed or differential without positing or *reading* some origin or ground of which the system would be an expression. The second way of pursuing questions then is not that of substituting system or text for life and nature, it is not imagining that 'we' are effects of language and must therefore always be literary or aesthetic. Such a position would be what de Man refers to as a 'relapse', an imagination of some ground or origin that would account for the emergence of the texts that we are given.

The second path is that of self-annihilation or willed extinction, acknowledging that readings or positings of sense are always relapses that conceive some whole of which fragments would be signs or expressions. De Man's mode of deconstruction is radically futural in that it aims to imagine a text without us, or a text that would not be redeemed in some future where meaning would be revealed. Surprisingly, perhaps, this places his mode of questioning closer to that of Deleuze and Guattari than to the philosopher with whom he is usually coupled, Jacques Derrida. For Derrida all texts or concepts have a futural dimension: concepts like justice and democracy, for example, are at once given in this world of the present in a determined manner – justice as defined by the US supreme court, justice as defined by John Rawls and so on – but there is also a potentiality or intentionality to the concept of justice that opens it beyond any given context (Derrida 1992, 15). What, we might ask, is justice *in general,* or the promise of justice? This would allow us to appeal to a promised sense of justice not already revealed or determined by any actual instance. This is what Derrida refers to as a messianic dimension that is without messianism, as though all experience harbours a promise, even if we cannot posit a messiah who would fulfill such a promise. For de Man, by contrast, history and futurity are inhuman – not promised by our concepts and therefore not at all messianic. He quite explicitly regards *literary* textuality as a positive deletion of messianism, for a literary register considers the text itself *not* as a promise of another dimension. (So in de Man we have *positive negation* in the manner of Nietzsche, a joyful refusal of anything other than radical contingency and a force without promise. What we certainly do *not* have is a *negative theology,* an idea that many Derrideans have claimed as crucial for deconstruction: in the absence of any given spirit or presence we can only imagine an absolute secrecy or withdrawal intimated by language's or meaning's incapacity never to rest within itself [Hart 1989].)

Just as de Man's specifically literary or rhetorical analysis radicalizes the usual impact of these words – because 'literary' becomes an attention to the detachment of the letter, while 'rhetoric' grants a force to textual or tracing systems *per se* that is irreducible to intention – so de Man's focus on the aesthetic needs to be understood in a highly singular manner. The aesthetic is not 'art' in its usual sense (of valued and consecrated art objects). For de Man the confrontation of the aesthetic register requires that a certain temporality be deconstructed. Any imagination of the future will tend to return to the figures we already have, and in this sense would be bound up with the ideology of the aesthetic – would be always translated back into present forms. But reading the text historically or in terms of the future would be to read *as if* it were detached from all humanity, as if – to use Deleuze and Guattar's terms – it was without a people, as though its population were still missing (Deleuze and Guattari 1994, 176). The series of oppositions de Man sets up in his lecture on Benjamin is not a series of choices, and is not ideological in the usual sense (where ideology refers to political intentions or interests). Rather the oppositions are *aesthetic*: the opposition between poetry and translation is between a text as it is in itself (as *poeisis* or detached object) and text as sign of something other than itself, even if this otherness can never be given (so that translation is unavoidable but impossible). The oppositions are unavoidable at the same time as they are unthinkable.

It is not the case then that de Man posits the situation of the translator as simply better than that of the genuine or sacred relation of the poet. Whereas there would be the possibility of a genuine relation between language and the world revealed (poetry), de Man (referring to Benjamin) explores the implications of the supposedly secondary mode of translation. Poets would name authentically, in a manner that is sacred, whereas translators and critics *merely* work from language to language, without any sense of the original. Benjamin had elsewhere (in his widely quoted 'Critique of Violence') been highly critical of what he seemed to regard as the fallen nature of modern democratic language (Benjamin 1996). Contemporary parliamentary democracies have lost all relation to the original, founding and constitutive violence that allowed the social order to emerge. Politicians now simply allow language to circulate in an almost bureaucratic manner, without any sense that they are *saying* anything, without any sense of the force of language, of what language might do. This idea – of an original and founding violence that opens or inaugurates the political and that is distinct from an administering violence that merely manages life as it is already formed – now has a widespread currency through the work of the Italian philosopher Giorgio Agamben.

Drawing on Benjamin's work, Agamben seeks to retrieve *the* opening of *the* political, which for Agamben (following Benjamin) occurs not with this or that act of speech but with the very opening of speech in general, or the event *that man speaks* (Agamben 2000). This understanding of 'the political' has, in turn, been seen as significant for the present because it allows for the theorization of a 'state of exception' (Agamben 2005) and the modern mode of 'biopolitics.' Our political world of an already determined system whereby the state has the power to manage life has, according to Agamben (who wants to retrieve something like Benjamin's sacred-poetic-original relation to language), forgotten and erased the sense that our political system of law must have emerged as a system via some event whereby life was determined as subject to regulation and management. Certain moments of the twenty-first century – such as Guantánamo and the war on terror – expose once again that we are not born into law. Law occurs both with a split between lawful and non-lawful life (for terrorists can be tried as those who threaten the law and therefore cannot be accorded the same rights) and with an originating violence; for the everyday 'policing' violence of a polity can only proceed legally if there has been a violence subjecting the polity to law in general. Agamben suggests that we, following Benjamin, think again about this genesis of law-language-system *in its original violence*. This will allow us once again to expose ourselves to the inauguration of the political and the status of man as one who has the power of speech but whose powers may not be actualized in conditions of terror or – in modern bio-politics – when man becomes merely managed life.

De Man's re-reading of Benjamin and his deconstruction of the opposition between sacred-poetic and translating modes of language relates directly to current theorizations of the political, and this is for two reasons. First, within 'theory' the reaction against something like de Man and a widely noted 'linguistic idealism' appeals to a materiality or life that would bring us back to politics. (In addition to Agamben there is a more widely noted *return* to life, materiality or affect against linguistic idealism, with Manuel de Landa's reading of Deleuze being the most trenchant [de Landa 2005, 4; 155], although this occurs alongside attempts to 'correct' theory by restoring it to affective life [Hansen 2003].) Second, and more generally, it is possible to see a broader turn to life and immediacy beyond academic discourses in ecological politics: 'we' are, supposedly, *not* privileged linguistic or cultural beings whose world is at our disposal for representation and manipulation, for humans are aspects of one inter-connected, dynamically self-producing and self-organizing life. The earth is one vast organism (Lovelock 2000). De Man's work was tirelessly critical of organicist aesthetics. The positing of a single self-productive whole of which texts would be fragments, could only occur through narcissistic projection: the imagination of life as 'our' living unity or wholeness. Further, the supposed possibility of retrieving an original event of political naming would not be an overcoming of contemporary managerial or state-sanctioned violence but itself a blind or violent retreat from our condition of textual fragmentation. At the same time, however, what de Man described as an oscillation between blindness and insight is constitutive: we can only criticize (or see as blindly faith-based) a positing or original life – such as Lovelock's positing of Gaia or Agamben's projection of 'the' political – if we see those positings as secondary or belated, and that will lead us to posit (blindly) our own position of reading as faithful and proper. The only way in which a mythical origin or natural foundation can be criticized *as mythical* is by showing the ways in which it is secondary or fabricated; but that demonstration of the illusory origin *as illusory* will also have its blind or originary presuppositions, its moments of aesthetic ideology where it falls back into some already-given figure.

It might seem that a cautionary critical position, such as de Man's, that stresses the illusory and reactive nature of any positing of life would need to give way to an urgent attention to the living systems of the earth, systems that are currently under extinction threats that go beyond species extinction to the possibility of an annihilation of life in general. How could de Man possibly be relevant today when we have not only abandoned old textual models to take up new modes of digital media and visual culture, but also when we face cataclysmic spectres of such a disastrous magnitude that 'theory' and attention to rhetorical registers might appear as irresponsible indulgence? Again, we are back to the de Man affair: the problem of responsibility and realism that was seemingly effaced by de Man the textually enclosed nihilist. But what if *not* leaping into the political, or the real, or life were – however discomforting – more responsive, if not responsible, to the present? What if thoughts of responsibility, of what we owe to the earth, of our deep connectedness, of our inescapably ecological existence or our participation in one unified network of immaterial labour were a reaction formation, a repression of the fragmented, dispersed, disarticulated and punctuated problem of existence? Consider, again, what the vogue for Agamben and questions of sovereignty might indicate: Agamben explicitly suggests that we return to the problem of the sovereign, to the problem of how *the* law establishes itself as relevant to an organized body. In doing so he is not content to remain within language or systems but wants to ask about the inauguration of systems. In this respect his work not only resonates with a general tendency in all academic disciplines to return to questions of life, nature, embodiment and the emergence of systems; it also accompanies a popular trend of stepping back from fragmentation to some type of inaugurating opening of the proper polity – ranging from 'Tea Party' returns to the founding moment of the constitution to ecological appeals to the organism of this great earth of ours. De Man's criticism of theocracy, most clear in his work on Rousseau (de Man 1976), becomes highly pertinent today when it comes to posing problems of the future. Should we be retrieving theocratic models of how *the* law relates to *the* body politic, *or* should we confront the possibility that there is no sovereign – no single, localizable body of authority that we might be able to liberate from a non-linear history of textual traces and fragments – and, more importantly, that there is no earth: there is no nature as such, no great organism that might offer 'us' a foundation or future?

When de Man reads Benjamin he therefore seems to be operating with a simple distinction between looking backwards or forwards in time: should we see translations as secondary texts that might be grounded by an animating original? Or, are we always within translations never able to get back to some first poetic act of naming? De Man notes that there have always been two readings of Benjamin, both as a naïve and messianic writer in search of a pure speech *and* as a modern practitioner of hermeneutics aware of the textual and historical nature of scripture. Rather than argue for either one of these modes of reading de Man regards both as unavoidable: one can neither answer nor vanquish questions regarding the speech of poetry or its emergence from a living voice, and yet any reading or sense of that voice will always displace that voice into some other register.

So, as de Man notes, there is one way in which Benjamin appears to be a rather naïve writer, believing that one might take systems of language and return or refer them to some sacred moment of origination. And this would run against the grain of what 'we' have come to accept. For 'we' – and de Man refers to the contemporary voices of his own time, such as his colleague Geoffrey Hartman but (more importantly) Hans Georg Gadamer – 'we' now know that we always work within language and that we must be reflective (Gadamer 1975). There is no primary knowledge or origin, only that origin as mediated by systems such as language. On such an account Benjamin's reference to some original or sacred naming would appear to be regressive. We should pause here to look at the problem de Man is outlining in his reading of

Benjamin, for it allows us to approach what became the de Man affair. It is widely accepted – at a level that is journalistic and never fully thought through – that de Man is the scandalous figure that he is *because he was so caught up in the primacy of texts and language that he lacked all moral judgement.*

> … de Man, with his emphasis on the 'autonomy' of language, is unable to see the relation between such autonomy and (social) determination as anything but purely oppositional. The reason is that de Man understands such determination only in the most simplistic way, as a monocausal relation between 'signs' and 'things' which is essentially self-evident without the mediation of theories, cultures or paradigms. The conception of reference which underlies de Man's theory of the productivity of language is narrowly empiricist.
>
> (Mohanty 1997, 34–35)

> De Man, as always, concludes that 'performative and cognitive rhetoric don't converge. Irony is the systematic undoing of understanding.' The systematic undoing of understanding becomes the aim of literary studies, their destruction not merely their deconstruction.
>
> Admitting the acumen of some of these readings, one cannot help reflecting that a terrible impoverishment of literary study is being propagated. It is limited to a rhetorical analysis that does nothing else than to reveal over and over again that there is an irreconcilable contradiction in every text that leaves one in doubt, undecided, with a matter left forever 'undecidable,' their favourite catchword. Literary studies would become a speciality, a new antiaesthetic ivory tower that would deprive literature of its human and social meaning as a representation of reality, as stimulation, admonition, and simply enjoyment.
>
> (Wellek 1990, 83)

> Who is Paul de Man and why does he matter? He is the central figure in a movement that argues that there is nothing outside a literary text and that literary texts are simply linguistic tropes which have no meaning beyond themselves.
>
> … As we use a narrative approach to the de Man story, we shall see the folly of ignoring historical contexts and the power of language to affect action. If the de Man narrative makes us more aware that writing cannot be divorced from its historical contexts, it will be helpful in refocusing literary study away from overemphasis upon complex tropes – what de Man calls rhetoric – which ignores author, theme and context. In other words, the combination of putative compensation, atonement and disguise in de Man's deconstructive phase paradoxically underlines how texts do refer to prior reality. The de Man narrative creates a necessary and probable plot which enacts both the hubris and arrogance of cultism and how language always has moral implications …
>
> (Schwartz 1990, 180, 181)

Rhetorical readings contain *in ovo* all other defective forms of their own defective selves, and de Man frankly acknowledges that they are 'totalizing (and potentially totalitarian)'(19). They totalize, however, only the refusal of totalization that is theory: they are 'universals' only in the sense that they are 'consistently defective models' of 'language's impossibility to be a model language' (19). Thus there is no position external to theory, no position that can be held 'in the name of ethical and aesthetic values,' from which theory might be challenged, and no position within theory that can serve as a model for anything other than theory's own self-sustaining resistance to itself.

(Morrison 1990, 59)

What is at issue is just the sort of problem de Man's own work addressed, in a number of different ways. Are texts signs or symptoms of anything? Or is our tendency to posit a natural order behind the difference of signs itself symptomatic? When we read texts and take them to have emerged from (or lead us back to) a single intent and origin, how do we pass from the sign to the history or humanity of which it is supposedly an expression? Today these questions might seem at once anachronistically and absurdly indulgent *and* utterly timely. It is possible to say that any questioning of the reference, truth or reality behind texts is today highly irresponsible when what is called for is action and belief, not cynicism. Alternatively, now might be the time – finally – to abandon our smug self-confidence that there are reliable ethical foundations, and that such foundations could be retrieved through processes of reading that disclose or uncover a proper sense. For can we be so certain today that good thinking and good reading will lead us to ethical norms? Has there not been a surfeit of such faith, and might not a dose of nihilism alert 'us' to all the ways in which our morality has been destructive or, at least, violent with regard to this good earth that we have treated as our ethical environ?

What needs to be noted is that the cartoon figure of Paul de Man – the theorist who came and doubted reality and was then shown to have been a collaborator (and therefore not surprisingly a perpetrator of nihilism) – is precisely the sort of figure that de Man destroys in his essay on Benjamin. De Man begins by noting that 'we' are supposedly now wise enough to know that there is no life in itself, no pure experience, and no truth as such that would not be mediated by language, history and cultural horizons. De Man cites Gadamer's work on modernity to this end. Gadamer claims that modernity is a condition of recognizing the distance and reflection required for any experience of truth and the world; we are always within some cultural, linguistic and historical horizon, and can reflect upon relations among horizons but never anything like truth or life in itself. It is precisely *against* this assurance that we are always already located within cultural-historical-linguistic horizons – and therefore that we can only reflect and interpret – that de Man raises the importance of reading Walter Benjamin for what he *really did say*. So, de Man is neither a simple textualist who accepts that one can simply abandon the thought of what lies beyond human conceptuality, nor a willful advocate of creative misreading that would allow us to have Benjamin's text say what we want it to say. On the contrary, the inability to read Benjamin indicates a force or violence that Benjamin's text touches upon but that remains – symptomatically – unreadable. Why, de Man asks, has Benjamin been read both as a naïve thinker of the sacred advocating a pure language and as a theorist of the necessarily written, textual or scripted nature of the word? What does such a divide indicate or conceal?

Given that this lecture was one of de Man's last words on the topic it is worth noting that the opposition he sets up is precisely of the kind that would be important for the archiving of de Man's own corpus. It was de Man who would be remembered for having pushed theory into an overly linguistic and reality-denying form of aestheticism. After de Man there would be a return to ethics and history. As Martha Nussbaum archived this 'ethical turn': 'It is striking that in the last few years literary theorists allied with deconstruction have taken a marked turn toward the ethical. No doubt a part of this change can be traced to the scandal over the political career of Paul de Man, which has made theorists anxious to demonstrate that Deconstruction does not imply a neglect of political and social situations' (Nussbaum 1992, 29). And yet, in his work on Benjamin de Man begins by arguing that the idea that one might simply accept the secondary and mediating condition of language could not be adopted or preferred without question. De Man opens the question of reading Benjamin with reference to some of the key concepts that today – after de Man – have been targeted as just the sort of issues that deconstruction supposedly avoided. For de Man, reading Benjamin, the problems of life, history, nature and humanity – all those problems that were deemed to have been ignored by 'high theory' and that require a new vitalism or materialism – are encountered in any reading of Benjamin (and possibly any understanding of what it is to *read*).[2]

Received readings of Benjamin, de Man notes, are divided between two contradictory tendencies. On the one hand Benjamin's 'The Task of the Translator' would evidence a pre-modern, sacred or 'purist' naïveté that believed in an attainable and present origin; on the other hand, the same text would also offer a mature and enlightened recognition that we only know the world as given through language, culture and history. We are always lost in translation, even if translation as such seems to require some original sense behind the various codes of one language or another: ' "The Task of the Translator", appears at first as both regressive (and has been attacked for this) and *messianic* in a way that may well appear to be a relapse into the naïveté denounced by Gadamer.' De Man notes that the question of translation opens up broader questions regarding the status of language, which he approaches first through Gadamer (who is an advocate of the inevitability of always being in a position of interpretation) and then through de Man's then colleague Geoffrey Hartman (2007, 78) for whom Benjamin offers something like a form of hope that might break through history. De Man quotes Hartman, 'The foundation of hope becomes remembrance, which confirms the function, even the duty of historian *and* critic. To recall the past is a political act.' (It is de Man who adds the emphasis on historian *and* critic, precisely because for de Man these duties would go in conflicting directions – towards critical fragmentation as opposed to historical narration.) For de Man Benjamin opens the question of historical closure (for we are always within texts) *and* historical redemption, for we can always re-read and open those texts. For Gadamer, Benjamin would be regressive in his inability to locate experience within cultures, while for Hartman he would offer a hope for exceeding closed histories. For Gadamer, there is an intelligent belatedness or secondariness to modernity – a recognition that we can only *read* experience as mediated through some symbolic frame, never as it is in itself. And so Gadamer's position – a position that would place Benjamin as seemingly naïve – is exactly the point of view that would be attributed to de Man. That is, it was de Man who was most often cited as denying any truth or reality beyond texts, and yet that position of simple textualism (or a form of linguistic idealism) is just what de Man would ceaselessly question.

Benjamin's theory of translation seems, says de Man, to provide a clear opposition: on the one hand an idea of poetry, pure experience, descriptive discourse or imitation and on the other translation, criticism, philosophy or theory. It seems at first as though Benjamin may be read in two ways, *both* as regressive – in his appeal to poetry and sacred language – *and* as literary or theoretical when he acknowledges that sacred texts are texts and have to take on the form of language. De Man then asks two questions: given the reading of Benjamin both as regressive and as textually self-aware, what did he *really* say? Further, why has what Benjamin really said not been heard? Why has he been split, carefully, between a naïve Benjamin of a pure poetry and messianic revelation on the one hand, and a critical theorist sensitive to the impossibility of translation?

De Man's 'answer' to these questions seems at once to support and destroy the figure of de Man that has been archived in the history of literary theory. De Man explicitly 'concludes' by not concluding; but this is because there is something essentially unreadable in Benjamin that we continually approach only (inevitably) to relapse. De Man begins by noting the impossibility of translation. This is odd given that the opposition that opens the lecture is that between poetry as some pure and immediate naming, and translation as some transition from language to language that bypasses all those things that we refer to as history, nature, life or reality. Surely translation – from language to language – is possible while pure or poetic speech could only be an ideal, never achievable. But the reason why translation is impossible is also because it is all we have. If the poet believes that language may refer directly to some pure experience, if the poet believes in a messianic fulfillment or moment when life will be revealed as it is, the translator works *after poetry* with the fragments of poetic texts. All poetic texts are fragments insofar as they are never *life itself* but only life as given through these moments of supposedly immediate expression. This complicates the opening opposition between the position of inevitable translation – where all we have are texts – and pure poetry, where we might refer texts back to some original pre-linguistic sense. The translator, when confronting a text that she must transfer to another language must consider what the text to be translated is aiming to say, to what it refers. When she does this she is not brought close to singular names but to differential complexes. De Man's example is the deceptively simple noun, 'bread.' In French, 'pain' can be tied up with a series of phrases, and this series is quite different from the associations of the German *Brot. Brot* would be aligned with phrases such as '*Brot und Wein';* but if you translate '*Brot und Wein*' into French as 'pain et vin' you get – de Man notes – an association with what you get in cheap restaurants. The same applies to the English word bread, which we can tie to phrases such as 'daily bread,' 'knowing what side your bread is buttered on,' 'being short on bread' or – for Americans at least – a series of food franchises such as *Le Pain Quotidien* or *Au Bon Pain.* The translator can only move from one language to another – knowing to use 'pain' for 'Brot' – if she knows that both terms refer to bread (so translation requires seeing language as a sign *of* something), but when she does go to the other language she brings in a web of associations that do not reside in the original language, *but which neither she nor the original author can control.* This forces translation to confront that any single name in a language, such as the noun 'bread' (or 'pain' or 'Brot'), is never just the noun itself but a fragment of a system that the translated word must leave behind. So the translator, unlike the poet, does not just work with language and its relation to 'the' world, but confronts language as something that in any poem, phrase or text can only offer itself as a fragment of sense. The translated word leaves behind the differential web of the original, and brings in another differential web; and this is because of what de Man refers to as 'materiality.' What *this* word means in de Man is itself untranslatable, and brings us back to the problem of reading (or not reading) de Man.

Materialism, today, is deemed to be something quite other than deconstruction, especially de Man's deconstruction. The return to materialism, after a too-linguistically oriented theory, is now accepted as a standard preamble to various claims for life, history or affect (de Landa 2006, 45–46; Hekman 2010, 4; Barad 2007, 42). And yet it is the materiality of language – not some socially or culturally constructed system of signification – that de Man focuses upon. Various modes of 'linguistic idealism' concentrate upon the ways in which language maps, organizes or constructs the lived world, and can therefore be rightly attacked as humanist or Cartesian (because the world is always the world *for* man – and this would apply to Gadamer and hermeneutics as much as to the Richard Rorty who claims de Man as a textualist) (Rorty 1982, 139). But, as the essays that comprise this volume demonstrate, de Man's materiality or what he referred to as language was neither empirical – that is, available to experience – nor ideal (a consequence of the human organism's way of mapping its world.) Materiality, both in the Benjamin lecture and throughout de Man's corpus, is a necessarily *resisted* non-phenomenon. We approach materiality when we come up against the fragmentation or dispersal of language: when we translate a text (or read a text) and accept that any meaning or sense is *not* the text itself. Translation cannot exhaust the text that will always be different from, and resistant to, any of our assimilations of it. Materiality is inhuman, but the inhuman for de Man is different from, and opposed to, what has come to be known as the post-human. Although the word post-human, like humanism, has an unmanageable range it has tended to refer recently to the overcoming of man's self-enclosure within the bounds of his own supreme and world-constituting rationality in favour of the thought of an ecology of all bodies that interface with living systems, animality, technology and what is left of nature and history (if we take away the ways in which these terms have been co-defined in relation to 'man.') (Hayles 1999, 287). This 'posthuman' liberation from cognitive or linguistic models – the liberation, more generally from the human notions of 'mind' as some thinking machine – precludes a consideration of what de Man referred to as rhetoric and figure. It seems then that his work was, right up to and including the lecture on Benjamin, linguistic, aestheticist and literary. Herein lies the scandal of what has come to be known as the de Man affair. For it wasn't de Man's collaboration and early published suggestions of anti-Semitism that were at stake; it was the apparent link one could make between moral failure and intellectual postures. Briefly, it was seen as inevitable or causal that anyone who insisted – as de Man would always do – that affect, life or nature could never be grasped in themselves would also negate problems of suffering and responsibility to others. Derrida's deconstruction, by contrast, would take an ethical and political turn by insisting that it is because we are always already within differential systems that there will be some messianic promise of that which lies beyond the determinations of any limited (compromised) conception of justice, democracy or the other (Rosenfeld 2006).

Both Derrida and de Man would both rule out – and deem to be violent – the reference to a messiah or any form of messianism, any idea that there might be an actual appearance or fleshed out conception of what lies outside the relations within which thinking takes place. De Man however insisted that the messianic – promise, futurity, life and affect – occurred through rhetorical, linguistic or aesthetic relapses: 'this differential structure engenders an affectivity and a valorization, but since the difference is one of epistemological divergence between a statement and its meaning, the affect can never be a reliable criterion of political value judgment' (de Man 1976, 672). That is, it is because of linguistic systems, which include human language but also encompass figures or images of unified bodies (such as the imagination of nature or humanity), that it is possible to posit something like a proper foundation of which language would be an effect. But there is no foundation in general, no life or nature in general, *no history in general if history is taken to be a narrative time within which humanity is located and upon which humans (or the humanities) can reflect*. History is radically inhuman, lived and known in a narrative mode even if it is a temporal or futural force that will always be experienced (aesthetically) as naturally coherent. There is nothing outside that force or violence of history, nothing that might allow us to redeem or renew the present on the basis of some proper notion of life to which we might appeal. Violence lies on both sides of this predicament, and this is why Benjamin becomes the figure to whom de Man will address questions of nature and history.

The de Man affair lies not, then, in de Man's complicity with certain notions and rhetorical strategies that were associated with some of the worst atrocities of human history; the scandal and horrific truth of de Man's work is what it said and what it revealed. Every event of speech and writing is at one and the same time blind and insightful; it must both rely on already given and received figures – for how can one *say* anything without a language in common? – at the same time as every new speech act in a system deviates, distorts and alters the system. Positively, one can say, then, that speaking at the time of the war and in a context of general violence and complicity, there was no such thing as an innocent or pure speech act. As Shoshana Felman (1989) so astutely noted, *that* was the horror of the Holocaust, its contamination and destruction of what we might have felt to be some reliable bedrock of humanity. Anyone today who *simply* denounces de Man fails to respect the degree to which the terrors of Nazism – of an unthinking, violent rhetorical automatism – swept up so much 'humanity' in its aesthetics. (As Derrida [1992] noted in his own work on Benjamin: Benjamin's disdain for the idle chatter of modern parliaments, for the unthinking markets of language that operate without genuine creative thinking would also resonate with a broader trend of anti-democratic and anti-Semitic rhetoric. The same would apply today to anyone who denounced the ungrounded or merely 'aesthetic' nature of theory, and who would seek to return theory to the political, history, life or bodies. The desire to return to foundations and to destroy the fallen corruption of language in favour of a full speech would always be a striving for purity. Any desired and violent break with the supposedly ungrounded and empty language of the present would at once criticize and mirror certain strategies of Nazism.)

To conclude: the de Man affair was never the *de Man* affair. The discovery of de Man's wartime journalism allowed many journalists, critics and commentators to include the entire movement of deconstruction in the discovered a-moralism. (So the causal relation was established: you don't have to be anti-Semitic to be a deconstructionist; deconstruction is just a general nihilism that allows for something like de Man's complicity, which should be read as a symptom of cultural malaise, or a 'sign of the times' [Lehman 1991].) The affair allowed for a certain definition of deconstruction – a deconstruction that supposedly denied reality, reduced everything to text, displayed a wanton disregard for history, ethics and suffering and evidenced a complete abandonment of truth and meaning. The de Man affair enabled a purification of deconstruction. Supposedly, it was the de Man affair that exposed a weakness of abandoning all foundations and messianic potentials; after de Man there would be deconstructive critique – for no foundation could be simple or determinate – but there would also be affirmation: one would not remain at the level of text alone, but would take the risk of *promising* some messianic outside. De Man's work therefore offers us today, should we wish to read it, the audacity of a future without promise.

One arrives at Paul de Man always too late. As de Man claims in his work on Benjamin and translation: it is not the original, in its canonized sanctity, that allows for or demands translation; it is the translation that creates an original *as canonical, as generative, as a productive original.* De Man is received today, if at all, as both too late – for he is often marked as holding theory back, keeping it too literary or too textual – and as already surpassed and displaced. It was de Man, even before the de Man affair, who domesticated and contained literary practice denying its potential radicalism and political activism. When we approach de Man there is already a temporal sequence, a narrative and a moralism. Temporally, de Man was an offshoot of Derridean deconstruction but a son who was far too literary and textual to realize the full fruits of theoretical radicalism. This standard temporality is a time of genealogy, where de Man's father is (or should be) Derrida, and where de Man's offspring is the dead end of 'high theory' that would be supplanted by a proper living theory of political engagement. The de Man narrative is almost Byronic in its agonistic figures and counter-redemptive fortunes. De Man appeared as a literary critic, concerned with the formal rigors of the text and with a scrupulous attention to reading that would make any quick transition to history and context impossible. When de Man was found to have been (some say) a fully-fledged anti-Semitic Nazi sympathizer or (as others claimed) an imprudent and possibly unwitting subject of a complex scene of restricted expression, then this allowed us to recognize something about deconstruction that was there all along if only we had not been seduced by the pleasures of the text. With its attention to reading and instability deconstruction was symptomatic of a failure to engage with decisive political events. At its worst deconstruction was complicit with the denial of the claims of history and suffering; at best it was partial, requiring a later deconstruction that would attend to justice as undeconstructible, to literature as essentially democratic, to an unassailable messianic dimension to all life and, ultimately, to a hypertrophy of political responsibility that would preclude all good conscience.

De Man would never be a simple character or figure within the history and narrative of literary theory: the figure of de Man would be required to allow theory to become a narrative. De Man (1976) makes this clear when he reads Rousseau and distinguishes between constative-narrative dimensions and performative-theoretical modes. In the mode of narrative and statement one can always give a ground and origin to a series or system: a good humanity precedes the law; a profound and fruitful origin precedes the offspring of translation; and a sequence of events in natural time precedes the archiving of history. In order for narrative, series, teleology or natural growing life to appear, take form or exist, one must have established points of reference and stability. There can only be a narrative *of,* translation *of,* growth *of,* or valuation *of,* some relatively stable point, and it is that process of producing stability and fixing referents that de Man refers to as 'grammar.' Before there can be a sequence and order there must be some establishing of terms. Grammar, then, is not the system we use in order to express what we want to say, for there must always have been a grammar – a distribution of relations, and the distinction between a 'before' and 'after' – from which something like intentionality and selfhood might emerge.

In the narrative that is the de Man affair the terms are clear. There was a Belgian literary critic, writing during the German occupation who failed to resist, or passively embraced, anti-Semitism. When that same critic arrived in the United States, a scene in which literature was already shielded from political and historical questions by being treated as a text unto itself, it is not surprising that he turned to deconstruction. Deconstruction was already a theory flirting irresponsibly with play and undecidability – and rendered post-structuralism even more scandalously nihilistic (if such a thing is possible). De Man enabled theory to become a form of high textualism, and he did this by insisting that history, far from being something akin to a natural process, was actually an inhuman and archival mechanism that should provide the lead for the ways in which we think of nature. (Nature, after all, was for de Man not a process of natural growth and progression leading to some final form and realization; nature was a surreptitious effect *of deconstruction.* Any attempt to expose a sec-ondary or derived text *as secondary* would necessarily produce nature as some presupposed but unattainable 'before.') This narrative, of de Man as the immoralist who came and destroyed theory's politics, as de Man's own theory suggests, is only possible after some 'grammar' or distribution that can never justify itself. So, here is a double scandal. De Man is a figure in the narrative of theory, the point we can mark as a zone of irresponsibility, the point at which an attention to text, rhetoric and the performative power of language pre-cluded an attention to history, politics and responsibility. De Man is also a symptom of so much more than himself – of an academy that was seduced by ideas from the continent that had been badly translated and divorced from their philosophical and rigorous home. That is scandal number one. It was overcome only by another narrative: one in which the originator of deconstruction – Jacques Derrida – took part in an ethical turn, allowing deconstruction to be justice itself: 'deconstruction is justice.' Literature would not be 'play' or a dis-solution of all moralisms, but democracy or a scene in which 'anything can be said'. And life would, in its distinction from any actualized lived form, be intrinsically messianic, always open to the not-yet or 'to-come.' But if the first scandal is de Man's existence in the history of literary theory, a scandal that will then enable a great deal of soul-searching, the second scandal is the way this narrative might be read from a de Manian point of view.

A moral story, an attribution of guilt, and a promise to redeem the future is, de Man insists, an act of justice that is essentially unjust, just as the striving for the promise of a messianic future is a lure and figural effect that cannot be sustained. Are we really saying, then, that the first naïve stage of accounting for de Man is to see him as guilty within a moral historical narrative, while the point of view of theory, rhetoric and deconstructive reading is to see that moral tale as an effect of a textual performance that cannot be read, grounded or justified? What would it mean to say such a thing? Part of the problem lies in the very nature or non-nature of meaning. One of the easier ways to consign de Man to the past is to read him, and to find him as a writer that offers us a meaning or message. On a certain account de Man argues that we only know nature or history through texts, we cannot get outside these texts. Any grounding beyond textuality – history, morality, suffering, politics – would be either illusory or ungraspable. The meaning of de Man's text is that he would refuse meaning; he would insist that all we have are texts without ground. Once we have established that that is what de Man says we can take several comforting steps. We can bring back justice, history, politics, democracy and the spirit of the future. There would be many ways in which one might do this, but perhaps the most interesting would be by looking to the very decon-struction that lived on after de Man (having mended its ways after the de Man scandal). For this deconstruction, justice is not – as de Man would have it – *unjust* for justice is the one undeconstructible. Here is the opposition. For de Man justice must be unjust because justice (as universal) must occur at the level of grammar, as something like a pure text or system freed from any particularity.

So what could such a bleak theory offer us today, precisely when distinctions between law and lawlessness appear to be urgently required? It might seem as though a pragmatic approach would be called for. At the level of theory we might acknowledge that justice and law cannot be given any ultimate grounding; at the *practical* level we must do all we can to maintain, and work within, the legal and justice systems we have. A Derridean approach that accepted the concept of justice as a promise of a future 'to come' might be better today than de Man's constant destruction of such concepts, even as he notes their inevitable return and relapse. In the essays that follow we pose the question of de Man *today,* in this context of crisis, urgency, destruction and (seemingly) required pragmatics. We suggest that it is because of the very nature of twenty-first century horizons – of ecological, cultural and financial catastrophe – that de Man's very inhuman and *unpromising* theory might have something to offer. Perhaps models of justice, rights, democracy and the hor-izon of promise have blinded us to the encroaching but inassimilable horrors of timelines and logics that are outside calculation and intention.

The three chapters that follow pursue, in different ways, the singular nature of resistance to (and within) de Man's work. In all cases we argue that what remains of de Man in 'theory' today, including the various versions of his work on Rousseau and Benjamin, cannot simply be redeemed, recuperated or included within the canon of theory or literary criticism. De Man's work remains as a resistant cipher to an emergent set of twenty-first century horizons in which the predicates of history and justice that mobilized twentieth-century energies have stalled. If de Man exists as a peripheral or problematic figure this is neither a simple accident nor something that can be remedied by arguing for the relevance of his work. De Man not only theorized but also performed a *resistance to theory*. If aesthetic ideology marks the machine-like tendency for reading to be captivated by figures, to remain happily content with the percep-tion of a posited presence, then theory is a distancing, disturbing or alienating manoeuvre that begins by disfiguring all the figures that seem at first to offer coherence. In this volume the examination of the de Man archive at once accepts that de Man is a historical figure whose work has, to some extent, been read, absorbed, criticized and extended; but we also argue that de Man's work evidences a problem of the archive that exposes the sort of forces that twenty-first century horizons have brought to the fore. A work or text (and also any sense, experience, meaning or identity) only survives or can be said to be if it possesses some material form, some quite specific inscriptive *body*. In the texts de Man examines the meaning of both Rousseau's and Benjamin's work survives in the form of a text, but both Rousseau and Benjamin were also concerned with the production of such surviving bodies of sense. Rousseau asked how something like a body politic could come into being, what forces or traces led to its stabilization, and then how members of that body politic (individual wills) experienced their own being through the figure of the sovereign.

In a similar manner, de Man reads what Benjamin has written about texts, focusing – as in Rousseau – on the material markers Benjamin employs (such as the German words *Aufgabe* or *Übersetzung*). The working of de Man's own material text is itself a negotiation of the archive of the English language: de Man uses terms from linguistics (such as constative and performative), from rhetoric (such as allegory and irony), from philosophy (critique, phenomenality, *Aufhebung*) and from political theory (State, sovereign, contract, general will); but he does so with an attention to their archival materiality. These terms are given to us and organize the moves we can make, what we can say, and the sense of the world to which they refer. J. Hillis Miller's attention to de Man's manuscript shows that the *impossibility* that de Man identified in these terms – that ultimately one could never grasp *justice itself* – is something we also have to confront in de Man's own archive. Yes, we have authoritative versions, and yes we have the manuscripts that can be traced back to the active working or practice of de Man's own hand. But when we look at the archive what we see is not the origin of a pure intent, but a splitting: de Man's crossing out or alternation of central terms, precisely when de Man is himself 'reading' the governing or founding terms of another text. For Miller this impossibility of the archive – the brute fact that the meaning or sense of our history of texts can always be drawn back to this disturbing non-identity in the text at hand – is not an accident or feature of purely academic culture, nor a problem of texts in the narrow sense. The fact that humanities academia is grounded on a type of archival authority, with 'research' being valued if it can draw closer to original sources, testifies to a broader investment in authority.

For Miller this is why de Man, among other things, is also a reader of Marx, and of the 'theotropism' of ideology: theotropism is the necessary deviation of the textual mark from its referent, which means that all marks are tropes (never the thing itself) and all referents ultimately have the status of some sort of theological (that is, mystical) ground. If, as a reading of de Man would make clear, the origin that grants research its force and precedence is actually always and necessarily suffering from *mal d'archive* (or essential disturbance) then this pertains to authority in general. Foundations, originating acts or referents are at once required by any trope or figure, and there could only be language or the positing of something that *is* if the differences of signs have some preceding ground; and yet any turn back to that ground must remain undecidable: it can neither abandon faith in that pre-differential precedence nor grasp some moment before the splitting of difference. The force of rhetorical reading and mis-reading therefore goes well beyond literature in the narrow sense, or – following Miller – one can note that literature needs to be taken in more than a narrow sense. There is a difference between the rhetorical deflections in literary texts – the ways in which novels such as *Pride and Prejudice* stage dissimulation – and the lures of political deceit; but the difference is undecidable. That is, it requires decision. Just as rhetorical literary readings need to labour to distinguish registers, analyzing whether the text is marking out a reference *or* placing referential language at one remove, so our reading of political figures needs to gauge what Gilles Deleuze referred to as the 'powers of the false.' How does the real appear *as real*? How do oil companies present corporate procedures and complexities as natural and self evident wholes? If theotropism is present explicitly in Jane Austen's staging of the ways in which characters are required to *read* social relations (rather than assume them as some natural organic whole), theotropism is also present in *any* event of politics. And this is because the *polity* – what is presented as 'ours' or, as Miller analyses, as 'human energy' – occurs through rhetorical substitution.

Tom Cohen's chapter on Toxic Assets also looks at the impossibility or unreadability of de Man: reading de Man would be destructive, resulting in an abandonment of what Miller identifies as the theotropic. More specifically, though, what had been played out in the brief family story of deconstruction – the relation between an ethical Derrida and discomforting de Man – is symptomatic of a more general cultural blind. Derrida, ostensibly defending or celebrating de Man, refers to him curiously through the trope of nuclear waste. In contrast with the comforting biodegradable – that which could emerge from and return to the earth – nuclear waste remains. Again, here we are at the *mal d'archive*: a material remainder that cannot be digested, humanized, recognized or assimilated. De Man's text was not, Cohen argues, accidentally or even *intentionally* sidelined to make way for a more ethical Derrida. With Derrida's attention to hospitality, democracy, justice and the messianic or ethical future, the radically inhuman materiality confronted by de Man simply could not even be recognized as something that would be refused and set aside. Rather, like nuclear waste, de Man would intimate a force that would go beyond human and narrative timelines, beyond ethics (if this could be read in terms of *ethos,* habitability and the proper names and homage that increasingly marked Derrida's work, and that of his followers). What Derrida seemed only fleetingly to address – the climate change of a waste or destruction that would exceed any of 'our' moral concepts or figures – could only (by Derrida) be imagined in the form of de Man as nuclear waste. Yet it was de Man – the supposedly literary, apolitical and de-historicizing de Man – whose strategies signaled a nature that was *not nature*. This nature is absent from any talk, today, of climate change, for the latter can only imagine an anthropomorphic world or environment, and not a horizon of waste and destruction that well exceeds the images and narratives 'we' have of climate change in its meteorological (or mapped, predicted and measured) sense. Any talk, then, of saving America or humanity by an appeal to what has come to be known as 'the humanities' would be one more lure or relapse, for it is precisely this figure of a moral and redemptive humanity that has precluded facing the abyss of what Cohen identifies as de Man's ruthless unnatural nature.

The final chapter to this volume – ostensibly on what has come to be known as the financial 'crisis' – bearing Miller's and Cohen's work in mind, refuses the very figure of *crisis*. Capitalism and economic 'management' appear to have run off the rails, but narrating the present as an accident or mishap would be (to follow Miller) the worst of theotropisms, or (in Cohen's terms) typical of a certain theoretical or critical stupidity. For there is no capitalism: no intrusion of inhuman exchange into an otherwise human and ethically proper world. Or, there is *only* capitalism: only substitution, dissimulation and theft. There is no such thing as *proper* property. 'A' property is a rhetorical event, a marking of something as belonging (properly) to a subject. But such events require a grammar, and such grammars have histories, and these histories are multiple, and can only be figured in the remarkably unhistorical forms of narration. To aim to *return* the crises of the twenty-first century to some more human or proper foundation is a rhetorical gesture, and one that is widely enacted today – from Glen Beck and the Tea Party's mourning of the real America, to the 'turn' of theory to ethics, life, the body, emotion or affect. What the de Man of this volume offers is neither a theory of rhetoric nor the reduction of theoretical reflection to mere rhetoric; beyond that impossible divide, what remains, is both inhuman and futural. Inhuman: it is precisely now, when we are amidst (but not witnessing) climate change, political chaos and economic disorder that we can not seek to restore the supposed 'man' or 'humanity' who would lie at the origin of what has come to be known as civilization. Futural: de Man offers a notion of history that takes into account our imbrication in, and blindness to, multiple systems that we tend to narrate and organize; but the future lies beyond narrative and the organism. In this respect the future lies beyond lived chronologies but can nevertheless be encountered as a resisting force in any attempt to read what has not yet been assimilated.

## Notes on the task of the translator

*Paul de Man: Transcription by Claire Colebrook*

Benjamin (Dupré)

H.G. Gadamer: die Grundlagen des XX Jahrhundert

Naivität des Zeitgeist concept of the

In the critique of the subject concept, which is being attempted in our century, something else than a mere repetition of what had been accomplished by german idealism — and, we must admit, with, in our case, incomparably less power of abstraction and without the conceptual strength that characterized the earlier movement? This is not the case ...

Naivität des Sehens        critique of pure perception and of
                           pure Derivation discourse

           the subject does not dominate his utterances, yet they
           are accessible to hermeneutic understanding
           ( hermeneutic circle - (Heidegger)

Naivität der Reflexion
                           separation between reflexion
           critique of Hegel's absolute
           historicity of understanding which is not accessible
           to individual self-reflexion

Naivität des Begriffs
           interrelationship between concept and language
           (as shown in f.  Wittgenstein (Nietzsche)
                conceptual and ordinary language are not
                simply separable

Benjamin (Dupré)

H.G. Gadamer die Grundlagen der xx Jahrhundert

[Naivitat des Setzens]

Is the critique of the concept of the subject which is being attempted in our century, [different from the] something else than a mere repetition of what had been accomplished by German idealism – and, we must admit, with, in our case, incomparably less power of abstraction and without the conceptual [effectiveness power] strength that characterized the earlier movement? This is not the case ...

[*De Man appears to be translating Gadamer and differing from the translation that will appear in English, given that he has to search around for the right word.*—C.C.]

Naivität des Setzens

Critique of *pure* perception and of *pure* descriptive discourse

The subject does not dominate his utterances, yet they are accessible to hermeneutic understanding

(hermeneutic circle – Heidegger)

Naivität der Reflexion

[separation between reflection

critique of Hegel's absolute]

historicity of understanding which is *not* accessible to individual self-reflection

Naivität des Begriffs

interrelationship between *concept* and language

(as rhetoric etc.) Wittgenstein (Nietzsche)

conceptual and ordinary language are not simply separable

Kantian in its critical outlook
Hegelian in its historical claim

This scheme of modernity is Hegelian and (as modernity) critical
overcoming of a non-awareness by Hegelian which then
allows for the establishment of a novel discourse, which
claims to overcome or to renew a problematic

piece ends with positive reference to Hegel:

the concept of Spirit, that Hegel took out borrowed from the christian
spiritual tradition, is still the ground of the critique of the
subjective and of subjective Spirit that appears as the main
work of the post-Hegelian (i.e. modern) period. This
concept of Spirit, which transcends the subjectivity of the ego,
finds its true abode in the phenomenon of language, which
becomes stands more and more as the center of
contemporary philosophy.

Compared to this critical, dialectical, and non-essentialist
concept of modernity and of language, B.'s text on language,
The Task of the Translator, appears as first as both regressive (and has been
attacked for this) and messianic in a way that may well
appear to be a relapse into the non-critical demanded by Gadamer,
but in a much earlier stage even than that of Kraus, Hegel and
German idealism

indeed, the messianic tone, the figure of the poet as
sacred, as echoing sacred language, is much in evidence in this
text. Poets cited are Mallarmé, George & Hölderlin

   impact of George circle (Pannwitz)
   impact of Hölderlin, as seen by George

this scheme of mourning is
kantian in its critical outlook
Hegelian in its historical claim
*hegelian* [and] (as modernity)

overcoming of a non-awareness by critical negation, which then allows for the establishment of a *novel* discourse, which claims to *overcome* or, to renew a problematic

piece ends with positive reference to Hegel:

the concept of Spirit, that Hegel [took out] borrowed from the Christian spiritual tradition, is still the ground of the critique of the subject and of the subjective spirit that appears as the main task of the post-hegelian (i.e. modern) period. This concept of Spirit, which transcends the subjectivity of the ego, finds its true abode in the phenomenon of language, which [becomes] stands more and more as the center of our contemporary philosophy.

Compared to this critical, dialectical, [and] non-essentialist concepts of modernity and language, B's text on language, The Task of the Translator, appears at first as both regressive (and has been attacked for this) and *messianic* in a way that may well appear to be a relapse into the naiveté denounced by Gadamer, but in a much earlier stage even than that of Kant, Hegel and German idealism

indeed, the messianic tone, the figure of the poet as *sacred*, as echoing sacred language, is much in evidence in this text. Poets cited are Mallarmé, George + Hölderlin

impact of George circle (Pannwitz)

impact of Hölderlin, as seen by George

critique of (his) dogmatic assumption of non-reader by
Rezeptions ästhetik (Jauss, ca., Pirk, Riffaterre) which
claims modernity

or, on the other hand, support of Benjamin as re one who
has returned the dimension of the sacred to literary language
or at least considerably refined
and thus overcome the historicity of literature on which the
notion of modernity depends    Habermas: redemption critism
                         Hartman: p. 78

What does B. actually say in this essay?

very difficult to establish ; even the translators
                    didn't know or couldn't see what
                    he said, so much does it go against
                    received ideas ; which is nevertheless turns to
                    write
        translating rather than reading
Why is translation the exemplary figure? rather than just
                         or reader or pair p. 2
he was himself a translator
translation fails        Aufgabe   (to give up)

why is this failure, with regard to an original text,
exemplary?

the translator differs ; is ambiva ; the past and artist
in a radical way

        Grund Uber missraumlentein:  § 8   John p. 75
                           unlike art
                   unähnlich der Kunst
                Grund Uber p. 267 bus de page

p. 69 Zohn

critique of his dogmatic assertion of non-reader by Rezeptionsästhetik (Jauss, etc., Fish, Riffaterre) which claims modernity

or, on the other hand, support of Benjamin as the one who has returned the dimension of the sacred to literary language and thus overcome or at least considerably refined the *historicity* of literature on which the notion of modernity depends. Habermas: interpretive criticism

Hartman p. 78

*What does B. actually say in this essay?*

Very difficult to establish; even the translators didn't know or couldn't see what he said, so much does it go against received ideas, which it nevertheless tends to evoke

*translating* rather than *reading*

Why is translation the exemplary figure? rather than poet or reader or pair p-2

he was himself a translator

translation fails     *Aufgabe*          (to give up)

why is this *failure*, with regard to an *original* poet, exemplary?

The translation differs, is unlike, the poet and artist in a radical way

Gandillac mistranslates β 8 Zohn p. 75

unlike art

unähnlich der Kunst

Gandillac p. 267 bot [?] the page

Only the messiah himself ~~includes all historical events~~ puts an end to history, ~~and~~ in the sense that he ~~it~~ frees ~~history~~, completes and ~~accomplishes~~ fulfills the relationship of history to the messianic. Therefore, nothing that is truly historical can relate, ~~to the end~~ by its own volition, to the messianic. Therefore the kingdom of god is not the telos of the dynamics of history; it cannot be posited as its ~~target~~ aim (~~Ziel~~ end). Seen historically, it is not its aim but its end, its termination. Therefore, the order of the profane cannot be constructed in terms of the idea of the sacred, therefore the theocracy does not have a political but only a religious meaning. (To have denied the political significance of the theocracy with with all desirable intensity is the great merit of Bloch's "Spirit of Utopia" "Geist der Utopie")

p. 280

Only the messiah himself [concludes all historical events] puts an end to history [and] in the sense that [it] he forces [history] completes and [accomplishes] fulfills the relationship of history to the messianic. Therefore, nothing that is truly historical can want to relax [to the me? Word illegible] by its own volition, to the messianic. Therefore the kingdom of God is not the telos of the dynamics of history; it cannot be posited as its [target purpose] aim (Ziel end) Seen historically, it is not its aim but its end, its termination. Therefore, the order of the profane cannot be constructed in terms of the idea of the sacred, therefore the theocracy does not have a political but only a religious meaning. (To have denied the political significance of the theocracy [with] with all desirable intensity is the great merit of Bloch's 'Spirit of Utopia' 'Geist der Utopie')

[*De Man is quoting and translating Benjamin's 'Theological and Political Fragment' here—C.C.*]

This chiasmus of hope and catastrophe is what saves hope from being unmasked as only catastrophe: as an illusion or unsatisfied movement of desire that wrecks everything. The foundation of hope becomes remembrance, which confirms the function, even the duty of historian and critic. To recall the past is a political act: a "recherche" that involves us with images of peculiar power, images that may constrain us to identify with them, that claim the "weak Messianic power in us. (Thesis 2). These images split off from their fixed location in history, undo concepts of homogeneous time, flash up into a reconstruct the present ...

(p.78 -- Or in the broadness)

This chiasmus of hope and catastrophe is what saves hope from being unmasked as only catastrophe: as an illusion or unsatisfied movement of desire that wrecks everything. The foundation of hope becomes remembrance, which confirms the function, even the duty of historian *and* critic. To recall the past is a political act: a 'recherche' that involves us with images of peculiar power, images that may constrain us to identify with them, that claim the '*weak* messianic power in us. (Thesis 2). These images split off from their fixed locator in history, undo concepts of homogeneous time, flash up into or reconstitute the present ... [*De Man is quoting Hartman, 1980 here.*—C.C.]

   p. 78 Criticism in the Wilderness

good ~~translators~~ translators are not good poets and vice versa

when poets are also translators (Hölderlin - George)
they are more than poets
         not    Dichter ⊃ er Dichter
         but    Übersetzer der Dichter

~~what are translators take~~
    §9         p.76 Zohn ( correct )

      translation is relation from language to
      language, not to an extra-linguistic
      meaning which could be copied, imitated, paraphrased
not imitation, hence              not ~~paraphrase~~
          Abbildstheorie ( p. 60 )
what is translation like?

      it is like philosophy, specifically epistemology as
        critical philosophy ( i.e. Kant ) which undoes the
               idea of art as imitation
   §6    Zohn p.73
   German: p.60    top of page           ( p.76 Zohn )

       + theory        F.       p.63
      it is like criticism, in the sense of F. Schlegel (German)
      "ironic" gesture of undoing the stability of the
       original by giving it a definitive, canonical, form in ~~translation~~
       this was the task of Jena romanticism   the theorization

the same in
translation; what
survives is sense
of the original

      it is like history, and this is the most difficult to
          understand , like history to be existent but
       history is not to be understood ~~by a~~ by analogy with a natural

good [translations] translators are not good poets and vice versa

when poets are also translators (Hölderlin – George)

They are more than poets

not Dichter der Dichter

but *Über*setzer der Dichter

[what are translators like]

β 9 p.76 Zohn (is correct)

translation is relation from language to language, not to an extra-linguistic meaning that could be *copied*, imitated, *paraphrased*

*not* paraphrase

not imitation, heine

*Abbildstheorie* (p. 60)

*What is translation like?*

It is like philosophy, specifically epistemology as critical philosophy (i.e. Kant) which undoes the idea of art as imitation

β 6 Zohn p. 73

German p. 60 top of page

It is like *criticism* + theory, in the sense of Fr. Schlegel)(p/76. Zohn) (p. 63 German)

'ironic' gesture of undoing the stability of the original by giving it a definitive canonical form in [translation] the theorization

This was the task of Jena Romanticism

the same in translation, which canonizes in revision of the original

It is like *history*, and this is the most difficult to understand, like history to the extent that history is not to be understood by analogy with a *natural*

process (of ripening, organic growth, dialectic)
but as something else (nature to be understood
from the perspective of history)

this is the burden of the reading

all these activities are derived from original activities
(perception, poetry, action) and all these activities are
singularly inconclusive, aborted — yet the mode of
derivation is not that of resemblance or imitation

they are not metaphors
    yet übersetzen means metapherein
                  translates
    metaphor is not metaphor

these activities resemble each other in the fact that they
do not resemble

they are, however, inter-linguistic: they relate to what,
in the original, belongs to language and not to meaning
as the extra-linguistic correlate susceptible of paraphrase
and imitation

they disarticulate the original, or rather, reveal that
the original was/always already disarticulated — dead

they read the original from the perspective of a
pure language that would be entirely freed of the illusion
of meaning and, in so doing, they bring to light
the dismemberment of the original    De-canonization

process (of ripening, organic growth, dialectic)

but as something else (nature is to be understood from the perspective of history)

this is the burden of the reading

all these activities are *derived* from original activities

(perception, poetry, action) and all these activities are singularly inconclusive, aborted – yet the model of derivation is *not* that of resemblance or imitation

they are not metaphors

yet übersetzen *means* metaphor

translates

metaphor is not metaphor

these activities resemble each other [by] in the fact that they

do *not resemble*

they are, however, inter-linguistic: they relate to what, in the original, belongs to language and not to meaning as the extra-linguistic correlate susceptible of paraphrase and imitation

they disarticulate the original, or rather, reveal that the original was always already disarticulated – dead

They read the original from the perspective of a *pure* language that would be entirely freed of the illusion of meaning and, in doing so, they [reveal] bring to light the dismemberment of the original *de-canonization*

Danger of translation
on Hölderlin

p. 69
2hm p 81/82

Translation, by reference to the fiction of a pure language to which it implies, brings to light what Benjamin calls die Wehen des eigenen (p. 60, bottom)

2ohm mistranslates Nach-reife as "maturing process"

Ombres
obstetricales        Wehen   as   birth-pangs        Nachsommer
( p. 26 ) Gandillac .)                                  überleben
de-canonisation         also   death-pangs ( as in Hölderlin)
of the original   the "process" (?) is one of change and of motion
                  this has the appearance of life, but as after-life,
                  because it also reveals the death of the original

Why is this?   what are the birth/death-pangs of
               the original?  Why does it suffer?

        certainly not for subjective reasons, as pathos of a self
(1)     the sufferings are not human ( also very hard to
        admit for translation: 2ohm p. 70
               §3      if they are referred exclusively to man
                       Gandillac p. 262  is wrong
                       original is unambiguous  p. 57
                                          n dürftiger Zeit
(2)  not as a pathos of history, a werden im vergehen,
     a sacrificial, dialectical  genre of, be  elegiac
     genre   ( cf. Hartman)

*danger* of translation
on Hölderlin
p.69
Zohn p.81 / 82
[Thus] translation, by reference to the fiction of a pure
language which it [refers] implies, brings to light
what Benjamin calls *die Wehen des eignenen* (p.60, bottom)
Zohn mistranslates Nach-reife as 'maturing process'
Nachsommer
überleben
Wehen as birth-pangs
*also* death pangs (as in Hölderlin)
*Douleurs obstétricales* (p. 267 Gandillac)
de-canonization of the original
The 'process' (?) is one of change and of motion
that has the appearance of life but as after-life,
because it also reveals the death of the original
Why is this? What are the birth/death pangs of the original? Why does it suffer?
(1)   Certainly not for subjective reasons, as pathos of a self
the sufferings are not *human* (also very hard to
admit for translators: Zohn p. 70
β3   if they are referred exclusively to man
Gandillac p. 202 is correct
original is unambiguous p. 57
(2)   not as a pathos of history, a werden im vergessen or durftige Zeit
a sacrificial, dialectical [gesture of] elegiac
gesture (cf Hartman)

the *terms* are specifically linguistic and are
shared with comparable ~~structural~~ precision, so much so that
the *abyss* ~~to #~~ referred to with regard to it. also means
the non-aesthetic, technical version of the *mise-en-*
*abyme* by which the text becomes itself an example
of what it exemplifies (namely untranslatability)

(1) disjunction of   *das Gemeinte* (what is meant)
              from *Art des Meinens* (how it means)

        Gandillac : p. 266        *visée intentionnelle*

"*vouloir dire*" and "*dire*"        *ce qui est visé de la manière*
                        *dont on le vise*

cf note p. 272      Zohn p. 74      intended object
                        mode of intention

*phenomenological*   the problem is precisely this. Whereas the
*assumption — what*   *meaning-function* is intentional, it is not a-priori
*Benjamin stands*   certain that the mode of meaning is intentional at
*beyond*   all, since it depends on linguistic properties that are
        not only not made by us, as historical beings, but
        perhaps not even made by humans at all

    f. ex.   ~~pain~~ Brot      pain      (pain de noix)
        Brot + Wein      pain et vin
                    champ restaurant
                    baguette, ficelle, bâtard

the reasons are specifically linguistic and are
stated with considerable / structural precision, so much so that
the *abyss* [is] referred to with regard to H. *also* means
the non-pathetic, technical notion of the mise-en-abyme
by which the text becomes itself an example of
what it exemplifies (namely untranslatability)
(1) disjunction of *das Gemeinte* (what it means)
from *Art des Meinens* (how it means)
Gandillac p. 266 visée intentionelle
'vouloir dire' and 'dire' ce qui est visé de la manière
dont on le vise
cf note p. 272 Zohn p.74 intended object
object of intention
phenomenological assumption – which Benjamin moves beyond
the problem is precisely that, whereas the meaning-function is intentional, it
is not a-priori certain that the mode of meaning is intentional at all, since it
depends on linguistic properties that are not only not made by *us*, as historical
beings, but perhaps not even made by humans at all
f. ex. [pain] Brot   pain   (pain de ? [word illegible])
Brot + Wein   pain et vin
cheap restaurant
baguette, ficelle, batard

I now turn to "aporia" in Brood

express the mobility of quotidien — in daily bread

best understood as relationship between
 _hermeneutics_ and _poetics_
 is it complementary? complementarity achieved
 always at the expense of poetics

(2) disjunction of Wort and Satz   p. 66 end of § 10
   statement (Satz)    message
   and the apparent agent of the statement (Wort)
   as lexical units but also as syntax and
   grammar

   *grammar +*
   *meaning*

   compatibility of grammar + meaning is in
                                        question

   *↓*
   *letter / word*

   *word / Satz*

   ~~but~~ understood as slippage of word (Aufgabe ...)
   and also as complete slippage of meaning when
   the translation follows the syntax, the priority of
   the word over the Satz   As the beginning was the **word**

   *p. 65*
   *p. 78  2 times*
   *(Hölderlin)*

   literalism of the _wörtliche_ Übersetzung  [Hölderlin]

   best compared to relationship of **letter** to **word**
   in which the letter is a-semos

(3) disjunction of Symbol and symbolized   *p. 66 bottom*
                                *p. 79 something that symbolizes*
   *type*                        *a meaning symbolized*

   *types*

   and meaning as totalizing power of tropological
   substitutions

I now hear the 'batard' in Brood
Upsets the stability of quotidian in *daily* bread
best understood as relationship between
*hermeneutics and poetics*
is it complementary? complementarity achieved
always at the expense of poetics
(2)   Disjunction of Wort and Satz p. 66 end of β 10
Statement (Satz) Aussage
and the apparent agent of the statement (Wort)
as lexical unit but also as syntax and grammar
*Grammar and Meaning* → letter / word
word/ Satz
compatibility of grammar and meaning is in question
understood as slippage of word (Aufgabe, [?; illegible word])
and also as complete slippage of meaning when
the translator follows the syntax, the priority of
the word over the Satz. At the beginning was the *word*
p.65 p. 78 Zohn (Holderlin)
literalism of the *wörtliche* Übersetzung Hölderlin
best compared to relationship of *letter* to *word*
in which the letter is a-semos
(3)   disjunction of symbol and symbolized p. 66 bottom
trope p.79 something that symbolizes
or something symbolized
tropes
and meaning as totalizing power of tropological substitutions

here is the main difficulty of the text, but it uses
tropes and illustrates the illusion of totality they
they convey; it seems to relapse in the topological
errors that it denounces (f. ex. read and bind; but
Keim, harmony, etc.) but displaces in fact the
traditional symbols in a manner that acts out the
discrepancy between them and their meaning

one striking example is the amphora

p. 65          read it in Zohn . p. 78

Scholem ( Jacobs p. 765   note 9)

Jacobs translation

system of tropes          folgen    nicht gleichen

metonymical & metaphoric
resemblance

but insistence is on fragmentation

on persistent fragmentation despite the
illusion of totality conveys by the metonymic

disjunction   symbol / symbolized ( a version of (1) and
(2) indicates the unreliability of rhetoric as a system of
tropes, productive of a meaning that is always displaced
with regard to the meaning that is ideally intended

B. approaches the question in terms of the aporia of
freedom and foreignness that harms translation

symbol as
symbolizer

here is the main difficulty of the text, that it uses
tropes and illustrates the illusion of totality that
they convey; it seems to relapse in the tropological
errors it denounces (f.ex seed and rind; but
Keim, harmony etc.) but displaces in fact these
traditional symbols in a manner that acts out the
discrepancy between them and their meaning
one striking example is the amphora
p.65 read it in Zohn p. 78
Scholem (Jacobs p. 765 note 9)
Jacobs translation
system of tropes folgen nicht gleichen
symbol as symbolon
metonymization of metaphoric
resemblance
but insistence is on *fragmentation*
on persistent fragmentation despite the
illusion of totality conveyed by the metonyms
disjunction symbol / symbolized (a version of (1) and
(2)   indicates the unreliability of rhetoric as a system of
tropes, productive of a meaning that is always displaced
with regard to the meaning that is ideally intended
B. apprehends the question in terms of the aporia of
freedom and faithfulness that haunts translation

the faithful translation is literal
    how can it be free?
by revealing the instability of the original as the
linguistic tension between hope (figure) and meaning
pure language is ~~present~~ implied in the translation (more so
than in the original) but as hope (as the hope (image,
face) predominates in B.'s sense), that is as a ~~displace~~
displacement of meaning, a movement of the original

this movement, which is a wandering, an "errance",
a permanent exile, if you wish, but it is not an
exile for there is nothing one has been exiled from,
least of all a Reine Sprache which does not exist
except as a permanent disruption that inhabits all
languages as such, including and especially ~~this~~ the
language one calls one's own

*it is not even a theoretical fiction*

this motion, this errancy of language, which is the
illusion of a life that is however only an after-life
is history

        history is neither human, nor natural, nor
                phenomenal, nor temporal (not even in
                (Heidegger's sense)

        the dimension of futurity is not temporal but the
        correlative of the figural pattern and its disjunctive power

        it is certainly not messianic, since it consists in the
        rigorous separation, the ~~messaging~~ acting out of the
        separation of the sacred from the poetic, of Reine Sprache

the *faithful* translation is *literal*
how can it be free?
by revealing the instability of the original as the
linguistic tension between trope (figure) and meaning
pure language is [present] implied in the translation (more so
than in the original) but as trope (as the trope (image,
Bild) predominates in B.'s text), that is as a
displacement of meaning, a movement of the original
this movement, which is a wandering, an 'errance',
a permanent exile, if you wish, but it is not an
exile for there is no homeland / nothing one has been exiled from,
least of all a Reine Sprache which does not exist
except as a permanent disjunction that inhabits all
languages as such, including, and especially [one's] the
language one calls one's own
it is not even a theoretical fiction
this motion, this errancy of language, which is the
illusion of a life that is however only an after-life
is history
history is neither human, nor natural, nor
phenomenal, nor temporal (not even in
Heidgger's sense)
The dimension of *futurity* is not temporal but the
correlative of the figural pattern and its disjunctive power
it is certainly not messianic, since it consists in the
rigorous separation, the [bringing] acting out of the
separation of the sacred from the poetic, of Reine Sprache

from poetic language

necessarily nihilistic moment / active moment ~~commonly occur~~

B. nail this, in the clearest terms, in relation to
political action; clear only in German because the English
translation (end/aus) messes it up!

    p. 2∂0      Theological-political fragment

        (whose nihilistic conclusion is left behind in
        the Task of the ~~the~~ Translator)

    for ~~~~ political, we can substitute poetical
for we now see that the non-messianic, not
sacred, i.e. political aspect of history is the results
of the ~~~~ poetical (in the sense of a poiesis).
structure of language

to the extent that such a poetics (such a history) is
non-messianic, not a theocratic but a rhetoric, it
has no room for the notion of modernity, which is always
dialectical, finally theological. You remember that
we started out from Gadamer's ~~~~ claim to modernity
in terms of a dialectic explicitly associated with
Hegel. I was gratified to find that Hegel himself, in the
notion of the Aesthetics on the sublime, is actually much
closer to Benjamin, in the Task of the Translator, than to
Gadamer. But that is another paper, and another
story

from poetic language

necessarily nihilistic moment /*active* moment [can only occur]

B. said this, in the clearest terms, in relation to

political action; but only in German before the English

translation (end/end) messes it up!

p.280 Theological political fragment

(whose nihilistic conclusion is left behind in

The Task of the Translator)

for [historical and] political, we can substitute *poetical*

for we now see that the non-messianic, not

sacred, i.e. *political* aspect of history is the result

of the [linguistic] poetical (in the sense of a poetics),

structure of language

To the extent that such a poetics (such a history) is

non-messianic, not a theocracy but a rhetoric, it

has no room for the notion of modernity, which is always

dialectical, i.e. essentially theological. You remember that

we started out from Gadamer's claim to modernity

in terms of a dialectic explicitly associated with

Hope. I was gratified to find that Hegel himself, in the

section of the Aesthetics on the sublime, is actually much

closer to Benjamin, in The Task of the Translator, than to

Gadamer. But that is another paper, and another story.

# Part II

# Theory and the disappearing future

# 1    Paul de Man at work

In these bad days, what good is an archive?

*J. Hillis Miller*

> What we call ideology is precisely the confusion of linguistic with natural reality, of reference with phenomenalism. It follows that, more than any other mode of inquiry, including economics, the linguistics of literariness is a powerful and indispensable tool in the unmasking of ideological aberrations, as well as a determining factor in accounting for their occurrence. Those who reproach literary theory for being oblivious to social and historical (that is to say ideological) reality are merely stating their fear at having their own ideological mystifications exposed by the tool they are trying to discredit. They are, in short, very poor readers of Marx's *German Ideology*.
> (Paul de Man, "The Resistance to Theory" [de Man 1986, 11])

My questions in this essay are the following: In these bad days, what good is a Critical Theory Archive? What good is studying literature or literary theory? By "these bad days" I mean the many ways things are not going at all well in the world, and in particular in the United States. We are experiencing global climate change that may soon make the species *Homo sapiens* extinct, but that is still denied by many. We are in the midst of a deep global recession, with catastrophic unemployment in the United States. Twenty to thirty million people in the United States are out of work, if you count those who have stopped looking for a job or who are employed only part time. The global financial meltdown was brought about by the folly and greed of our politicians and financiers. We have highly influential news media in the United States, such as *Fox News*, that are more or less lying propaganda arms of our right wing party but are believed in as truth by many citizens. We are mired in an apparently endless and unwinnable war in Afghanistan. New global tele-communication devices are putting people in touch with one another worldwide, thereby weakening local communities. These devices—computers, iPhones, iPads, Facebook, Twitter, video games, and the like—are rapidly diminishing the role literature plays in most people's lives. Our universities are, like glaciers worldwide, also in meltdown mode, especially the humanities.

We all know these frightening realities. How can we justify spending time, in such a dire situation, with something so marginal or even trivial as literature or literary theory? My colleagues in this volume, Claire Colebrook and Tom Cohen, have brilliantly confronted this question, with special attention to how useful or even indispensable it is to read Paul de Man carefully today, no easy task. Colebrook suggests that de Man may be *the* theorist for the twenty-first century. I agree.

Even if reading de Man's work is necessary now more than ever, what possible use in aiding this can be the Paul de Man Archive as part of the Irvine Critical Theory Archive? We tend to assume that an archive is a self-evident good in itself. It is good to store safely in one place all the "remains" of a distinguished writer or critic, to organize these, to inventory and index them, to make them available to qualified researchers. It is more and more coming to seem good to digitize such materials and to make them available online, as is the case with the example I shall discuss in the first section of this essay. (See de Man 1973 and de Man 2010.) Archives hover uneasily between a commitment to restricted access and a commitment to "open source," universal dissemination. Putting archived materials online is the best way these days to achieve the latter.

To borrow speech act terminology, archiving in any of its modes is assumed to be constative, not performative. It just neutrally gathers together such materials, saves them from harm, and lets researchers decide what use to make of them. These uses would include the study, transcription, and perhaps print publication of hitherto unpublished materials; the searching out of biographically interesting and relevant information; the checking of published work against early drafts, manuscripts, or proofs to be able to follow and evaluate a process of genesis; the study of letters, diaries, notebooks, annotations in books, coffee stains or tear stains. Any slip of paper may be important, such as the famous Nietzsche note: "I have forgotten my umbrella." You never know—until you have looked at the remains and thought about them. More and more these days archives include other things than written papers: photographs, films, videos, tapes, computer files of texts as well as emails, and so forth, all the artifacts of our ecotechnological age. A recent conference at the University of California at Irvine celebrated the acquisition of Richard Rorty's digitized materials. More than one of de Man's major essays is a transcription of a taped oral delivery without an extant written text, for example, "Conclusions: Walter Benjamin's 'The Task of the Translator'" and "The Concept of Irony." The first of these is one of my focuses in this essay.

Researchers who use archives are obeying more or less unselfconsciously a set of widely established protocols: 1) Using archives shows you are a really serious scholar. 2) Such scholars have the vague assumption and hope that they will find something truly surprising and important in an archive, something that will transform the hitherto accepted understanding of the author in question. Some stray slip of paper will hold a vital revisionary key. 3) You will become famous as the scholar who found that stray slip of paper and understood its importance. 4) An under-theorized and unstated penchant not just for historical or contextual explanations, but, more specifically, for biographical explanations, for "de Man at work," as opposed to just reading de Man's published essays. 5) Somewhere in the background is the idea that the works the author revised and published during her or his lifetime cannot stand on their own. They need the supplement of the archive to be fully understood.

These assumptions are extremely powerful, as well as extremely problematic. They might be called the ideology of the archive. I do not exempt myself from submission to their force. Nevertheless, it is well to remember the challenge to this ideology in Jacques Derrida's *Mal d'archive* (Derrida 1995), somewhat unsatisfactorily translated as *Archive Fever* (Derrida 1996), since that loses the moral force of *mal*. In a striking and counter-intuitive formulation Derrida argues that archiving is not just constative. It is a performative act that does something to what is stored. Derrida makes a scandalous comparison to what the news media do to the "objective facts."

> The archive, as printing, writing, prosthesis, or hypomnesic technique in general, is not only the place for stocking [*stockage*] and for conserving an archivable content *of the past* which would exist in any case, such as, without the archive, one still believes it was or will have been. No, the technical structure of the *archiving* archive also determines the structure of the *archivable* content even in its very coming into existence and in its relationship to the future. The archivization produces as much as it records the event. This is also our political experience of the so-called news media.
> (Derrida 1996, 16–17; Derrida 1995, 34)

If Derrida is right, an archive is not at all innocent. Far from objectively storing materials that would be the same if they were somewhere else or in some other format, an archive changes what it archives. It even in a certain sense creates what it archives, just as a given medium determines what can be said by way of that medium. Derrida's example is the way the institution of Freudian Psychoanalysis depended on belonging to a time of the telephone and of what we today call snail mail. In what he calls a "retrospective science fiction" project, Derrida tries to imagine what psychoanalysis would have been like "if ... Freud, his contemporaries, collaborators, and immediate disciples, instead of writing thousands of letters by hand, had had access to MCI or AT&T telephonic credit cards, portable tape recorders, computers, printers, faxes, televisions, teleconferences, and above all E-mail" (Derrida 1996, 16; Derrida 1995, 33). Derrida's list already sounds a bit old-fashioned. Today we would be likely to include Facebook and Twitter, iPhones, iPads, and blogs. Derrida himself steadfastly resisted email. De Man's time did not have it. His *Nachlass* exists in hand-written, typed, printed, taped, Xeroxed, and photographic form, except when it has been digitized after the fact.

*

Well, what help can the de Man Archive be in making us better readers of de Man's published essays? With that question and with Derrida's warning not to take an archive as neutral storing or *stockage* in mind, I turn now to my two examples. To some degree they go in opposite directions. One example is the various versions of de Man's essay on Rousseau's *Profession de foi*. The other example is the various versions of de Man's essay on Walter Benjamin's "*Die Aufgabe des Übersetzers.*" The first exists as:

1   A hand-written manuscript written in Zürich in 1973, and now "stored" in the Irvine Critical Theory Archive, entitled "Theotropic Allegory" (de Man 1973). The manuscript shows that de Man considered and discarded (by crossing out) other titles: "Allegories of politics and religion," "Allegories of religion and of politics," and "Religion and the politics of Allegory." Here is a reproduction of the first half of this page:[1]

One might spend a long afternoon here in Deer Isle, Maine, where I am writing this, or anywhere else, meditating on the implications of those changes. The citations from Rousseau in the manuscript version are in French, whereas they are in English in the revised published version.

2   A scanned and digitized facsimile of that manuscript, available online (de Man 1973): http://dspace1.nacs.uci.edu/xmlui/handle/10575/1092 (accessed March 23, 2011).

3 A recent and admirably exact computer file transcription by Erin Obodiac of that handwritten manuscript, with "blank" put in for words she could not read (de Man 2010).

4 The transcription as put on line and available in open access. De Man's manuscript and the transcript are now available virtually all over the world, to anyone who has a computer connected to the Internet. They are floating in cyberspace, available at http://dspace1.nacs.uci.edu/xmlui/handle/10575/1092 (accessed March 23, 2011).[2]

5 The revised printed chapter on the *Profession de foi* in *Allegories of Reading* (de Man 1979). This is called "Allegory of Reading (*Profession de foi*)." Though the manuscript is followed closely in the final version, many small changes were made. These were often, but not always, as far as I can guess, for increased clarity and crispness, not because de Man had changed his mind about what he wanted to say. One must be careful in passing such judgment, however. Whatever de Man's intentions may have been (they are unrecoverable now), even an apparently insignificant change makes a change in meaning, perhaps an important one.

I do not know whether manuscripts or proofs of the printed version still exist, in the Irvine Archive or elsewhere, for example at the Yale University Press or in Patricia de Man's collection. If so, it would be interesting to see them. They would constitute additional versions in different media.

My second example, de Man's essay on Benjamin's essay, "Conclusions: Walter Benjamin's 'The Task of the Translator,'" exists:

1 In two sets of notes in a de Man notebook of 1983, in my possession, though it will ultimately be deposited in the Irvine Critical Theory Archive. William Jewett apparently had access to the first sketchier set when he transcribed the tape of the Cornell lecture. He speaks of "eight pages of rough manuscript notes," which describes the first set of notes in the notebook I have, but not the second set, which is eleven pages long and not exactly "rough." We are extremely grateful to Patricia de Man for granting us permission to include in this book a facsimile and transcription by Claire Colebrook of this second set of notes.

2 As the tape of the oral lecture de Man presented at Cornell in March 1983.

3 As Jewett's "edited transcript" published as "Conclusions: Walter Benjamin's 'The Task of the Translator'" in de Man's *The Resistance to Theory* (de Man 1986). This includes a transcript of the discussion period after the lecture. De Man never, so far as I know, wrote out this lecture, so we do not have a version he authorized for printing. He also gave a version of the lecture at the Whitney Humanities Center in the same spring of 1983, but no tape of that exists, to my knowledge. I was present at the Yale lecture, as were some others who were also present at the Irvine conference for which I wrote this essay. The two lecture versions must have differed somewhat, however, both because both were improvised from notes and because de Man was self-consciously speaking to somewhat different audiences.

If Derrida is right, each of these versions of each composition has a different meaning just because it is in a different medium from the others, handwritten as against a typescript or computer file, handwritten notes as against a tape, a tape as against an edited transcript of that tape, and so on. Just what those differences in meaning are, however, might be hard to specify. Contradictory ideological, institutional, or disciplinary assumptions certainly play a big role. On the one hand, we in the humanities ascribe great value to research that involves archival work. Using archives, as I have said, means research must be really serious. Something in an author's own hand has authority because he or she so evidently wrote those words at such and such a time and place. On the other hand, we tend to assume that only the results of research printed in a peer-reviewed journal or book count. A thick square book has tangible, material solidity. It also often has the august authority of a university press, as well as the printed indication that the author authorized it, intended it to be published. Who knows, on the contrary, who may have written something that is published online, or have decided to publish it that way, even if peer review is claimed? Anyone could do it.

In any case, an online text, many still think, is fragile and changeable, just so many zeroes and ones flitting here and there on the ghostly filaments of the World Wide Web and dependent on a rapidly changing technology that may in time make a given file unreadable, just so much cyberspace junk. You can change an online text any way you like on the screen, cut and paste it, change the fonts and type size, and so on. The reluctance of tenure and appointment committees to let online work "count" is one symptom of this resistance to new media, as is the disparagement by many academics of that marvelous collective invention Wikipedia. If anyone anywhere in the world may contribute to it, it must be completely lacking in authority, as opposed, say, to the *Encyclopedia Brittanica*, where the articles are signed. In the case of Paul de Man's *Nachlass*, some people apparently feel anxiety about taking seriously early drafts or notes or tapes that de Man never authorized for transcription and publication, much less approved for digitizing and making freely and universally accessible. I do not feel that anxiety myself. Who cares, at this point, what de Man might have thought if he were still around to pass judgement? We must make our own decisions about his remains.

One essential mediatic or "mediotic" (playing on "idiotic" as "idiomatic," singular) difference in meaning between digitized writing, such as this essay I am at this moment writing, and hand-written manuscripts is that revisions in the former vanish, unless you go to awkward lengths to save all intermediate versions. Part of the fascination of de Man's manuscripts is that you can see him at work changing a word or a phrase, for example, as I have already mentioned, in the several earlier titles he wrote down and then discarded for "Theotropic Allegory," though even that title vanished in the published text. These visible changes are, no one can doubt, part of the meaning of the manuscript. They disappear in Obodiac's digitized transcript. Our only access to them at this point is by way of the manuscript or its scanned digitized facsimile.

I have said that the two sequences in my examples go to some degree in opposite directions. The *Profession de foi* essay goes from a first draft to a finished printed text. The final version is not only revised substantially in detail, almost sentence by sentence. It is also shorter, tighter, and more forceful. The Benjamin essay goes from those two sets of notes, to a taped oral presentation that expands on those notes to produce the relative informality of an improvised lecture, to the printed transcription of the lecture and of the ensuing discussion in *The Resistance to Theory* (de Man 1986, 73–105). In a sense the tape is even less a finished product than the notes, since it records something that was made up at the time and not intended for publication, whereas the printed version of the *Profession de foi* essay in *Allegories of Reading* is definitive. It is an end product, the last word. De Man, for example, improvised on the spot the translations he made from Benjamin and others in the "Task of the Translator" lectures, though some prepared translations exist in the notes. De Man in any case had a quite extraordinary ability to work out a lecture elaborately beforehand, in his mind, and then deliver it on the basis of notes. That was the way he prepared and presented his graduate seminars.

\*

Well, what good is judging the differences in the archival sequence for reading "Allegory of Reading (*Profession de foi*)" or for understanding and then doing something about our sad plight in these bad days? De Man's target in the essay is previous interpretations of the *Profession de foi* by such famous and authoritative scholars as Pierre Burgelin and Jean Starobinski. These worthies have tied themselves in hermeneutic knots to explain in one way or another the discrepancy between the apparent theism of the *Profession de foi* and the forceful repudiation of such religiosity elsewhere in Rousseau's writing. De Man, for all his superficial respect (after all he needs worthy antagonists), wants to persuade us, as is usual in his work, that these previous scholars are very bad readers of Rousseau. De Man's initial "naïve" question is the following: Is the *Profession de foi* a theistic text or is it not a theistic text? That looks like a question that ought to be answerable with a yes or a no. Powerful ideological presuppositions within the discipline of humanistic studies reinforce the assumptions that a good text is unified and that a unified author stands behind the text. Therefore you can make a univocal reading.

Careful readers would agree, or ought to agree, that the centre of de Man's essay is the claim that what Rousseau calls "judgment" works by metaphorical comparisons to produce structures that are linguistic but aberrantly referential. This is a way of saying that the apparent referents do not exist. The structure has no basis in reality. Its illusory referents are created by language, specifically by unwarranted metaphors. "Summarizing the characteristics of 'judgment' (*Urteilskraft*)," writes de Man in the manuscript of 1973, "we can say that Rousseau describes it as the power to set up politically aberrant systems of referential relationships that deconstruct the referentiality of their own elaboration; this description warrants the equation of judgment with figural language, extensively conceived" (de Man 1973, 118). This becomes in the printed chapter: "We can conclude that the vicar describes judgment as the power to set up potentially aberrant referential systems that deconstruct the referentiality of their own elaboration. This description warrants the equation of judgment with figural language, extensively conceived" (de Man 1979, 234–35). "Say" becomes "conclude." The definition of judgement is now ascribed explicitly to the Savoyard Vicar, not to Rousseau. This is a narratological assertion that reminds the reader that Rousseau speaks through a mouthpiece in the *Profession de foi*, therefore not necessarily for his own opinions and judgements. He speaks, that is, by way of just the sort of "metaphorical" displacement that is being deconstructed. "Politically" in the manuscript becomes "potentially" in the final version. One might make a lot out of that change. Just why did he drop "politically"? Unfortunately for that tempting move, the manuscript clearly (to my eye at least) says "potentially," just as does the printed chapter, not "politically." The transcription errs.

First formulations crossed out in the manuscript give one much to think about. For example, de Man first wrote "the characteristics that circumscribe judgment" and then changed that to "characteristics of judgment." "Potentially" in the citation I made in the previous paragraph is inserted above the line in perhaps slightly heavier ink, as though it were an afterthought added later. I suppose, on the basis of formulations elsewhere in de Man, that he means you cannot decide for sure whether they are aberrant or not. They are just potentially aberrant. They might just by accident be on the mark. You never know. Following through the implications of all these small changes would be an intellectually delightful process. It would also be an exceedingly long business, and the payoff in cases like the ones just adduced would not be all that great. I hazard to say, however, that when a great many words and phrases are crossed out in a given place in the manuscript and new words substituted, this is a sign that de Man at work was having some difficulty getting it right. This might justify looking closely at the changes. I shall later give one interesting (to me at least) example of that.

Though the word "deconstruction" is frequently used in the *Profession* essay, even in the 1973 version, explicit reference to Austinian speech act theory is missing, though the Austinian words "perlocutionary," changed to "illocutionary" (in the manuscript [de Man 1973, 131]) and "exhortative performatives" (in the printed text [de Man 1979, 245]) are used in crucial places, as I shall show. Moreover, de Man's definitions of Rousseau's concept of judgement lead to formulations that would correspond to a claim that judgement is performative, not constative. Judgement, however, is a misleading performative, unauthorized by pre-existing institutions, which masks as a constative, impartial, statement of fact. The transcript says: "The scene of judgment is that of a verbal pronouncement, an oracular verdict, like in the plays of Kleist" (de Man 2010, 116). The manuscript shows that de Man first wrote "The primal scene of judgment" and then crossed out "primal." I suppose he did this to avoid a misleading allusion to Freud's "primal scene," the parents' copulation that engendered the self, the "moi," though he may have at first intended that allusion, and then thought it would be a diversion to justify it. The primal scene of judgement engenders all the aberrations that follow it, just as the "I" may feel that his conception by his parents was a big mistake. "That of a verbal" is added above the line, and "of a verdict" was changed first to "of a verbal verdict," then to what looks to me like "of a suspended verdict," and then to "an oracular verdict" (de Man 1973, 116). The printed version is: "The scene of judgment is a *verbal* pronouncement and that of an oracular verdict" (de Man 1979, 233). The term "verdict" reminds de Man of the judicial verdicts in Kleist's stories and plays. In Kleist's work, de Man asserts, the verdict repeats the crime, in a feedback reversal that is essential to de Man's formulations in the *Profession de foi* essay, as well as in the essay on Kleist in *The Rhetoric of Romanticism* ("Aesthetic Formalization: Kleist's *Über das Marionettentheater*") (de Man 1984, 263–90) and in other references to Kleist's work. The claim that mechanical, unintentional repetition of the linguistic or ideological error that has just been denounced necessarily occurs is a primary theme in "Theotropic Allegory," as in de Man's work generally. Another especially intransigent example appears at the end of "Shelley Disfigured":

> *The Triumph of Life* warns us that nothing, whether deed, word, thought, or text, ever happens in relation, positive or negative, to anything that precedes, follows, or exists elsewhere, but only as a random event whose power, like the power of death, is due to the randomness of its occurrence. It also warns us why and how these events then have to be reintegrated into a historical and aesthetic system of recuperation that repeats itself regardless of the exposure of its fallacy.
>
> (de Man 1984, 122)

Here is the climactic formulation about judgement, several pages later in "Theotropic Allegory," as transcribed by Erin Obodiac. As you can see, it gives what de Man calls "the aporia of judgment" the widest presence as the fundamental rhetorical structure of the *Profession de foi*, whatever its ostensible topic at a given moment may be—sensation, nature, will, freedom, God, politics, or whatever, in their interlocked and chiasmic inside/outside pairings and reversals:

> The logical structure of each of these judgments is the same and repeats the aporia of judgment. The same concept operates deconstructively as the principle of differentiation but then, because of the referentiality inherent in its linguistic structure, re-integrates by an act of the mind (noema) what it had taken apart on the level of intuition. [The terminology here is Husserlian.] As the referent of a linguistic sign, the noematic correlative of this second operation (regardless of whether it be called the *meaning* of a judgment, the *subject* that controls the will, or the *god* that freely invents), regains in its turn the attributes of a (natural) existence, and can therefore be deconstructed by means of the same conceptual system. The original denominative metaphor is said (blank [it looks like "judged" in the MS to

me]) to be based on a misleading assumption of identity, but the utterance of this negative insight [the MS clearly says "the enoncé of this utterance"; I do not know where "negative insight" came from; it's not in the MS, to my eye at least] is itself a new metaphor that engenders its own semantic correlative, its own proper meaning: we move from sensation to judgment, for example, or from nature to God, but what appears to be a hypostasis ["of a phenomenon" is written above the line and then crossed out] is in fact even more vulnerable, logically speaking, than the entity it claims to supersede.

(de Man 2010, 123–24)

The version of these sentences in "Allegory of Reading (*Profession de foi*)" (de Man 1979, 239–40) is essentially the same, but differs somewhat, and some variants exist in the manuscript, as well as differences between the manuscript and the transcript, as I have indicated.

I conclude this all too sketchy indication of what happens when you set manuscript, transcript, and printed version side by side as an exemplification of de Man at work and of the use of the Archive, by referring to three other passages. Most readers of the printed text will have noticed the remarkable extension toward the end of de Man's essay of the results of reading the *Profession de foi* to a universal declaration of the work "deconstructive readings" perform. The passage, which would need to be read in detail, begins, in the transcript version of the manuscript, "Deconstructive readings can point out the unwarranted identifications achieved by substitution, but they are powerless to prevent their recurrence and to uncross, so to speak, the aberrant exchanges that have taken place, in a gesture that would merely reiterate the rhetorical defiguration that caused the error in the first place" (de Man 2010, 127). The printed text differs only slightly: "Deconstructive readings can point out the unwarranted identifications achieved by substitution, but they are powerless to prevent their recurrence even in their own discourse, and to uncross, so to speak, the aberrant exchanges that have taken place. Their gesture merely reiterates the rhetorical defiguration that caused the error in the first place" (de Man 1979, 242). "Even in their own discourse" is added, in case you did not get the point. De Man is not talking just about Rousseau's discourse, which might by a stretch be called a deconstructive reading of its own rhetoric, but about deconstructive readings in general, such as his own. "In a gesture" becomes "their gesture," to make sure you understand that he is talking about what happens, by an irresistible fatality, in all "deconstructive readings" whatsoever.

The other classic de Manian formulation comes three pages later in the printed version, as its last sentence, its final touché of the lighthearted reader who may hope nothing of great importance is at stake in this "theoretical" exercise, nothing that would touch on ethics, politics, economics, gender, religion, or history, those serious matters that concern those who have turned from theory to cultural studies: "One sees from this that the impossibility of reading should not be taken too lightly" (de Man 1979, 245).

These portentous words just hang there in the air, followed by the blank before the next chapter. They seem to be a definitive conversation stopper, leaving nothing more to say, just meditative silence.

In the manuscript and transcript this was: "One should not take the inability to read too lightly. It leads to a great deal of trouble, all the worse for not being tragic trouble" (de Man 2010, 132), and so on, for another five pages. You will note that "inability" in the MS becomes the much more intransigent "impossibility" in the printed version. "Inability" suggests a correctable deficiency. It implies that with a little training, perhaps in a remedial reading class, or even in a speed-reading class, you could learn to read perfectly well. "Impossibility" indicates the blank wall of an aporia, a no thoroughfare, over which it is impossible to learn to climb, however rigorous the training.

Well, why should I not take the impossibility of reading too lightly? Why should I care? Who cares? "What, *me* worry?", as the anti-hero of *Mad Magazine*, Alfred E. Neuman, says.[3] The sentences that precede de Man's quite amazing statement suggest the answer. The manuscript puts this verdict under the aegis of a claim that after all this deconstructive reading, "The link between Rousseau's theory of rhetoric and his religious thought should now become a little more apparent" (de Man 2010, 131). This follows several sentences in the manuscript that have vanished in the printed version. In the printed version, the context is two sentences not in the manuscript that return to de Man's initial question, derived from the critical tradition, about the *Profession de foi*. The sentence asserts categorically that we cannot know whether or not the *Profession* is a theistic text: "The naïve historical question from which we started out—should the *Profession de foi* be called a theistic text?—must remain unanswerable. The text both is and is not the theistic document it is assumed to be" (de Man 1979, 245). Rousseau's text both proclaims theism and denounces it as aberrant. The consequence is that "A text such as the *Profession de foi* can literally be called unreadable. It leads to a set of assertions that radically exclude each other" (de Man 1979, 245). "A text such as the *Profession de foi*" suggests that lots of such texts exist, so what de Man is saying is of wide applicability, perhaps of universal applicability. "Literally" is an odd word here, as de Man probably intended, since I may well be able to read the words all right and make sense of them sentence by sentence. I should think a "literally" unreadable text would be, for example, a text in a foreign language that I "ignore," to remember de Man's quaint Gallicism about how he "ignored" Russian. Trying to make coherent sense of Rousseau's *Profession de foi* is like trying to read a foreign language of which one is ignorant. What de Man says about the unreadability of such texts as the *Profession* depends on an unstated assumption that it is easy not to notice. It assumes that only a text of which one can make verifiable and univocal sense is "readable."

Just why does this particular form of unreadability matter? Who cares? The coherence of a given text is something we have come in recent years habitually to put in question without worrying too much about it. What de Man goes on to say gives the answer. These assertions that radically exclude each other are not just contradictory constative assertions. They are what de Man calls in the manuscript "illocutionary utterances that, as a consequence of their referentiality, necessitate the passage from speech to action. They force one to choose, but, on the other hand, they undermine the grounds of all choice" (de Man 2010, 131), and, in the printed text, are "exhortative performatives that require the passage from sheer enunciation to action. They compel us to choose while destroying the foundations of any choice" (de Man 1979, 245).

De Man appeared, in my judgement, about as lacking in religious belief as anyone I have ever met, but he once said to me, "Religious questions are the most important ones." In the paragraph in question, we must choose whether or not to be theists, and we cannot choose. If we decide to become theists, the *Profession de foi* shows us what fools we are. If we decide that we are too enlightened to be taken in by such foolishness, then we foolishly miss the fact that we have fallen into a trap like that of the verdicts in Kleist's plays that repeat the crime: "But if we decide that belief, in the most extensive use of the term (which must include all possible forms of idolatry and ideology) can once and forever be overcome by the enlightened mind, then this twilight of the idols [*Götzendämmerung* in the manuscript, a reference to the title of a book by Friedrich Nietzsche] will be all the more foolish in not recognizing itself as the first victim of its occurrence" (de Man 1979, 245). In the manuscript the last phrase is "all the more foolish in not perceiving that [it] is itself the primary target of its execution" (de Man 2010, 132). Either by believing or not believing we have had it, and had it big time, since matters of the utmost importance are at stake. Later this came in "deconstructive" critical theory to be called "undecidability."

The somewhat comic impasse here (de Man says its pathos is that it is not even tragic, therefore by implication comic) is parallel to the one de Man, following Friedrich Schlegel, identifies as the trap of irony. The person who is certain he understands irony and will not be fooled by it is the most likely or even the most certain to be taken in by it. Then after the remarks about theism at the end of the printed *Profession du foi* essay follows that resounding clunk or clank of the final sentence, like the fall of a guillotine's blade, followed by silence, at least for the victim: "One sees from this that the impossibility of reading should not be taken too lightly."

What is the difference between the manuscript or transcription version and the printed version, besides the not insignificant small differences I have identified? The answer is that the two climactic passages are made unmistakably salient in the printed version, whereas they are diffused and a little fuzzy in the manuscript version. The last sentence in the printed version comes in the middle of a paragraph in the manuscript. It is followed not only by the rather flat remarks I have cited about how the impossibility of reading "leads into a great deal of trouble, worse for not being tragic trouble," but first by several sentences that are full of crossed out phrases and changes. It looks as if de Man felt he should go on talking but could not decide, in some embarrassment, just what to say. Then follow the five final pages that wander off into more remarks about religion and politics. These are of interest primarily as preparation for the next chapter of *Allegories of Reading,* "Promises (*Social Contract*)." De Man wisely decided when he was revising to stop at the point when he was still ahead. The result is that we have in the printed essay one of the great classics of deconstructive reading and theory combined.

I am not quite finished yet, however, with what we can learn from watching de Man at work in turning the manuscript of the *Profession de foi* reading into the finished essay. The manuscript is entitled with a striking phrase, "Theotropic Allegory." The word "theotropic" appears just once in the manuscript, two pages after the sentence about how the inability to read should not be taken too lightly. The word "theotropic" vanishes from the printed essay. Why? That disappearance is surely significant.

One explanation might be that de Man remembered that he had at first, and perhaps still, at that point, named the essay in the manuscript version with one of another of several combinations using the words "politics" and "religion": "Allegories of politics and religion," "Allegories of religion and of politics," and "Religion and the politics of allegory." The title "Theotropic Allegory" may have been an afterthought, added after he finished the manuscript. What de Man meant by "allegory" we know from "The Rhetoric of Temporality," written well before the Rousseau manuscript. For de Man, all allegories are in a sense allegories of (the impossibility of) reading, since allegories are constituted by a temporal relation between signs and are about their own working or not working, their *désoeuvrement*, as texts:

> ... this relation between signs necessarily contains a constitutive temporal element; it remains necessary, if there is to be allegory, that the allegorical sign refer to another sign that precedes it. The meaning constituted by the allegorical sign can then consist only in the *repetition* (in the Kierkegaardian sense of the term) of a previous sign with which it can never coincide, since it is of the essence of this sign to be pure anteriority. ... allegory designates primarily a distance in relation to its own origin, and, renouncing the nostalgia and the desire to coincide, it establishes its language in the void of this temporal difference.
>
> (de Man 1983a, 207)

So far so good, if you think you can understand and accept this definition of allegory, including the wonderfully enigmatic phrase "*repetition* (in the Kierkegaardian sense of the term)." Just how did de Man read Kierkegaard on repetition? Not much evidence exists about that. The *Profession de foi* essay claims to show that this text is an allegory in the de Manian sense of the term, that is, something intralinguistic that crosses out or disqualifies any referential meanings, and something built unreadably on the void between sign and anterior sign, i.e., a sign that is "pure anteriority."

It looks to me as if those additional five pages in the manuscript, pages that so blunt the force of the sentence about the impossibility of reading, were added when de Man remembered his implicit promise to focus on the allegorical relation between religion and politics, as opposed to the relation between Rousseau's "theory of rhetoric and his religious thought" which leads to the climax of the essay in the printed version. He got himself in a jam, however, when he tried to make that shift. When he returned to the essay he may have seen that and have decided just to cut all those pages. Saying that, however, is of course pure speculation. Who knows what went on in de Man's mind when he went to work to write the final essay?

What was that jam? That at least can perhaps be identified from the words on the page, though the pages are among the densest, most condensed, and obscure that de Man wrote, which is saying quite a lot. In the excised pages de Man begins by saying once more that "The deconstruction of rhetorical models that base the referential power of a language on a substantial relationship between sign and meaning (and thus on their implied polarity) [that would be "symbol" as defined in "The Rhetoric of Temporality"], is an invariant of Rousseau's thought. It articulates the political to the linguistic code in the *Second Discourse*" (de Man 2010, 132–33). De Man goes on to claim that this invariant structure can be found not only in the *Second Discourse*, but in *Julie*, in the second Preface to *Julie*—and in the *Profession de foi*.

In the paragraphs that follow de Man proposes, rather exceptionally, a metaphor of his own, or rather two metaphors if you include "double-faced." Someone who is two-faced is duplicitous. De Man makes a comparison between "the double-faced notion of referentiality that we keep discovering" (de Man 2010, 133), and the opposition between the busy world of society and the *hortus conclusus* of Julie's garden: "The topographical agitation < vagaries > of the first part of the *Nouvelle Heloïse* becomes the static and clearly marked-off < delimited > world of Clarens" (de Man 2010, 133). On the one hand, referentiality is so broad and so vague that it might refer to almost anything outside language. Referentiality is "transcendence" of the linguistic in general. On the other hand, it narrows down to "the finite horizon of a specific semantic 'space.' Like Julie's garden, it sets up a fence, and it provides the key with which the properly initiated readers can open the gate that leads into the privileged, private property of the referential meaning" (de Man 2010, 133). The sentences that follow define this narrowing down as a process of spatial and temporal movement and turning. This leads in turn to the sentences that contain the exceptional neologism, "theotropic." The four final pages then turn to the relation between religion and politics in Rousseau ("The possibility of practical action is inherently linked to the [fallacious] coinage of the word 'god'" [de Man 2010, 134].), and to the binary opposition between public person and private person that is of such enigmatic importance in Rousseau's political thought. Here are the theotropic sentences:

> As such, referentiality is constitutively metaphysical, in the Nietzschean sense of the term as taken over by Heidegger and his best French reader, Jacques Derrida. It is also constitutively theotropic, since the only

conceivable name for transcendental signification that would no longer be itself a sign, the only word that would have a truly proper meaning, is "god". The only "meaning that one can give the word to be" (Profession, p. 571) is that of "god". Yet, at the same time, the referentiality resulting from this paradigmatic denomination must lead to the performance of a finite, practical or, as we say, "historical" act—such as, for example, the acts performed or the emotion experienced by the readers of the second part of the *Nouvelle Heloïse* under the impact of their reading. The possibility of practical action is inherently linked to the (fallacious) coinage of the word "god". [This close relationship between practical action and transcendental meaning is what is referred to, in the *Social Contract,* as justice.] Hence the redoubtable instrumental effectiveness of any political action (conquest, colonization but also legislation) combined with religious faith.

(de Man 2010, 134)

These sentences have such clarity and power that one understands why he named the essay "Theotropic Allegory." Reading them also leads the thoughtful reader to wonder why de Man cut them and did not, so far as I know, use them elsewhere. Here are my guesses at the over-determined reasons why.

One reason: the powerful metaphor of the opposition between the space of vagary, wandering, and the space of the locked garden violates two of de Man's prohibitions. One is the prohibition against spatial as against temporal thinking. The other is the prohibition against metaphors in general. Always fallacious judgement in Rousseau is said again and again to depend on false metaphorical comparisons and claimed similarities between things that are fundamentally unlike. Here is de Man himself doing just what he condemns so forcefully and persuasively, and claims, in the printed part of the essay, that Rousseau deconstructively condemns. It looks to me as if he is inadvertently proving his dictum, already cited, about the reader or critic: "Deconstructive readings can point out the unwarranted identifications achieved by substitution, but they are powerless to prevent their recurrence even in their own discourse, and to uncross, so to speak, the aberrant exchanges that have taken place. Their gesture merely reiterates the rhetorical defiguration that caused the error in the first place" (de Man 1979, 242). De Man may have realized he had been caught in the trap he had described and so erased the evidence of that in the printed version. He always just smiled enigmatically when students asked him how he could claim to escape the fatal misreadings he ascribed to others and claimed were inescapable.

This may also be the case with the sentences that contain the word "theotropic." We understand what is meant by saying any judgement is only a sign, such as the signs that compare narrowed-down reference to an enclosed garden. We also understand what is meant by saying such a reference is a "movement of transgression or transcendence" that "turns always again into a signification that radically differs from it by its (fallacious) claim < of > to be a meaning" (de Man 2010, 134). Another way to put this would be to say that a judgement, based on a baseless metaphor, is a performative enunciation that creates the appearance of the pre-existence, external to language, of what it actually creates by the fiat of a speech act. "Metaphysics," in the sense the word has, in different ways in each case, for Nietzsche, Heidegger, and Derrida, is a name for the age-old system of ideological mystification that Derrida calls "logocentrism." This is the assumption that a pre-existing "logos" or "Being," *Sein*, is at the basis and origin of all beings. De Man's climactic claim, however, is that this movement of fallacious transgression or transcendence is "also constitutively theotropic." At one level, this is a shorthand version of Marx and Engels' claim, in *The German Ideology*, referred to by de Man in a famous put-down of what today we call "cultural studies" (see my epigraph from "The Resistance to Theory"), that the basis of all ideological mystifications in Western culture is the Christian belief in the Incarnation, in which divine spirit, the Word, the Logos, became matter (Marx and Engels 1976, 152–60). Commodity fetishism is secretly a form of belief in the Incarnation.

In the reference to *The German Ideology* cited in my epigraph, de Man accuses the opponents of literary theory of being "very poor readers of Marx's *German Ideology*." What would it mean to be a good reader of Marx (such as, he insinuates, de Man himself is)? Though de Man never wrote directly about *The German Ideology*, I claim the section about "theotropic allegory" I am discussing gives the answer. It brilliantly employs the same mode of critical reading that Marx and Engels use to "deconstruct" Max Stirner, as well as Ludwig Feuerbach and Bruno Bauer. This includes a use of ironic parody that is one of de Man's chief tools of rhetorical reading. De Man may have learned that from Marx. Marx is, among other things, a devastatingly funny writer in ridiculing his opponents and in making them look like idiots. I shall discuss de Man's irony in the second section of this essay.

One could make a better case for claiming that de Man was a socialist, in the old-fashioned nineteenth-century sense, or even a Marxist of sorts, than one can for saying he was a Nazi sympathizer. He once told me, for whatever my testimony is worth, that he did not need to lose his Christian faith, since he was brought up in a non-churchgoing Belgian family that had been socialist and anti-clerical for generations. De Man, however, was neither what we call a "vulgar Marxist," nor a sophisticated one like Louis Althusser. For example he evidently doubted, as against what Marx apparently believed, that a change in the material bases of society would alter the ideological superstructure, the fatal duplicity of language that generates history. *Die Sprache verspricht (sich)* ("Language (falsely) promises and at the same time makes a slip of the tongue."), for de Man, would still be true in any conceivable social order. I shall discuss this phrase further later in this essay. De Man did, however, I speculate, learn a lot about rhetorical reading from being a good reader of *The German Ideology*. A full reading of the long section of *The German Ideology* (Marx and Engels 1976, 117–450) on Max Stirner, whom Marx derisively calls "Saint Max,"[4] in its relation to de Man's procedures of rhetorical reading in his Rousseau essays, would be a lengthy, though rewarding, task. Doing that, however, is beyond the scope of this essay. A productive presupposition for such a reading might be the hypothesis that as Marx is to Stirner, so de Man is to Rousseau. Deciding whether that hypothesis is true or false, or partly true, would require that "full reading." It might be one of those metaphorical comparisons that produces structures that are aberrantly referential linguistic substitutions.

De Man dismantles (or does he?) mystified belief in the Incarnation in all its incarnations by arguing that all referentiality is theotropic. Whatever a referential judgement appears to name is, says de Man, only a covert trope for God. The word "theotropic" has a double meaning. It can mean both turned toward God, and, since a trope is a substitution, turned away from God, apotheotropically, toward some specific semantic referent that is a cryptic cover for God, a hiding of God. You can be a commodity fetishist, as we all are under capitalism, without being consciously a Christian, but commodity festishism, at least in the West, is a derived form of belief in the Incarnation. The fetishized object, a certain fashionable automobile or running shoe, for example, is experienced as the concrete embodiment of spiritual value.

De Man's expression of what he means by "theotropic," however, is curious, to say the least. Kenneth Burke, himself no mean reader of Marx, argued powerfully in a number of places that any system of language has what he called a "God term" (Burke 1945, 101–13, esp. 105), for example, the word "money" in capitalism, the word "honor" in medieval and Renaissance chivalry, or the word "gentleman" in Victorian novels and in Victorian class society, or, one might argue, the word "judgment" in the *Profession de foi*. Such terms are localized in a given culture and historical moment. "Such reduction to a simplicity," said Burke, "being technically reduction to a summarizing title or 'God term,' when we confront a simplicity we must forthwith ask ourselves what complexities are subsumed beneath it" (Burke 1945, 105). A god term is, for Burke, by no means necessarily the word "God." It is whatever word in a given language system that is the basis of the meaning of all the other words while not being definable itself by any of those words. You can tell when you have encountered a God term when someone says something like, "I can't define the word 'gentleman,' but I know one when I see one, and I can identify someone who is not a gentleman." Marx himself says something of the sort in a scornful formulation at the end of the long section on Max Stirner in *The German Ideology:* "This great problem ['the transition from thought to reality'], insofar as it at all entered the minds of our ideologists, was bound, of course, to result finally in one of those knights-errant setting out in search of a word which, as a *word*, formed the transition in question, which, as a word, ceases to be simply a word, and which, as a word, in a mysterious superlinguistic manner, points from within language to the actual object it denotes; which, in short, plays among words the same role as the Redeeming God-Man plays among people in Christian fantasy" (Marx and Engels 1976, 449).

The peculiarity of what de Man says about theotropic allegory, with however much or little irony, or with however much or little of just mimicking what he claims Rousseau says, is that he limits God terms to one single, sole, possibility, "the (fallacious) coinage of the word 'god.'" He does this, moreover, without explicit authority from Rousseau. Referentiality is constitutively theotropic, says de Man, to cite the crucial sentences again, "since the only conceivable name for a transcendent signification that would no longer be itself a sign [such as all words are in the sign/sign relation of allegory], the only word that would have a truly proper meaning [as opposed to all other words, that are tropes for the word "god" (my insertion: JHM)], is 'god.' The only 'meaning that one can give the word to be' (Profession, p. 571) is that of 'god'" (de Man 2010, 134). If one turns to page 571 in the volume of the Pléiade edition that contains Rousseau's *Profession de foi*, one finds no such thing. Rousseau says rather that what distinguishes man from other creatures is his ability to give a meaning to the word "is": "Selon moi la faculté distinctive de l'être actif ou intelligent est de pouvoir donner un sens à ce mot *est*" (Rousseau 1969, 571). ("According to me the distinctive faculty of the active or intelligent being is the power to give a meaning to this word 'is'" [my trans.].) Nothing whatsoever is said about God by Rousseau in this passage. Rather the reverse, since the power to give a meaning to the word "is" is said to be the basis of the ability, unique to man, to superimpose one sensation on another and say they are similar or the same, thereby creating the fallacious metaphors that are the basis of judgment. One might even say that the god term here is "is."

I conclude that by limiting god terms to the word "god," however "fallacious" he says that linguistic projection is, de Man has demonstrated, perhaps inadvertently, the truth of his own climactic proposition in the printed version about not taking the impossibility of reading too lightly. It is impossible to decide whether what de Man says by way of the word "theotropic" is theistic or not theistic. Does he really mean it or does he assert it only ironically when he says "the only word that would have a truly proper meaning is 'god'"? If de Man literally means what he says, without irony, then he is accepting the existence of a transcendent god who, as transcendent, is beyond wordplay. The name "god" literally names god. The word has a truly proper meaning, unlike all other words. If what de Man says is ironic, his assertion would mean that the word "god" fallaciously hypothesizes or performatively creates the illusion of an independently existing transcendent deity who would be above all wordplay.

In generating this uncertainty, de Man thereby demonstrates the truth of Derrida's reproach to Jean-Luc Nancy that it is impossible to deconstruct Christianity. It reforms itself out of the ruins of its *déclosion* or "dis-enclosure," or "dis-explosion" (Derrida 2000, 68; Derrida 2005, 54; Nancy 2005; Nancy 2008). The meaning of what de Man says about the way all referentiality is constitutively theotropic is undecidable, though the reader needs urgently to decide in order to know what use, if any, to make of de Man's procedures, or in order just to understand what he says. I also somewhat hesitantly hypothesize that this may have been what made de Man uneasy when he went back to this passage. This hypothetical uneasiness may then have led de Man to drop the whole five pages and change the title from "Theotropic Allegory" to "Allegory of Reading (*Profession de foi*)."

\*

What, at this stage of my chapter, can I say about the utility of reading literary theory and of using archival materials in aid of doing that better? I have shown that much is at stake in the section of de Man's *Allegories of Reading* on Rousseau's *Profession de foi*. If de Man is right in his claim that the "linguistics of literariness" is of more use than economics as a way of understanding ideology, his reading of Rousseau, with its culmination is his warning not to take unreadability lightly, and his subsequent, perhaps inadvertent, exemplification of that in the pages cut from the published version of the *Profession de foi* essay, may perhaps give the careful reader some understanding of why politicians are so given to telling lies, why their lies tend to use the rhetorical strategy of unwarranted metaphorical substitutions that are taken as referential truth, and why even when the lies are exposed they are repeated as though those who speak them were somnambulists.

In the interview of March 1983 by Stefano Rosso that followed the six Messenger Lectures de Man gave at Cornell in February and March 1983, less than a year before his death, de Man asserted that, "It was in working on Rousseau that I felt I was able to progress from purely linguistic analysis to questions which are really already of a political and ideological nature" (de Man 1986, 121). In a brilliant essay on the articulation (or disarticulation) of literary theory, philosophy, and politics in de Man's writings, Kevin Newmark has shown how the word "progress" in this statement clashes ironically with questionings in the Messenger Lectures themselves of progress, development, and articulation (Newmark 2009). Nevertheless, the Messenger Lectures, like the Rosso interview, work out in detail de Man's assumptions about how the linguistics of literariness can help understand politics and ideology.

One possible use studying literature and literary theory (including the detailed reading archival comparisons allow) might have, or ought to have, in these bad days is just that unmasking of ideological aberrations and an accounting for their occurrence de Man promises in the sentence cited in my epigraph. United States citizens are inundated these days with distortions and outright lies from politicians, the news media, and advertising on television and radio. Even my local Public Television station, supposedly objective, used to run, daily and repeatedly, an advertisement in which the giant oil company, Chevron, pro-motes itself under the slogan of "The Power of Human Energy." The phrase is solemnly intoned as the Chevron logo is shown. A moment's thought reveals that Chevron's interest is in energy from oil, not human energy. Chevron is devoted to getting as much money as it can (billions and billions of dollars a year) by extracting fossil fuels out of the earth and thereby contributing big time to global warming. The advertisement is a lie. Learning how to read literature "rhetorically" is primary training in how to spot such lies and distortions. This is so partly because so much literature deals thematically with imaginary characters who are wrong in their readings of others, for example, just to stick with one recurrent theme in British fiction, Elizabeth Bennett in her misreading of Darcy in Jane Austen's *Pride and Prejudice*, or Dorothea Brooke's misreading of Edward Casaubon in George Eliot's *Middlemarch*, or Isabel Archer's misreading of Gilbert Osmond in Henry James's *The Portrait of a Lady*.

Literature is also training in resisting lies and distortions in the skill it gives in understanding the way the rhetoric of tropes and the rhetoric of persuasion work, as de Man demonstrates in the various versions of the *Profession de foi* essay. Such expertise as literary study and the study of literary theory gives might be translated to a savvy resistance to the lies and ideological distortions politicians and talk show hosts promulgate, for example the lies of those who deny climate change, or the lying claims, believed in by a high percentage of Americans, that Barack Obama is a Muslim, a socialist, and not a legitimate president because he was not born in the United States. The motto for this defense of literary study might be the challenging and provocative claim made by Paul de Man in my epigraph from "The Resistance to Theory." Let me cite part of it again apropos of the point I am making at this stage of my essay: "What we call ideology," says de Man, "is precisely the confusion of linguistic with natural reality, of reference with phenomenalism. It follows that, more than any other mode of inquiry, including economics, the linguistics of litera-riness is a powerful and indispensable tool in the unmasking of ideological aberrations, as well as a determining factor in accounting for their occurrence" (de Man 1986, 11).

The chances that literary study would have this benign effect on all that many people are slim. One can only have the audacity of hope, and believe that some people who study literature and literary theory might be led to the habit of unmasking ideological aberrations such as those that surround us on all sides in the United States today. The chances are slim because it is difficult to transfer what you might learn by a careful reading, say, of *The Portrait of a Lady* to unmasking today's dominant ideologies. Such unmasking might lead a thoughtful person to conclude that he or she should only vote Republican if her or his income happens to be in the top two per cent of all Americans and if maximizing your wealth in the short term is your only goal, without concern for the long term consequences, even for yourself and your heirs.

Another great difficulty is the actual situation in American universities today. Derrida's *The University Without Condition* (Derrida 2001; Derrida 2002) force-fully argues that universities, and especially the divisions of humanities and law within the university, should be entirely without outside influence from gov-ernment or corporations. Professors should be free to put everything in ques-tion, even the right to put everything in question. In a proper university, the university *sans condition,* everything should be "up for grabs," as we say. Derrida's intransigent plea was not exactly greeted with shouts of joyful assent when he presented it as a lecture at Stanford. In spite of their lip-service to teaching so-called "critical thinking," the politicians and corporate executives who preside today over both public and private American colleges and universities are unlikely to support something that would put in question the assumptions on the basis of which they make decisions about who teaches what. They need colleges and universities these days, if at all, primarily to teach math and science, technology, engineering, computer science, basic English composition, and other skills necessary for efficient work in a technologized capitalist economy. The ability to do a rhetorical reading of *Pride and Prejudice*, much less of Marx's *The German Ideology* or of de Man's *Allegories of Reading* or of his "Theotropic Allegory," and then to transfer that skill to politicians' and advertisers' lies, is not one of those necessities.

*

I turn now to consideration of the other archival sequence, the one that goes from the two sets of notes for the "Task of the Translator" essay, to the tape of the oral presentation of this at Cornell, to the "edited" transcription of that by William Jewett, with help from Roger Blood, to the publication of that transcription in *The Resistance to Theory* as "Conclusions: Walter Benjamin's 'The Task of the Translator'" (de Man 1986, 73–105). What, if anything, can we learn from this sequence about the uses, if any, of Paul de Man's work today, at this moment of catastrophically accelerating global climate change; widespread species extinction, including possibly the human species, as our own suicidal actions make the planet more and more uninhabitable for us human beings too, not just for the polar bear; worldwide financial meltdown and the accompanying widespread unemployment and human misery likely to lead eventually to insurrections by the hopeless; the increasing world dominance of digital-mediatic-teletechnologies like the Internet; and, as a minor concomitant, the rapid meltdown of the "humanities" in our colleges and universities, as we in the humanities become more and more like one of those Pacific islands about to be inundated by rising ocean waters? "The humanities are a lost cause," one Harvard administrator, perhaps Lawrence Summers, is reported to have said. In this situation, who needs to read Paul de Man? What possible good could it accomplish, as our coastlines vanish and our cities are submerged, and nothing adequate is done, or appears at all likely to be done, to limit the $CO_2$ emissions that are changing the world's climate big time?

I have in my possession, as I said earlier, the notebook of spring 1983 in which de Man wrote two sets of notes for his Benjamin essay. The shorter set is headed "Benjamin (for Dupré)." The longer set, reproduced in facsimile and transcribed in this book, is headed "Benjamin (Dupré)." It was Louis Dupré, de Man's colleague at Yale, who had invited de Man to give such a lecture. It was presented at the Whitney Humanities Center in the spring of 1983, as well as at Cornell that same spring. I was present for the Yale version and can remember that what de Man said was not only a powerfully revisionary reading of Benjamin's essay, but was met with a good deal of resistance by members of the audience like Peter Demetz, as happened again at Cornell with scholars like Meyer Abrams, Dominick La Capra, and even Neil Hertz. De Man had (and his writings still have) a remarkable ability to send people up the wall. The scholars in question are not dumb-bells. They could see that something serious was at stake, such as much of the scholarly work they had done, if de Man happened to be right. Some weeks or months later, either late that spring or early the next fall, when I used to visit de Man once a week at his home where he lay on his deathbed (he died in December, 1983), I asked de Man if he had a copy of that lecture. He said it was never written out, but that I was welcome to have the notes. He then gave me the notebook. Eventually it will go into the de Man archive, but I am fetishistically keeping it—for the moment.

The first set of notes is six pages long, with an inserted page containing in de Man's handwriting the citation from Geoffrey Hartman that figures in the lecture (Hartman 1980, 78), as well as de Man's own translation of the segment of Benjamin's essay that culminates in the admiring allusion to Bloch's "Spirit of Utopia." A xerox of this set of notes was apparently available to Jewett. The second set of notes is eleven pages long and matches the published essay closely, with many passages written out. A xerox of Gandillac's French translation of Benjamin's essay is stuck in the pages. The two sets of notes are not dated, but they are sandwiched between notes for class lectures in "Lit 130," one of the three introductory courses for the Literature Major at Yale, and what appear to be notes for a graduate class on Diderot and Baudelaire, the last graduate class de Man gave. I suppose hypothetical dates might be determined from that placement. I can see why de Man thought I could reconstruct the lecture from the second set of very full notes.

Well, what is the difference between the notes and the published transcript? I shall work around to an answer to that question. "Conclusions: Walter Benjamin's 'The Task of the Translator'" is one of de Man's most challenging essays. It seems more and more challenging the more you think about it, read it and reread it. It characteristically begins with discussion of a couple of distinguished fall guys who are set up in order to be rather casually knocked down, in this case Hans-Georg Gadamer and Geoffrey Hartman. These worthies are stand-ins for the whole humanistic-messianic-phenomenological way of reading Benjamin. De Man's rhetorical strategy is to show that both, in different ways, argue that modernism has responded to the modern political and cultural situation and has gone beyond German idealism. Gadamer does this by claiming that we have lost four forms of naïveté present in idealism. Hartman does it by claiming that our sober view of history plus what Benjamin called our "weak messianism" (whatever, exactly, that means; it is not an easy concept to understand, for me at least) have made us better able to deal with our troubled modern times. On this basis, de Man can then assert that, "at first sight, Benjamin would appear as highly regressive. He would appear as messianic, prophetic, religiously messianic, in a way that may well appear to be a relapse into the naiveté denounced by Gadamer" (de Man 1986, 76). This apparent regression to a pre-idealist credulity is supported by Benjamin's seemingly admiring references to the prophetic view of poetry in Stefan George, in Friedrich Hölderlin, and even in Stephane Mallarmé, one of whose obscure pronouncements is cited (Benjamin 1969a, 64; Benjamin 1969b, 77). I think, by the way, that de Man perhaps exaggerates the degree to which Benjamin's essay can easily be taken as endorsing a vatic view of the poet as unmediated spokesperson for the divine *Geist*. Of course de Man is right to say that the essay has often been read that way, for example by Hartman and others. The reader will remember that the subtitle of Benjamin's "The Task of the Translator" is "An Introduction to the Translation of Baudelaire's *Tableaux Parisiens*." Benjamin's essay is prefatory to his fulfillment or non-fulfillment of one example of the task of the translator.

After this beguiling prefatory material, calculated to lull the listener into acquiescence, as well as dazzle them by de Man's knowledge of an obscure essay by Gadamer, not to speak of Hartman's then quite recent work, de Man draws himself up and asks "the simplest, the most naïve, the most literal of possible questions in relation to Benjamin's text, and we will not get beyond that: what does Benjamin say? What does he say, in the most immediate sense possible? It seems absurd to ask a question that is so simple, that seems to be so unnecessary … " (de Man 1986, 79). In the notebook, this is an underlined sentence: "What does B. actually say in this essay?" (de Man 1983b, 3). This is a characteristic move in de Man's teaching and writing. First make a plausible recapitulation of received opinion and then go on to show it is radically mistaken.

The answer to the question, "What does B actually say in this essay?", says de Man in the notes, is "very difficult to establish" (de Man 1983b, 3). One reason is that the standard translators into French and English "don't seem to have the slightest idea of what Benjamin is saying; so much so that when Benjamin says certain things rather simply in one way—for example he says that something is *not*—the translators, who at least know German well enough to know the difference between something *is* and something *is not*, don't see it! and put absolutely and literally the opposite of what Benjamin has said. This is remarkable … " (de Man 1986, 79). Yes, you can say that again. Two more of de Man's strategic targets, then, in addition to Gadamer and Hartman, are the translations of Benjamin's essay into French by Maurice de Gandillac and into English by Harry Zohn. Both know German extremely well, but that does not prevent them from over and over making Benjamin say the exact opposite of what he does say, making a yea into a nay, or vice versa. This suggests, among other things, that you must read Benjamin for yourself, in German, or trust de Man's improvised translations to be more accurate than the published translations. Another help is the quite literal translations of key passages, with the German juxtaposed, by Carol Jacobs in her brilliant essay, "The Monstrosity of Translation: Walter Benjamin's 'The Task of the Translator'" (Jacobs 1993). De Man refers admiringly to this essay, whose first publication in MLN preceded his own lecture.

The issue of translation's impossibility, ascribed to Benjamin himself, is constantly present in de Man's lecture, making that lecture like the serpent with its tail in its mouth. It does performatively what it talks about, that is, it manifests the impossibility of translation. Benjamin does not, strictly speaking, say translation is impossible. He says translation is always possible, though in different ways depending on the nature of the text to be translated, but that it always, in one way or another, fails, gives up, in another meaning than "task" for *Aufgabe*. The mistakes by the translators also imply that you or I, Demetz or Hertz, are also likely to be unable to read Benjamin's essay right, either by reading the original or by reading the misleading and failed translations. The translators, after all, had to look at the German text word by word and try to find French or English "equivalents." They ought to have noticed the absence of a *nicht* that turns yea into nay. How can we be sure we will not make similar errors? Ideological presumptions are so strong that they lead us to make a yes into a no. We cannot see clearly what the words on the page say. Ideological presuppositions blind readers.

What does de Man find when he tries to answer that naïve question: "What does Benjamin say?" Answering that fully would require a virtually interminable interlinear or marginal commentary, such as those the old Biblical commentators used to provide in the Middle Ages or Renaissance for the Bible, verse by verse. Benjamin mentions interlinear translation in the last sentence of his essay, and seems, though only "seems," to endorse it as an escape from the impossibility of translation (Benjamin 1969a, 69; Benjamin 1969b, 82). Not that de Man's essay is a sacred text. Far from it. I shall, however, provide a more or less succinct set of sequential, linked, and highly counter-intuitive propositions that de Man finds Benjamin asserting as the latter moves from stage to stage in his essay. They are counter-intuitive both in the sense that they go against what we think we know about translation and also in the sense that they go against what we think we know about what Benjamin says:

1  "No poem is intended for the reader, no picture for the beholder, no symphony for the listener" (Benjamin 1969a, 56; Benjamin 1969b, 69). There is a counter-intuitive proposition if there ever was one.
2  Translation, by definition, fails. *Aufgabe* should be understood not as meaning "task," but as meaning "giving up," as when a cyclist in the Tour de France leaves the race, does not compete any more.
3  The translator is not like the poet, but more like the critical philosopher, or like the literary critic, or, strangest similarity, like history (not the historian). All four of these are secondary in relation to their object, as the translator is to what he or she translates. All four are intralinguistic in relation to their object, whereas the poet strives to say something about the extralinguistic "real world." Translation is like literary criticism or like literary theory in the sense that it de-canonizes the original, puts its authority in question.
4  Though the German word for translation is *Übersetzen*, which also means metaphor, the translation is not like the original, metaphorically or otherwise. "It is a curious assumption to say that *übersetzen* is not metaphorical, *übersetzen* is not based on resemblance, there is no resemblance between the translation and the original. Amazingly paradoxical statement, metaphor is not metaphor" (de Man 1986, 83).

5   As intralinguistic, translations "disarticulate, they undo the original, they reveal that the original was always already disarticulated" (de Man 1986, 84). They do this by relating the original to a pure language (*reine Sprache*). This pure language is not a sacred speech in the sense of an aboriginal language that we might imagine Adam and Eve to have spoken to one another before the Fall. It is rather a language of pure form that is "devoid of the burden of meaning" and that causes suffering, "'*die Wehen des eigenen*'—the suffering of what one thinks of as one's own" (de Man 1986, 84). This suffering is not so much birthpangs, as the translators erroneously have it, as it is death pangs. It is the suffering of a linguistic failure that Benjamin expresses in a famous passage about the way meaning, in Hölderlin's translations of two of Sophocles's plays, tumbles from abyss to abyss into the fathomless depths of language: "In ihnen stürtzt der Sinn von Abgrund zu Abgrund, bis er droht, in bodenlosen Sprachteifen sich zu verlieren" (Benjamin 1969a, 69; Benjamin 1969b, 82). De Man understands this abyss, however, "in the non-pathetic, technical sense in which we speak of a *mise en abyme* structure" (de Man 1986, 86). This structure makes translation always a failure: "The text about translation is itself a translation, and the untranslatablity which it mentions about itself inhabits its own texture and will inhabit anybody who in his turn will try to translate it, as I am now trying, and failing, to do" (de Man 1986, 86).

6   This failure derives from the incompatibility between *das Gemeinte*, what is meant, and *Art des Meinens*, the way the meaning is expressed. Far from being a matter of human intention, this incompatibility is a consequence of the inhumanity of language. Language "is as such not made by us as historical beings, it is perhaps not even made by humans at all. Benjamin says, from the beginning, that it is not at all certain that language is in any sense human" (de Man 1986, 87). That is a truly scandalous proposition, one that, if true, would have far-reaching consequences. Language, it may be, is not in any sense human! The different connotations of the German word *brot* and the French word *pain,* "bread" in English, are examples of this lack of human control over language. This is Benjamin's example, picked up and expanded by de Man (Benjamin 1969a, 61; Benjamin 1969b, 74; de Man 1986, 87). As de Man says elsewhere, in a famous formulation, it is not so much that *die Sprache spricht* ("Speech speaks"), as Heidegger says, as that *die Sprache verspricht (sich)* (de Man 1979, "Promises [*Social Contract*]," 277). Language misspeaks. It makes a slip of the tongue, or it makes promises it cannot keep. *Versprechen (sich)* is an antithetical word or reflexive phrase that says these two contradictory things at once: "promise" and "make a slip of the tongue." It thereby exemplifies the inhuman duplicity of language. De Man puts this as follows: "This model is a fact of language over which Rousseau himself [de Man's essay is about Rousseau's 'Social Contract'] has no control. Just as any other reader, he is bound to misread his text as a promise of political change. The error is not within the reader; language itself dissociates the cognition from the act. *Die Sprache verspricht (sich)*; to the

extent that is necessarily misleading, language just as necessarily conveys the promise of its own truth. This is why textual allegories on this level of rhetorical complexity generate history" (de Man 1979, 277). The mechanical uncontrollable duplicity of language makes history happen, willy-nilly, whatever people may want or intend to have happen.

7   This duplicity means that hermeneutics and poetics can never be reconciled:

> When you do hermeneutics, you are concerned with the meaning of the work; when you do poetics, you are concerned with the stylistics or with the description of the way in which the work means. The question is whether these two are complementary, whether you can cover the full work by doing hermeneutics and poetics at the same time. The experience of trying to do this shows that this is not the case. When one tries to achieve this complementarity, the poetics always drops out, and what one always does is hermeneutics. One is so attracted by problems of meaning that it is impossible to do hermeneutics and poetics at the same time. From the moment you start to get involved with problems of meaning, as I unfortunately tend to do, forget about the poetics. The two are not complementary, the two may be mutually exclusive in a certain way, and that is part of the problem which Benjamin states, a purely linguistic problem.
>
> (de Man 1986, 88)

> If de Man is right about this incompatibility, I might point out, it would be a disaster for the ordinary academic project of literary study. Some inkling of this may explain why mimetic, representational investigations of literature these days have said about poetics and literary theory: "Forget it." At stake in this incompatibility is the disjunction between *Wort* and *Satz*, between the materiality of the letter and meaning. This disjunction "means" that "all control over that meaning is lost" (de Man 1986, 89).

8   This assertion leads de Man, with the acknowledged help of Carol Jacobs's admirably exigent essay about Benjamin's essay (Jacobs 1993, esp. 136–37, 225–26), to a quite original reading of the famous metaphor in Benjamin's essay comparing the original text and its translation to the fragments of a pot. Far from seeing this as an organic metaphor posited on some presumed totality, the sacred *reine Sprache*, de Man sees original and translation as fragments that remain fragments and that are juxtaposed metonymically rather than being metaphorically similar:

> ... the fragments are fragments, and ... they remain essentially fragmentary, They follow each other up, metonymically, and they will never constitute a totality. ... What we have here is an initial fragmentation; any work is totally fragmented in relation to this *reine Sprache*, with which it has nothing in common, and every translation is totally fragmented in relation to the original. The translation is the fragment of a fragment, is breaking the

fragment—so the vessel keeps breaking, constantly—and never reconstitutes it; there was no vessel in the first place, or we have no knowledge of this vessel, or no awareness, no access to it, so for all intents and purposes there has never been one."

(de Man 1986, 91)

Just here a subtle difference between de Man and Benjamin may possibly be glimpsed. Benjamin often sounds as if he believes a *reine Sprache* really exists, as something toward which all languages point, as when he says "that which seeks to represent, to produce itself in the evolving of languages, is that very nucleus of pure language (Benjamin 1969b, 79). ["Und was im Werden der Sprachen sich darzustellen, ja herzustellen sucht, das ist jener Kern der reisen Sprache selbst" (Benjamin 1969a, 66–67).] De Man, on the other hand, leans more toward asserting that the *reine Sprache* does not exist as a separate entity. "Least of all is there something like a *reine Sprache*, a pure language, which does not exist," he says, "except as a permanent disjunction which inhabits all languages as such, including and especially the language one calls one's own. What is to be one's own language is the most displaced, the most alienated of all" (de Man 1986, 92). The difference between Benjamin and de Man is perhaps a nuance, but it is an important nuance.

9  The consequences of unavailability of the *reine Sprache* are a) that history is not human, because it pertains strictly to the order of language, which de Man argues, following Benjamin, is not a human creation; b) that neither history nor poetry is sacred or messianic. "It is within this negative knowledge of its relation to the language of the sacred that poetic language initiates. It is, if you want, a necessarily nihilistic moment that is necessary in any understanding of history" (de Man 1986, 92).

De Man may just here deviate a little from what Benjamin actually says. I think Carol Jacobs is right to say that Benjamin identifies only ironically *reine Sprache*, pure language, with sacred language, the Word or Logos in John's Gospel (Jacobs, 1993, 141). Benjamin's *reine Sprache*, as he more than once affirms, is a pure speech toward which all languages point, but it is pure in the sense of being absolutely meaningless. Here is one of Benjamin's most intransigent affirmations of the meaninglessness of the *reine Sprache*. I cite Carol Jacobs's approximately interlinear translation:

> To win back pure language formed in the flux of language is the violent and single power of translation. In this pure language—which no longer means anything and no longer expresses anything—but which, as expressionless and productive word, is that which is meant in all languages—all communication, all meaning, and all intention ultimately meet with a stratum in which they are destined to extinction.

(Jacobs 1993, 135)

[Die reine Sprache gestaltet in der Sprachbewegung zurückzugewinnen, ist das gewaltige und einzige Vermögen der Übersetzung. In dieser reinen Sprache, die nichts mehr meint une nichts mehr ausdrückt, sondern als ausdruckloses und schöpferisches Wort das in allen Sprachen Gemeinte ist, trifft endlich alle Mitteilung, aller Sinn und alle Intention auf eine Schicht, in der sie zu erlöschen bestimmt sind.

(Benjamin 1969a, 67)]

Benjamin means by "intention" here, as elsewhere in his essay, not the conscious aim of some ego or subjectivity, but rather is echoing the Husserlian or phenomenological use of the word as naming the orientation of a sign toward its meaning. Benjamin's pure language is perhaps closer to Derrida's *trace* or *archi-trace* in *Of Grammatology* (*De la grammatologie*) (Derrida 1997, 46–47, 61–63, 65; Derrida 1967, 68–69, 90–92; 95), though not quite identical to it, than it is to the sacred language of Holy Scripture. De Man's take on *reine Sprache* as "a permanent disjunction which inhabits all languages as such" may be closer than Benjamin is to Derrida's notion of *archi-trace* as not existing except as pure *différance*: "*The trace is in fact the absolute origin of sense in general. Which amounts to saying once again that there is no absolute origin of sense in general. The trace is the différance which opens appearance* [*l'apparaître*] *and signification*" (Derrida 1997, 65, italics in original). ["*La trace est en effet l'origine absolue du sens en général. Ce qui revient à dire, encore une fois, qu'il n'y a pas d'origine absolue du sens en général. La trace est la différance qui ouvre l'apparaître et la signification*" (Derrida 1967, 95, italics in original).] The differences among Benjamin, de Man, and Derrida are, as I have said, subtle, evasive nuances, but important ones.

Two other biblical passages, in addition to the opening words of the Gospel of John cited by Benjamin, hover over both Benjamin's essay and de Man's lecture about it. Neither cites these passages, so they remain unspoken, offstage. One is the story of the confusion of tongues by Jehovah that prevented the completion of the Tower of Babel (Genesis 11: 1–9). This is the biblical explanation of why so many different languages exist. The other passage is the repair of that confusion when the gift of tongues was bestowed on the apostles at Pentecost, so they could go forth throughout the world to preach the Christian Gospel (Acts 2: 1–12). The spread of Christianity has depended on the assumption that the Bible can be translated into all languages. That effort continues to this day. Benjamin seems to agree that the Bible is pre-eminently translatable.

Surely Benjamin does not mean, however, as a precondition of that translatability, that the Bible is meaningless? Or does he? It sometimes sounds as if he does, but at other times, sometimes in the same sentence, he speaks of Scripture as containing dogma and truth. An example is the famous sentence that Gandillac mistranslated, putting a no for a yes, "untranslatable" for "translatable": "Where a text is identical with truth or dogma, where it belongs to 'the true language' in all its literalness and without the mediation of meaning, this text is unconditionally translatable" (Benjamin 1969b 82, trans. altered).

[Wo der Text unmittelbar, ohne vermittelnden Sinn, in seiner Wörtlichkeit der wahren Sprache, der Wahrheit oder der Lehre angehört, ist er übersetzbar schlechthin" (Benjamin, 1969a, 69.)] For Benjamin, the superiority of translation over the original is that the translation approaches more closely the *reine Sprache* that means nothing. How a sacred text such as the Bible can simultaneously be identical with truth or dogma, *Lehre*, teaching, and at the same time be meaningless would take some explaining. It could be done, I suppose, by showing that what the Bible teaches is fathomlessly enigmatic, as often seems the case, as in the teachings of Jesus. Nevertheless, the Ten Commandments or Jesus's assertion that "If thou wilt be perfect, go and sell that thou hast, and give to the poor, and thou shalt have treasure in heaven" (Matt 19: 21) seem clear enough, however difficult it might be actually to obey the Commandments or to do what Jesus says.

Benjamin expresses the greater proximity of a translation to the *reine Sprache*, that is, to meaninglessness, in the figure of fruit and rind (for the relation in the original of content [*Gehalt*] to the art of stating that content) and in the figure of enveloping folds of a regal robe hiding the wearer (for that relation in translation):

> Unlike the words of the original, it is not translatable, because the relationship between content and language is quite different in the original and the translation. While content and language form a certain unity in the original, like a fruit and its skin, the language of the translation envelops its content like a royal robe with ample folds. For it signifies a more exalted language than its own and thus remains unsuited to its content, overpowering and alien.
>
> (Benjamin 1969b, 75)

> [Es ist nicht übertragbar wie das Dichterwort des Originals, weil das Verhältnis des Gehalts zur Sprache völlig verschieden ist in Original und Übersetzung. Bilden nämlich diese im ersten eine gewisse Einheit wie Frucht und Schale, so umgibt die Sprache der Übersetzung ihren Gehalt wie ein Königsmantel in weiten Falten. Denn sie bedeutet eine höhere Sprache als sie ist und bleibt dadurch ihrem eigenen Gehalt gegenüber unangemessen, gewaltig und fremd.]
>
> (Benjamin 1969a, 62)

About the status of the striking series of figures of speech that punctuate "The Task of the Translator"—the forest of language, the broken vessel, the tangent that touches the circle but at one point, the abyss beneath abyss, fruit and skin as against someone hidden in royal robes—there would be much to say, even in supplement to de Man's penetrating remarks in his Benjamin essay and elsewhere about symbolism and about the self-undoing of tropes. I refrain from that task, however, since my focus here is on the way, in de Man's essay on "The Task of the Translator," one by one the assumptions that critics like

Gadamer, Hartman, Abrams (and I) have made are somewhat scornfully dismantled. No wonder the lecture drove its Yale and Cornell audiences up the wall. What he said was truly hard to take. Neil Hertz, as the first questioner at Cornell, for example, went straight to the point and politely expressed his outrage by putting in question de Man's claims that language and history are "inhuman."

\*

All these scandalous propositions can be found in the longer, eleven page notebook version. As I have said, that is presumably why de Man thought I could reconstruct the lecture from the notes. What, then, is the difference? Why do we need the printed transcription of the tape rather than just the notes, which are, after all, in de Man's own hand, not at several removes? The printed version of the *Profession du foi* essay subtracts much material from the manuscript. The printed version of the "Task of the Translator" essay adds much to the manuscript notes.

What of most importance is missing from the notes, I claim, is essential. It is the pervasive irony of the spoken lecture. Almost no trace of that exists in the notes. Ironic formulations, however, are everywhere in the printed text. Here are some salient examples:

Having cited Benjamin's claim that "No poem is intended for the reader," de Man says, "You can see how this would have thrown them into a slight panic in Konstanz" (de Man 1986, 78). Konstanz is the home of *Rezeptions-ästhetik*, presided over in those days by Hans Robert Jauss and Wolfgang Iser.

Speaking of Benjamin's mentions of Stefan George, de Man says: "in George there was a claim made for the poet, again, as some kind of prophet, as a kind of messianic figure—George doesn't kid around with that, he sees himself at least as Virgil and Dante combined into one, with still quite a bit added to it if necessary—and therefore he has a highly exalted notion of the role of the poet, and incidentally of himself, and of the benefits that go with it" (de Man 1986, 77). The ironic formulation here is not in the notes. The hyperbolic inflation in the oral presentation makes George's claims sound absurd, as they are. You will remember that de Man at the end of his essay claims that this is just the view of the poet that Benjamin rejects.

A little later de Man asserts that the passage he has cited from Geoffrey Hartman refers to

> a historical concept which then dovetails, which injects itself into an apocalyptic, religious, spiritual concept, thus marrying history with the sacred in a way which is highly seductive, highly attractive. It is certainly highly attractive to Hartman, and one can understand why, since it gives one both the language of despair, the language of nihilism, with the particular rigor that goes with that; but, at the same time, hope! So you have it all: you have the critical perception, you have the possibility of carrying on in apocalyptic tones, you have the particular eloquence that comes with that (because one can only really get excited if one writes in an apocalyptic

mode); but you can still talk in terms of hope, and Benjamin would be an example of this combination of nihilistic rigor with sacred revelation.

(de Man 1986, 78–79)

The illusory possibility of a "marriage" of history and the apocalyptical-religious "seduces" Hartman, makes him really "excited." Again, the ironic undercutting of Hartman was added in the oral presentation.

The whole paragraph about asking "the most naïve, the most literal of possible questions in relation to Benjamin's text" (de Man 1986, 79) is steeped in irony. Far from being a naïve question, it is the most serious, the most devastating question one can ask of any text: "Stand, and unfold yourself," as Hartman puts it, citing *Hamlet*. "Tell me what you are really saying."

At the end of that paragraph de Man has great ironic fun with the hapless translators who cannot tell the difference between "Ich gehe nach Paris" and "Ich gehe nicht nach Paris." One wonders why Paris. Why did that particular joke come into de Man's mind that day in Ithaca, New York? He used to "gehen nach Paris" from Belgium during the war.

On the next page de Man in the lecture has some more ironic fun, this time by saying that he is sure Derrida could cover up his error made by following in a Paris seminar Gandillac's mistaken translation (Gandillac had put "untranslatable" for "translatable") by saying they are the same: "I'm sure Derrida could explain that it was the same … [Then de Man draws himself and adds:] and I mean that in a positive sense, it *is* the same, but still, it is not the same without some additional explanation" (de Man 1986, 80). Derrida was right, it seems, but without knowing it, by the accident of following a mistaken translation.

In the next paragraph, speaking of Benjamin's belief that translation always fails because it is secondary, de Man says, "The translator can never do what the original text did. Any translation is always second in relation to the original, and the translator as such is lost from the very beginning. He is per definition underpaid, he is per definition overworked, he is per definition the one history will not really retain as an equal" (de Man 1986, 80). Note the sexism, by the way, of those "he's." Lots of translators are "she's" rather than "he's," probably per definition paid even less than their male counterparts and even less frequently retained by history as an equal.

Later, speaking of the mistranslation of *Wehen* as "birth pangs," de Man says, "this is a magnificent moment, you'd be willing to suffer (especially easy for us to say)" (de Man 1986, 85). I suppose he means it is perhaps easy for us men to take birth pangs lightly.

Fewer of these ironic moments appear later on in the lecture, when de Man got down to the serious business of trying to identify what Benjamin really said, though "forget about the poetics" (de Man 1986, 88) as a way of describing the inevitable victory of hermeneutics over poetics, of *das Gemeinte* over the *Art des Meinens*, is a late example.

Well, so what? Might one not argue that these little ironic jokes, which will remind those who ever heard de Man lecture of his characteristic tone, are just there to add to the informality and to put his audience at their ease? Or might one argue that irony is primarily an intersubjective feature of language, a feature of direct address, so it does not appear in the notes, where he is writing for himself? I do not think either of these explanations is correct. Irony, for de Man in "The Concept of Irony," can be a feature of any sort of language, written, spoken, digitized, or whatever. "[I]rony," says de Man, "is the permanent parabasis of the allegory of tropes" (de Man 1996, 179), in whatever linguistic medium that occurs. De Man's irony is used primarily in the spoken version of de Man's lecture to ridicule the received opinions he is trying to confute. He uses irony as a weapon in that warfare. In a strikingly counter-intuitive and apparently contradictory assertion in his essay on Friedrich Schlegel, "The Concept of Irony" (also only available as the transcript of a taped lecture), de Man ascribes a powerful performative force to irony: "Irony also very clearly has a performative function. Irony consoles and it promises and it excuses. It allows us to perform all kinds of performative linguistic functions which seem to fall out of the tropological field, but also to be very closely connected with it" (de Man 1996, 165). Irony makes things happen. If de Man goes on to define irony, modifying Schlegel, in the cryptic phrase I have already cited, as "the permanent parabasis of the allegory of tropes," the claim that irony can pervade a whole discourse and permanently suspend ascription of any univocal meaning to it would seem to disable any performative force irony might have. How can it be a felicitous performative if we do not even know what it says?

The answer of course is that irony is performative just because it permanently suspends meaning in a prolonged hovering undecidability such as I have found in de Man's essay on the *Profession de foi.* How that allows irony to console, promise, and excuse might take some lengthy explaining, but the upshot would be that these particular performatives depend on the uncertainty of what Austin called their "uptake." You can never be sure a consolation will work, or that a promise will be fulfilled, and we know from de Man's "Excuses (*Confessions*)" that excuses never excuse. They just repeat the crime that required the excuse in the first place. In the case of de Man's "Conclusions: Walter Benjamin's 'The Task of the Translator,'" the ironies I have identified in it function to ridicule and therefore disable the forms of "aesthetic ideology" he wanted to exorcise in order to make way for his quite original (except for Carol Jacobs's essay) reading of Benjamin's "*Die Aufgabe des Übersetzers.*"

Of course, these mystifications inevitably reform themselves out of their ruins. They rise from their ashes. The other side of the irony is that what beguiled Hartman really *is* "seductive," for you and me too, as is the Georgian notion that poetry is sacred, prophetic. Heidegger, notably, was seduced by the latter in his readings of Hölderlin. Which of us can claim not to be the least bit attracted and seduced, for straight men, by that beautiful lady, or, for straight women, by that handsome prince—aesthetic ideology?

Irony's redoubtable performative force cannot succeed in permanently banishing aesthetic ideology. It even comes back in de Man's own language toward the end of the Benjamin essay. Having said firmly that no such thing as *reine Sprache* in the sense of a sacred language exists, de Man nevertheless goes on a few sentences later to paraphrase Benjamin, apparently without irony (though how could you be sure?), as saying "*reine Sprache*, the sacred language, has nothing in common with poetic language; poetic language does not resemble it, poetic language does not depend on it, poetic language has nothing to do with it" (de Man 1986, 92).

*

I conclude by claiming that study of the various versions of de Man's writings by way of the Archive does really help us to understand de Man. Well, so what? Why is that important now, when we have other things to worry about, from the melting of the Arctic icecap to global financial meltdown to the meltdown of the humanities? My shorthand answer is that de Man was prophetically aware of the way assumptions about "the human" and about related concepts such as pan-organicism can get us in big trouble. Paradigmatic within aesthetic ideology is the assumption that language is human and within human control, whereas language, as de Man patiently showed by way of what Benjamin is really saying, is an inhuman machine. Language is a machine that, performatively, *verspricht (sich)*, falsely promises and contradicts itself at the same time.

We have been beguiled, mystified, and bamboozled for centuries and millennia by a fetishism of the organic, most recently from the idolizing of organic unity in a good poem in romanticism up through more of the same in the new criticism to the present-day ideology of the human body in cultural studies and feminism as an escape from the abstractions of theory, with somewhere in the background the assumption that since language is human, language too must be an organic system; from the prizing of "organic" foods to present-day ecocriticism with its idea that the whole earth or the creation as a whole may be a vast organism ("Mother Earth"); all the way up to some hope that the Internet, as a prosthetic appendage to the human body, may also be a form of the organic, just as perhaps the global financial system may be organic, with its "toxic assets" that are like poisons in a human body.

All these organic metaphors, de Man suggests, as do I, are colossal ideological mistakes, the aberrant hypostatization of a metaphor. They are fueling our fallacious assumptions, these days, that we ought just to get finance capitalism back on track and all will be well, or that global climate change might be reversed with some carbon cap laws, or that the humanities can be returned to their former glory. The human or animal body, language, a poem, the financial system, the planet, the universe, the global ecotechnical new communications systems into which we are all, or almost all, these days plugged—all these should more properly be thought of as elaborately interconnected machines that just go on operating blindly according to built-in programs. These machines are out of our control, like robots gone mad, large versions of Kafka's Odradek (Kafka 1919; Kafka 2007), even if we have ourselves constructed a given machine, such as the Internet, or have, by way of our "quants," young mathematico-financial wizards, devised those computer programs that spin out worthless credit default swaps in "tranches" and "tranches of tranches." I suppose the French word "*tranche*" is used because it sounds more benign than "slice."

The human genome, with its inborn "bugs" (note the organic metaphor transferred to an automatic genetic program), might provide an excellent model for these self-acting machinal programs. The genome just does what its protein-reproducing templates tell it to do. All these machines, moreover, come equipped with an inherent auto-immune technology that will lead them sooner or later, inch by inch or all at once, catastrophically, to self-destruct, as the human immune system, generated by the genome, may destroy the body it controls, in auto-immune diseases, or as the Antarctic or Greenland or glacial ice worldwide may suddenly collapse rather than slowly melt, as is now happening. Reading Paul de Man, dead since 1983, may conceivably help us to understand all this by some set of sideways displacements or articulating transfers.

Do I think understanding the looming meltdowns will help avoid them? I doubt it. The human propensity for collective species suicide is too great, as in the disappearance of our cousins, the Neanderthals, or of the great Mayan culture, or of the Anastazi. But at least we may have a clearer understanding as the water rises up to our chins. The Mayan hieroglyphs for Christ's words on the cross, "My God, my God, why hast thou forsaken me," spell out, disturbingly, when translated literally back into English, at least according to a possibly fictive passage in a mystery story my wife has read but can no longer identify, "Sinking. Sinking. Black ink over nose." All the ink we have spilt will only add to the flood, but it is better, I claim, more human-inhuman, to know what is happening than to be naïvely surprised by the rising waters. Paul de Man's writings are a great help with that, though not at all a reassuring help.

# 2 Toxic assets

## de Man's remains and the ecocatastrophic imaginary (an American fable)

*Tom Cohen*

### Like nuclear waste in the deep sea

> This is the end game of our system. Our system is basically exhausted. Our authorities try to prolong the good times that we have been in for several decades by printing paper money, by going into more debt, etc., etc., to support the system and get it growing. But it won't get back to where we've come from. ... [A]nd the owners of those nominal values over the next ten years or so will be the big losers.
>
> Felix Zulauf, *Business Insider* (Zulauf 2010)

> One can say that, following the brief and violent return of Paul de Man after his death, thinking in America—or the quasi-mythical ambience that makes one sense the advent of thought—took a nosedive. I am not saying that everyone in the academic precincts suddenly became stupid (or that de Man was simply the opposite of stupid), but his ghost took something down with it ...
>
> Avital Ronell, *Stupidity* (Ronell 2002, 105)

Perhaps, there is something about *currency* in the recyclable genealogies of the "present" that creates a parallel to the financial vortex in the credit and credibility markets—including that of critical thought, whose primary claim is always not to be deceived.[1] The Ponzi scheme of the 2008 credit collapse indexed to projecting megadebt onto a deferred future, one that would be simultaneously drained of reserves and resources, has curious parallels with the "post-theory" moment of the critical market place. The smart money today tends to congregate in communal and phenomenological hedge-funds, doubling down in received discourse ideals and invested in master-texts, slow to turn to the new referentials of 21st century horizons. The particular forms of 20th century theotropisms of the human, the community, sovereignty, or the market merge with cognitive reflexes to double-down in self-extending programs. These "new" horizons (or ones which no cultural memory accommodates as reference) include: an imponderable *materiality* outside of the concept itself that is the domain of, say, "climate change," biomorphic and punctuated by mass extinction events passively incurred, an *irreversible* if cognitively delayed erasure of "life as we know it" (a worn phrase that deserves pages of commentary).

There is a kind of stupor that descends on reciting what is at once too apparent yet virtually bracketed as well today—a fascinating awareness of an exitless disjuncture between numbers, calculable futures, social logics and those of a materiality of the biosphere. America has become, in its way, the very poster child of this, and there are too many analyses available of its imperial unraveling, corporate feudal envelopment, post-democratic telecracies, and infantilization to require retelling.[2] It remains, nonetheless, a spectacle of cognitive impasses and, again, *disjunctures*. It is bankrupt and captured by rogue financial acceleration—deferring a collapse of the dollar's "sovereignty"—yet gives itself massive tax cuts; its military plans for climate wars while its senators mock the non-existence of climate change; it has no funds to restore a decaying infrastructure or plan beyond the appearance of peak oil (possibly, three to five years).[3] The dark prognosticators from outside our cognitive bubble point not only to what has become a sort of disaster-porn mantra, to what lies outside its perceptual vortices: to irreversible global heating and coastal inundation and calculation of megadrought, mass extinction events, agricultural collapse, resource wars, and late century "population culling." Such logics could still be called, in a sense shorn of conceptual binaries, *material* ones, like the $CO_2$ count, indifferent to man as geological time is to innumerable life-forms and extinction events.[4]

Was there a question, then, as to whether de Man had performed "deconstruction's" own death *productively*, or whether the latter would pass over that as an inauspicious roadbump in order to continue to weave a lasting, *hospitable* network? That would be a good survival strategy—counting on the heart of the institutional humanities to embed it as hosts (*the* theological, *the* ethical, *the* political). But in a way that one can only see today, perhaps, it would misfire. That is, if instead of an open future, a more monstrously banal future would disclose itself before which "9/11" appears a politically calculated distraction. It is a prospect that the theoretical mastertexts of the 20th century did not, strictly, anticipate. In this context, the *abjected de Man*, relinquished because he seemed to have turned against the anthropic "irreversibly" would appear to be indexed as something like a hermeneutic traitor to his species.[5]

*Scene 1:* Let's rewind. The year is 1989 and Derrida is caught in a bind. He had walked into a trap of his own making with his defense-nondefense of Paul de Man in his *Critical Inquiry* response to the "wartime journalism" flap, "Like a Shell in the Deep Sea: Paul de Man's War." (Derrida 1988) A swarm of critical hitmen responds, from whom Derrida, in "Biodegradables," the follow-up piece, finally just turns away. He describes the attack, just to recall the episode in its full savour and resonance:

> in the face of murderous caricatures, abusive simplifications, unjustified acts of violence by those … who have spoken out loud their dream of destroying once and for all the memory of de Man, of his work, and of all that can associate with him from near and from far.

> (Derrida 1989, 841)

It is "a scalp dance" (852). One of his responses will be to parody and outbid this desire to erase, to "purge" or occlude—by dropping de Man in the sea as "nuclear waste" outside the "ecosystem," with a remainder that would be indeterminable. The gesture will mark or even help produce the phenomenon of the *dead de Man* or the *abject de Man*, a figure all but suspended from the theory episode or trajectory closing out the 20th century.

May one re-inspect the logic of all this, at a remove and from the advantage or disadvantage of a certain "today"—let's say, the very different referentials of a 21st century traversed by other *materialities*, metrics, aporia, and temporalities (geological, say, or biomorphic)? If part of de Man's *abjection*—and not only by the moral brotherhood but, eventually, Derrida—were due to a certain *materiality* he was driven to solicit, and this "irreversibly" (a term central in his Messenger Lectures), a different toxicity need be addressed in the zone of occlusion in which one had last placed "de Man."[6]

But we are still in 1989. Derrida will mime the attacks on de Man in unusual terms, by drawing upon ecological and eco-catastrophic terminology. In fact, placing the "thing," de Man, outside the "ecosystem" (here, the archival one of libraries, reading networks), Derrida positions his "de Man" in the one domain he, Derrida, will never address or choose to—a lack some find puzzling today: the domain, aporia, and impasses of the eco-catastrophic, of the so-called "ecological crisis."[7] The lack is troubling to some, who wonder how the pre-ponderant horizons of transformation of the 21st century, the biospheric mutations of a closing hydro-carbon era with its entirely different time-lines and agency, had not made it into Derrida's work, which addressed almost everything else. This gesture of occlusion—of de Man, of "materiality," of climate change as a horizon—marks the strategy Derrida would adapt subse-quently. That is, the production of a "late Derrida," so called, that would purge *deconstruction*, on one level, of the clichés that seemed to have entrapped de Man, fairly or not. This adjustment resonates, still, in the recuperations and inertias of the *après-Derrida*, what sometimes calls itself "deconstruction" as a sort of family concern or corporate will to canonization.[8] Many have remarked, sympathetically, a spell of mourning, legacy-mongering, Vatican-like orthodoxies, various *naturalizations*. The resulting "deconstruction" appears, above all, to have difficulties orienting toward these other horizons, apparently since Derrida left no instructions or template or marked for himself a limit of the anarchival. What is ironic is that this *excluded* domain into which de Man would be dropped or disappeared, as if in order for Derrida to stage an aporetics of hos-pitality, an ethics of undecidability, "the democracy to come" or the prosthetics of religion, appears, as against these last, to define the coming century increas-ingly. That is, a *materiality* outside the conceptual narratives left over as remainder or waste of the great legacy from 20th century thought, a force outside of any model of sovereignty.

Derrida places his "de Man" in this choice chain of eco-catastrophic metaphors. The latter will be likened in "Biodegradables" not only to "nuclear waste," but to *oil* ("at the bottom of the little bit of oil remaining, a black stain" (1989, 819)), to what is cast outside the (literary) "ecosystem," to a "minuscule simulacrum of nucleo-literary waste" (866), to the (non)biodegradable, and so on:

> Yes, to condemn the dead man to death: they would like him *not to be dead* yet so they could put him to death (preferably along with a few of the most intolerable among the living). To put him to death this time without remainder. Since that is difficult, they would want him to be *already dead without remainder*, so that they can put him to death without remainder. Well, the fact is he is dead (they will no longer be able to do anything in order to kill him), and there are remains, something surviving that bears his name. Difficult to decipher, translate, assimilate. Not only can they do nothing against that which survives, but they cannot keep themselves from taking the noisiest part in that survival. Plus there are other survivors, aren't there, who are interested in survival, who talk, respond, discuss, analyze endlessly. We'll never have done with it. It's as if something nonbiodegradable had been submerged at the bottom of the sea. It irradiates …
>
> (861)

Derrida will wait. When a decade later he returns in "The Typewriter Ribbon" to write on de Man, he will perform a textual ritual that quietly repeats the "purge" he had confronted in the pieces mentioned above.[9] He will, discretely, delete de Man from the genealogy of "deconstruction," and this by essentially taking the *word* itself back from him, noting that it had been taken up always in quotes, and was not his. Or, as Andrzrej Warminski glosses: "Derrida steals back what had been taken from him, from his own text, in the first place." (2009, 1088). While it may be a matter of interest largely for genealogists of "deconstruction" and tourists, and seems parochial to dwell on, something appears marked here that remains unread and, potentially, relevant to today. There was a backstage *war* between de Man and Derrida more lethal than either let on, one effaced by how Derrida would strategize "deconstruction" henceforth.

What de Man conjures by the term *materiality* might have more in common with the oil plumes in the Gulf of Mexico than nuclear waste. One is tempted to think of oil as at the invisible core of hyperindustrial culture. *Toxic*, it is waste when exposed, draping itself around life forms. As a corollary to an ink pool or viscous entity, it suggests a carbonic link to writing, a fluid mass preceding or dissolving letteration. It moves as if into some pre-inscriptive or non-site in relation to what has been called "life as we *knew* it." At a supposed interface of the organic and the inorganic, viscous, the black storage of solar technics undergirds the hyperindustrial accelerations, the autophagy of "life" on its own waste.

*Scene 2:* Now fast forward. We are in 2009, the "twenty years" into the future which Derrida, at one point in "Biodegradables," asked us to look toward to see whether de Man survives or irradiates still. That is, from the perspective of the 21st century, as Timothy Clark puts it, in which things have become more political than humans (and it is as "thing" that Derrida had characterized de Man in "Biodegradables"). In the spring of 2009 Martin McQuillan and Erin Obodiac call a symposium together to discuss an unpublished manuscript of de Man from the early 1970s, parts of which would be used toward *Allegories of Reading* but others of which had not been published at all.[10] The invitation focused particularly on the question of de Man's missing contribution to contemporary discussions of sovereignty and the appearance of the term "theotropic." The pretext would be to ask what de Man's "contemporaneity" might be today, or in a certain "today," and that means evoking biopolitics, sovereignty, perhaps even the theological—aware, nonetheless, that there is a problem with this that is more than smuggling de Man back into the marketplace.

What comes out at once is something different. Not only that de Man seems to be useless on *sovereignty*, since he is interested in what cannot be encompassed by the term or seems to regard it as a perpetual imposition or recuperation. And he deleted the term "theotropic," one assumes because it was redundant (even "atheism" is a theotrope). What emerges instead is how much this text seems to have been, in 1972, erasing or deleting the term "deconstruction" *avant la lettre.* Erin Obodiac, in an excellent account of its archival migration, points this out with some surprise. In doing so, tactfully, she defers the most obvious implication: this occurs, we are told, again and again, but "not perhaps to erase or deface the encounter with Derrida":

> Although the Roman numeral in the title deems itself a second chapter, it symptomatically re-begins with a page "1," and spells out in the title a certain conflict or confrontation: the term "deconstruction" is crossed out in the title "II. The Metaphor of the Self and Its Deconstruction." In fact, the writing of "deconstruction" (often spelled "de-construction" by de Man) and its crossing-out serves as a certain authenticating watermark, or hypo-mark, of the manuscript: here / there / everywhere all over the manuscript the hand-writing of deconstruction must be crossed out, not perhaps to erase or deface the encounter with Derrida, but to hesitate rigorously. In many instances, "deconstruction" is entirely crossed-out, or there is an attempt to find another word. One would expect something like "undoing," yet surprisingly terms such as "system" or "structure" pop up, suggesting that this is how system or structure operate: "undoing" or deconstruction is its operation. This striking revision, which indicates that de Man is engaging not only Rousseau, but Derrida's reading of Rousseau, had already been pre-empted by another text by de Man (written perhaps in 1970 or 1972), i.e., his lengthy chapter on Derrida for *Blindness and Insight,* published in 1973.
>
> (Obodiac 2011)

Derrida posited a binary between himself and his "de Man," from which de Man would be deleted from "deconstruction." Yet the risk of such a strategic binary, staged in "The Typewriter Ribbon" (the machinal vs. the inventive, the dead vs. the living) is that it may appear, from the 21st century horizons marked, reversible at points. Today, the logics of *eco-catastrophism* render much that seemed disturbing in de Man, perhaps, unexceptional. Now that the *jejeune* theory wars of the 1980s have subsided as an episode in which to win was, also, to lose (the depoliticized, nostalgiac critical culture of today); and now that 21st century horizons have abruptly exceeded historicizing and humanist pre-occupations—well, a different backglance emerges.

Of course, one encounters the echoes of this de Man as nuclear waste, not to be gone near, today, and it even marks in a strange way what has happened to "deconstruction" or the *après-Derrida*. Of course, "deconstruction" has all sorts of new friends in its current phase. One of our foremost journalists who made a career in the pile-on on "de Man," Jeffrey T. Nealon, lends his support to the remnants of academic deconstruction by asking the question, "Post-Deconstructive?" (Nealon 2006) That this occurs in a volume supposedly bemoaning the "Discouragement" and paralysis of leftist paradigms may seem a sleight of hand (pull off the wings of dead deconstruction, sans Derrida, rather than account for your own slide into praxis-less moralisms), but it is still safe. Nealon begins by endorsing Negri's account of a deconstruction exhausted and, still, depoliticized, and he ends—after agreeing with that, and bemoaning how hard it is for the remnants mourning the death of Derrida, for whom he has great empathy of course—by positing that "deconstruction" has just barely begun. This is welcome news, that it has barely begun, but it comes with conditions. Since its past is to be read, as by Negri, as a near miss, the question is if it has learned its lessons. It had tried to be political, ethical, and historial, and that was also not enough or its present state would not be so unimpressive. Nealon agrees with Negri that "deconstruction" today is obsolete, yet he offers it two generous consolation prizes with Solomon-like clarity: either it appear in its current phase as fetishized and without traction ("Co-optation. It had to happen to deconstruction. Very discouraging" (78)), or be considered a general condition of hyper-capitalism (in which no recognizable practice of it makes sense). With friends like this any newly chastised "deconstruction" of academic stragglers should be glad to get a plug at all. All it has to do is ensure its de Manian side is deleted. Then it receives fulsome support, on certain further conditions: "deconstructive 'theory' in this sense is not dead, but just being born." So it is just being born in some "sense." Its present is clownishly disconnected, its past obsolete, its future barely beginning, but it is welcomed onboard (we have by now, moreover, forgotten about the "discouragement" of what calls itself the Left). This bright future of an undead and unborn "deconstruction," safely neutered, is only possible since it has been: "[f]reed from the restrictive job of having to show us again and again that we don't know the dancer from the dance" (79). And here is the got-ya line, since if nothing else "deconstruction" has at least stopped telling us about the disjuncture between "the dancer from the dance." Indeed, it has finally stopped that awful de Man stuff, but then, it had stopped that twenty some years before and its then "future" was, well, for

Negri at least, not impressive. But, no matter what else, it must have no "de Man" (in case he's still there, hiding). It seems Nealon sees this spectre everywhere, cannot forget it—having made a career playing whack-a-mole with this fearsome target when doing such involved no risk. We don't want that, not today, when reference lines up so well, and old memes of *praxis* are so very promising. It is good to be freed of this "restrictive job," even if one had been freed of it for decades. This nonetheless still traumatizes Nealon. It is a sobering measure of the decay and pathos of a "deconstruction" in mourning (for itself), one might say, to have such *friends* hailing the "post-deconstructive." At least, now that it is free (again, still, or clearly not) of "de Man"—as if this record got stuck, and for some *nothing had happened* in some obscure sense since then.[11] For instance, the 21st century.

## Entre Nous: suiciding "de-construction," or thirteen ways of looking at de Man … (notes for a lecture)[12]

> Toxic: from Fr. *toxique*, from L.L. *toxicus* "poisoned," from L. *toxicum* "poison," from Gk. *toxikon* (pharmakon) "(poison) for use on arrows," from *toxikon*, neut. of *toxikos* "pertaining to arrows or archery," and thus to a bow, from *toxon* "bow," probably from a Scythain word that also was borrowed into L. as *taxus* "yew."
>
> *Etymological Dictionary*

### 1

Would it make sense, reviewing these threads and where they played out as one looks back, today, to open up more daylight between de Man and Derrida altogether, perhaps tear open the term "deconstruction" itself—or would that be an *American* indulgence, having to do with the strange history, and strategic failure, of "deconstruction" in America? Might these histories be linked, even, to "America" as we find it here and now, today, to what cannot even be called its *suicidal auto-immune spiral*—in the after-time of a global credit collapse, of corporate and telecratic zombie "democracy," of the horizons of "climate change" broadly emergent?

I found myself interested in one sentence which appears both in "Textual Allegories" and, later, *Allegories of Reading*—in the chapter called "Promises."[13] It is simple in a way and, as often, graphs itself onto and through Rousseau: "Far from denoting a homogeneous mode of being, 'nature' signifies a process of a deconstruction redoubled by its own fallacious re-totalization." The sentence is viscous. It bars the extrication of a single outcome or translation. It folds back to re-absorb its point of citational departure (nature, deconstruction) in "a process" that it does and does not stand apart from, as one might from a suddenly post-binarized shore. What is called *nature* arrives as already auto-deconstructive and deconstruction finds itself (artificially) naturalized—in either case with no apparent point of exit from the folding ribbon. Much could be said about such a "deconstruction" that is redoubled by what is instantly called its "*own fallacious re-totalization*." De Man appears still to be transfixed by liqui-fying Derrida's initial "deconstructive" premises of undoing something some-times called metaphysics, of undoing a canonical author named "Rousseau," and so on. But I find myself stopping, am interrupted, as if by another hand. We know where such close reading will at first lead, to what games of unmastery and discipleship, if one cares for that. Rather, in still prefatory fash-ion, I would use the sentence to conjure a contextual outline or face that can barely be made out yet which the present query finds itself well situated within.

Contrary to *doxa*, de Man did not do "the same" as Derrida at all, and the latter knew it—thus he could never be excused, explained, defended or absorbed by the latter; and de Man's text does not demand of its reader imita-tion, absorption, the adoption of these "rhetorical" reading techniques mimed or traced. Contrary to *doxa*, everything in the writing seems to devise its own immolation at a border, as if it were de Man's task to make that *irreversible*, which also means to provoke *what comes beyond itself*. I am not sure academic protocols ever registered this implication: the implied injunction, not that you cannot possibly go where I do, in ironic mastery, but, you cannot repeat this but if you are able, you cannot go back either. It registers, in one of two senses I will give to this term, a *suicidal* and irreversible movement more related to Benjamin's "one-way street" than Derridean *hospitality*: one can follow that movement or abject it in its entirety—or, perhaps in reverse order today, both.[14]

What is this *irreversibility* which, de Man implied once, one cannot cross toward without perhaps being punished, abjected (you better have tenure, he tells his academic audience—and allow me to mark, for a moment, the world that is implied by this term "academic," in matters of collective temperament, pro-fessional resentments, academic cadres, arrested developments, and so on)? Moreover, *de Man* would be particularly marked: at a point when he signified "theory," he would be, I suggested, *abjected*, become, as Derrida tropes, "nuclear waste." This would occur at a time when the critical community would proceed differently to representational, historical, cultural, determinedly "political" narratives—as if, even in the 1990s, suspecting a "post-political" white-out as the curtains of the 21st century were drawn?

Would it be incidental that this same *American* critical community, collec-tively and otherwise, including the most politically advertised on the left, would strangely and without effect or resistance accompany the then Bush debacle up to its point of implosion—much as new historicism would be a covertly Reaganesque invention?

## 2

I can hear the protests to this narrative, but they would not be too loud today. Even brushing aside familiar cobwebs (but "de Man" was a *textualist*—?), or disinterest (so what if he differed from Derrida, the latter is the thing, so far as "deconstruction" goes and … ), one is still within a more general dilemma.

That would be that "deconstruction" appears to some dead in the water today, unable to address eco-graphematic horizons because, well, Derrida had not; without enemy, relapsed into an auto-co-immune phase of inadvertent recuperations and normatizations. Differently put, would there have been reason to link what de Man was doing not to "politics" as it was defined going into the 1990s, but as the non-anthropic horizons of 21st century climate change have begun to reveal themselves—according to another "materiality"? Something in this text, as it were, gazes back, solicits or reads the narrating present in turn.

Where Derrida would obsess over the survival of his corpus, his web of transformational writings and their chance or hypothetical mission, and would perhaps be seduced by the desire to program their *survival*, de Man seemed poised to extinguish in advance his intervention as its own premise. Would there be two "deconstructions" rather than one—that which prioritized survival and that which suicided the term in advance? It will always be a testimony to American infantilism and academic chicanery, the Glen Beck side in imaginary "theory wars," that it could not grasp that de Man's contamination—his exposure to *historical contamination*, rhetorical misalliance, self-deception ("the de Man affair")—would be an empowering dimension of his project, not the opposite, and particularly one reflecting on the self-deception and accelerating violence of a visibly totalizing cultural order, the global telecracies that emerged in the time-bubble of a supposedly *post* war period (after, that is, the "so-called" *world war*, as Derrida names it), that which in post-democratic *America* today is disclosing itself like some dance of the seven veils.

The phrase "toxic assets" can be displaced to illuminate a more general program of *reference* itself—what, through a network of real world metonymies, leads to the double logic by which terrestrial preserves, in being capitalized, convert into poisons, down to ground water, melt-offs, and spatio-temporal *locus*. It is with these thoughts that I use the phrase "toxic assets"—reflecting on the toxicity of "de Man." In the global credit collapse, *toxic assets* would have been *on the book* assets when caught in a general Ponzi scheme of deferred reference that mimes, today, that of the *real* itself (water depletion, species extinction, peak oil). Both megadebt and resource depletion are deferred to voided "futures" that would be drained, themselves dumped into as wasted, or cut off altogether (the Ponzi-scheme of referential currency). Benjamin's Angel of History is less likely to have his wings blasted by a *storm* from the future ("progress," the acceleration of the hyperindustrial today) than be ground to farmyard feed by Monsanto.[15]

## 3

Now I should add a personal note. If part of the issue of de Man today is pharmacological, my interest is not to restitute "de Man" or his techniques of reading and so on. Some appear very time-bound, others minimally usable (for the present, this might include the technicalities of "rhetorical" inventions), still others yet in advance. It is hard to imagine, were de Man's treatment of *face* fully digested, that an entire retrohumanist dossier on face from Levinas through Agamben ("The face's revelation is revelation of language itself" (Agamben 2000, 92)) would have been a necessary and confusing detour. De Man erased as he went—Derrida notes in "The Typewriter Ribbon" the former's dismissal of his own essays once cast off—accelerating as he approached his death, and I recall him quipping about tropes, "they are all the same." This would seem harsh for one who had labored to so retrieve their genome. And I have heard myself referred to as an "intolerant de Manian," whatever that means, and which I am certainly not (not "de Manian" at all, that is, as Andrzej Warminski, who certainly defines these domains, could attest). So one wants to raise some questions without falling into that trap, set up as a guardrail by a certain policing imaginary. Rather, I raise the question of de Man as a certain non-return that would have been itself programmed by the gesture of abjection (which in some ways he set up and would have half endorsed). This occlusion would be by a collective critical community, *American*, but also discretely by what would call itself "deconstruction" heard today as a kind of Derridean*ism*. So, I do not explore this opening out of nostalgia or even remote discipleship as such (for the record, de Man told me he did not recognize the nature of my "contract" to him, and called me, in his estimation, a "wild card"—as I preferred). Nonetheless, whatever way you turn it, as Avital Ronell remarked in a fairly critical piece on de Man, thinking in America took a plunge after his death, as if a sort of self-mutilation rather than a mere occlusion were involved. This said, the "de Man" that interests me is only one of several that can be generated today. I do not want to propose it is the only such, just one which we can pull certain threads from that seem to me still, if you like, radioactive.

### 4

Now, you might protest, it is a poor sign of the times if one turns to de Man as a *pharmakon*, however obscurely, or feels the need to open a crypt thought more or less closed, with relief, but you can (and no doubt will) decide. I invite you to think as if from *before and outside of*, as well as with, the temporal back-loops and accidents and events that closed out a certain episode—with the death of Derrida, yet already much beyond. The sentence I identified above on Rousseau's "nature" elicits a speculation on the loop a certain *then* (1972) forms with *now* (2011), or even the future conditionals that seem to crowd about us today. The de Man that interests me at the moment is not the one who *touched upon*, let us say, a point where a certain move that defined "deconstruction" appeared to him self-engendered and requiring a second that needed to undo the first, then a third, and on going. It is what proceeds from that in, for instance, what might be called the *post-binarized* sentence quoted above on "nature."

For de Man what we have got used to calling "metaphysics" did not exist. It could not have been an institutional or historial epoch—certainly not written *into* a text like Plato or Rousseau. Rather, "metaphysics" would both never have existed and be the *Nachkonstruction* of a perpetual relapse engineered by interpretive reflexes and tropes in a perpetual non-present's self-invention. If one needed evidence on his side, so to speak, one may look around one, since it would seem "metaphysics" would never be simply closed, reversed, or even dismantled, but rather with every such blow simply multiply and find new sites of residence, viral, not even uncanny—including the legatees of "deconstruction" today, for whom an auto-immune moment may have arrived (as predicted by Derrida, who proffered that within a couple of months if not days after his death, his literal death, well—you know). One might want to bring in some measure or *metrics* first, using American common sense of course, to ask how the world is or has been going across the decades, from the gaze of a certain de Man script of the 1970s—three, almost four, decades ago now. Does the historicity of the 1970s define and place de Man's project, or does the disheveled present see itself otherwise from within a new rhetoric of temporality?

## 5

It is here that I must ask everyone into a special consultation, even auto-critique *entre nous*, and it is not only (as one can say with good humour) because "deconstruction" in America could be called, as said, a strategic failure. And it is not because "it" never recovered from de Man's public abjection, however contrived, nor bizarre provincial schisms such as Gasché spun (whose desire to peel off Derrida for an ennobled discipline of philosophy, against the literariness of a "de Man," did nothing but feed the public *doxa* at the time and, putatively, get to separate out and self-anoint Gasché, in his sense, as a philosopher).[16] Today this template can be speculatively reversed. So what I ask, for a moment, is a certain indulgence, if for nothing else than to get rid, if it be, of my own curiosity—can I call it that?—in this regard. No doubt, you will tell me to shake it off.

The best way to frame this is to relay a dream that I had—it is not necessarily a nightmare, which I seem never to have or recall, though it involves a sort of *bizarre* vision or logic of which I am happy to be disabused. It keeps recurring nonetheless and is hard to awake from. I will ask you, imaginatively any way, to close your eyes and indulge this aberrant logic.

I dreamed, essentially, that the world had taken a sharp turn of self-disclosure, which delegitimized the passive progressive narrative of intellectual culture with it—parallel to the contemporary global currency schemes and the fall of American-led hypermodernity (where the fiction of reference is deferred into a hypothetical future which, in turn, is essentially robbed of its resources, wealth and, in some accounts, existence); that the figurative drape had been pulled back on the accelerated undoing of the support networks of terrestrial life— mass extinction events, glacial melt-off, agricultural collapse, unfolding oil and water wars, and so on, with the attendant unraveling of geopolitical (not to mention local) accords, mass immigration in the face, now, of predicted global "population culling" by century's end. What a dream, since none of it accords with the protocols and expectancies of 20th century thought, to say nothing of the retirement prospects of its middle-aged academic progeny? Today this template can be speculatively reversed. Pour money into this Ponzi scheme, it fuels the black hole, depleting futures; retrieve the "free market" system by restoring it to earlier functionality, it accelerates the impasse—ignoring that on the other side of the reality screen, the demands of dwindling reserves, global warming, and collapsing systems (transport, agriculture, currency) bars any such "return."

It is almost with nostalgia that one recalls the critical assumption, in the early 1990s, that the trajectory of "formal democracy" was on the infinite menu—what, in retrospect, appears to have been a clever attempt to co-opt the neo-liberalist triumphalism of the day, and become embedded in the host. It is something of this that Derrida wanted to transpose and *spectralize* as a non-existent "democracy to come." That is, at the price of being so caught up in this rhetorical duel as to have omitted any reference to or acknowledgement of climate change, global heating, disappearing resources, mass extinction events in his summary "ten plagues" of this new world order.[17]

## 6

Glancing back, the 20th century culmination in analytics of social justice and human-on-human depradations gives way, implicitly, before an anorganic hive of backlooping and chrono-metastasizing processes that, like de Man's chiastic reading of a "sublime," are irredeemably banal, of the mud, matters of shifting biomass.

What might be called a "time bubble" emerges. The current decade will have been, after all, that in which terrestrial habitats for unfolding aeons will have been irreversibly and negatively decided (the "anthropocene," as it will have been named). At one pole of such calculations, a James Lovelock posits at century's end a core remaining population (perhaps 700 million), under very altered circumstances that the planet can support, while Stephen Hawkings suggests off-world colonization as the only option in two hundred years if man wants to survive as a species. These are public memes that operate within the ecocatastrophic imaginary. The problem—and a species on the ecocatastrophic brink has, as we say, a problem—would necessarily include cognitive regimes, perceptual templates, organizations and technologies of memory, the manner in which reference is generated or codified, or phenomenality produced (itself captured or caricatured by telemarketing).

A totalized *disjuncture* appears almost normative. That is, between public acknowledgement and practical denial of eco-catastrophic logics among else. The latter denial is often referenced to the cognitive limits of human short-time memory, now rendered hyperbolic by digital media, news cycles, and markets, or the empirical experience of the *everyday* within developed societies. For the latter the incremental effects of "climate change" may seem imperceptible, denied by the senses or contradicted by the hard facts of wealth or technological comforts. It is the same sort of "time bubble" that Bernanke's quantitative easing generates by deferring default by counterfeiting trillions. This denial of the *obvious* is what Zizek, however, finds constitutive of *culture* itself: "One of the elementary rules of culture is to know when (and how) to pretend NOT to know (or notice), to go on and act as if something which happened did not happen" (Zizek 2009). Such culturalization can even deny perpetually this interpretation of culture itself, maintaining itself indefinitely in a sort of obverse *mise en abyme*. What might be called here a "prison house of (artificed) reference" creates the circumstance today, not of a time merely "out of joint," but one in which a radical disjuncture has become the premise of a *virtual* homogeneity, "a *fallacious* re-totalization."

## 7

Let me more fully enter with you the bizarre world of this dream, then, and draw our topic into play—what relevance, in this disturbed sleep or slumber, this suicidal acceleration, is de Man, mandarin of "close reading"? Let us assume, for the moment, that the purge or banning of de Man within critical culture had something to do with the extremity of a counter-gesture he would embody, a de-anthropomorphizing scan of the historial premises and *asubjectality* of this entire historial dossier, deriving as it does from the West. To this self-undoing spiral, one would have to add critical preferences within the humanities, semantic programs, and political definitions. Which is not to say these latter were not "good," or so intended—which is the problem, since it is the return of *the good* that is here suspect. Even definitions of "social justice" get confused here: the restitution or emancipation of the oppressed, like the neo-liberal fiction of raising the developing world to the state of American consumers, fuels representational *aporia*. The calculation of "futures" is perceived to be banned by Derrida, in the name of keeping an "openness" to the future formally. This literalization has left what calls itself "deconstruction" disoriented. Yet in current calculations of material resources the implications appear clear: "climate change" absolutely interrupts any progressive modernity, whether conceived of as national or "global." And the first to be passively triaged will be those at the bottom. That is, as survivalist pressures emerge (of groups, classes, corporate entities, nations, localities, and so on).[18]

Within this aberrant dream, relentlessly banal and *not* "apocalyptic" at all (no sudden impact, no redemptive flash or nuclear holocaust, no revelatory disappearance)—banal and irreversible and impacting non-human or geomorphic times—one might expect *a corresponding mutation of epistemographies*. The Xanax-ridden intellectual class would surely rise, in America at least, to this occasion, or at least within the bold "theory" set—in effect, this would be their moment. A materiality irresolvable to dialectical and Christian myths (Marxist) enters the frame. And surely this group or class, committed to politics in its muted way, no doubt liberal, would understand that in entering this promised economic order now resisting disclosure, everyone must *give up,* sacrifice, something, wealth certainly, but also consumption of a certain order, energy use, and so on, as a different calculus of futures, resources, and currency emerges (in its first phases). Surely, *they* know that. But this too does not occur: instead, the groups and stylistic investments circulating in neo-orthodoxies in the afterworld of 20th century theory (and else), share a first response with the bankers themselves: how to re-assert my province, my conceptual territory, in this new dispensation: how to recover what is threatened with loss.

Now again, I think here that I was already beginning to speculate on de Man's unpublished manuscript, mentioned above, in what some might call the unconscious (a term I personally don't have use for or experience of even—it seems to me all there all the time, and always readable, which I hope doesn't disqualify me as a voice here). In my dream, those wedded to tropes of "emancipation" soldier on; Lacanians, Deleuzians, historicists, cultural studies exemplars in its wonderfully hybrid evolvements—each, for the most part, double down on their investments; the mavens of what is still called "*the* political," what often conceals the most programmatic of representational faiths today, and the most casual presumptions of praxis, withdraw from categories that do not execute their inherited definition of *the* social as a 20th century phantom. Before an abrupt and not so abrupt *mutation of reference*, so far, general retreat into the gated communities of mannerist discourse (biopolitics, sovereignty) and academic deferral, even as programs close, presses diminish, public discussion is infantilized and courses through mediacratic arteries. As if this entire "global" turn, even at the expense of the planetary, had to do with orders of consumption linked to semantic fictions, inertia, ancient cognitive or mnemonic orientations (some returning to hunter-gatherers), a misreading of the "commons" or supposedly Enlightenment premises bound to the 20th century impersonations of the nation-state, of the mythemes of mere "world" wars past—premised, still, on human enmity, ideological (or specular) divide, and a radical blind. Well, here is where the dream gets uncomfortable—forget all the disappearing water sources or predictable catastrophics.[19]

## 8

Now, I realize I've been asking much of you but I may as well continue, so that we might speculate otherwise. That is, against our "selves" and our investments, these forms of capital, without concern for all the protocols of silence that shape academic sociality and currencies. I do not exclude myself from the most severe of these critiques. Pretending, for the moment, that other things are at stake today, let me solicit what the pre-moment of any "history of 'deconstruction'" might view scanning what lies between then and now, or even just *within* "now."

One of the things de Man seemed engaged in was what Derrida calls a "wager". In this, one can hedge one's bets, as we say, try to have it rhetorically both ways, or put all on the table. Unlike the "late Derrida," who seemed unable not to wish to program his own survival, that of his oeuvre and its import, and be contaminated by that—with fumes and results one will experience for a generation, specifically "this" generation, until (and as) hybrid readers arrive—de Man gambled an "irreversibility" which met one of its catastrophes, which would be being surrounded, neutralized, abjected. There would be good practical and cognitive reasons for this, but that is not the main logic, and amusingly, it is not until you get back to Gasché that you have overt complaint, for a while at least, of de Man's mere *incomprehensibility*. To be incomprehensible to Gasché (as *The Wild Card of Reading* shows he is surely not), what a symptom!

But let me suggest from within the non-dream proffered above—for let us take that dream for a moment as indifferently real—one would have to say that perhaps this was a "secret" of a pre-ordained suicide of deconstruction all along, or in any case, that the entire episode of critical thought cannot fail, today, to be reread as if from this cx-anthropic pivot (that is, *as if* from "without").[20]

*Internote: if one hears "reading" as a complex name for cognitive process, then the brake de Man engineered endeavoured to alter neural patterning as such. To what end? For one thing (or two): to mark aesthetic formalization as the site of power and the index of an exteriority without interior at all; to precede the generated programs of phenomenality; to form a wedge that blocks the reflexive generation of "reference" and semantic consumption—as if these mechanisms precede not only ideology (a mechanism that binds the "Left" and "Right" in a parallel theotropic structure) but concept or ideation.[21] To turn against "oneself" as itself the carrier is an extreme pharmacological gesture. It only appears suicidal in structure since the "I" is given up on in advance of its appearance, which is to say it enters as ghost in rehearsal, testifying to each blind and sandtrap it has been in despite its non-existence.*

**9**

Is the word "deconstruction" appropriate for de Man, who took up the term by in essence negating its promise? A rupture occurs within and before the word "deconstruction" takes hold which, subsequently, Derrida would have to walk around, clean up as a kind of mess, and as time went on (plain to see, not discussed) efface, resent, find toxic. And it has been argued, I think obversely, by Christopher Morris, that the example of de Man or rather his abjection propelled Derrida to lean the other way—and, inversely, in effect, become figural, literary.[22]

Derrida found himself harassed by de Man on two sides—pre-empting "deconstruction" in advance (the critique of *Grammatology*) and destroying the brand from after death. Derrida would decide to preserve the legacy by taking the word itself back (deconstruction), or try to, if one can take back what is taken up in quotes (and disowned in advance). And Derrida would experience a rancor here, a resentment increasing over time rather than the opposite, as if de Man not only had on some infinitesimal point sabotaged him (even in the choice to abject the latter in turn), or by default had as if coerced him to launch a "late Derrida" as a counter-toxin—as if he had been, due to this, delayed from getting back to the ex-anthropic column in his work. Of course, it was too much to expect of those seeing themselves as managing this capital to turn toward the one zone absent in Derrida, that Derrida did not show how to do. It would imply a very different conception of legacy and capitalization if a next step of "deconstruction" were willing to dissolve the premise in order to recast or supplement it, rather than be exegetically invested in a proper name. That is, the biomorphic and geomorphic anarchivism which no Levinasian trope can be applied to, which entered high media presence more or less just following Derrida's death.

## 10

I stop, or at least abandon this drift. It has all seemed to me preparatory to a deferred reading of one sentence. It is simple in a way and, again, piggy-backs Rousseau, an iconic misreading of whom would formalize a supposedly onto-logical trope of "nature" for modernity and, in its implications, hyperindustrial modernity in particular: "Far from denoting a homogeneous mode of being, 'nature' signifies a process of a deconstruction redoubled by its own fallacious re-totalization."

De Man knew his tapestry of reanimated classical tropes could not become a typology. What interests me is where, today, the disclosure of what we will pre-tend to still call *material* mutations, "climate change," has broken with the anthropomorphic histories decisively without providing any template. As a result, any language of tropes, of semantics, of hermeneutic relapse is beached or exposed not just as a deformedly constituted regime of history but a criminal and auto-immune enterprise—caricatured by the "American way of life." In this sense, de Man was "right," in that he turned against a certain doxological totality. And we are not speaking of a "late de Man," who went in the opposite direction to the tendencies of "late Derrida"—with consequences still today. Even before we get to the blanket diagnosis of *aesthetic ideology*—the recasting of the political as the epistemological—the essentials were there: the absolute dissolution of any "subject" effect into the forces and effacements of rhetorical agons without outside. Rather than mime the palatable illusion of an extension of empathy from subjects to various forms of "the other" (ethnic, racial, animal, inorganic), or even an "otherness of the other" Derrida relies upon, de Man dissolves into a certain asubjectality, shifting as if to that "inhuman" non-site he calls, misleadingly to today's ear, the "linguistic," "language," yet which, as the "inhuman," does not belong to man and is not excluded from the techno-genesis of life forms, anima-tion, *biosemiosis* without *bios*, the premise of atelic "evolution." What emerges in the sciences today as *biosemiosis* presents something different from a cutting off of "text" to return to the real, but rather the totalization of the latter, a "semiotic" or unbounded *textism* in advance of "life" on all levels. The "organic" itself would appear the effect of proto-semiotic agency (and thus, is the figural creation of a language itself decidedly not organic).[23]

The sentence above is intriguing, I suggested, both for its faux naturalization of "deconstruction" and the marking of "nature" as an auto-deconstructive process in advance, embedded in a folded ribbon effect which, nonetheless, the sentence stands back from. It opens up a conceit of "nature" that parallels an auto-deconstructive "process" and does so by a then inescapable relapse ("retotalization"). The stylistic hiccup in the phrase *"a* process of *a* decon-struction" (rather, say, than "the process") registers an internal slippage or fold in the mechanism of the repetition. Much could be said about a *nature* that assumes and effaces its own *technogenesis*, or about a "deconstruction" that is redoubled by what is instantly called its *"own fallacious re-totalization."* Too much. Yet de Man is also digesting, liquifying, Derrida's "deconstructive" precepts in this 1972 sentence—the rhetorical premise of vaporizing something sometimes called metaphysics, of undoing a canonical author named "Rousseau," and so on. It would be inconceivable to title a reading of de Man something like "radical atheism," as Martin Hägglund does of Derrida (2008), since even the latter term would appear entirely theotropic still. If Derrida could enter the theological labyrinth with fascination, flirt with soli-citing undecidably negative theologies or their investments from readers (really, "god" as trace?), de Man was—for better and worse—godless.

## 11

De Man's courteous way of describing some aporia he would disclose as *dilemmas*, or *predicaments*, is amusing today. Even what he terms undecidables one senses are not really that at all – one side of which (say, for brevity's sake, the hermeneutic, modernist, redemptive, theotropic, historicist straw man reading) has just been trashed. One understands these were in advance too *decidable* at least in one sense: the referent as constituted by institutionalized memes and aesthetic ideology broadly was not only artefactual, as Derrida might have it, but, how shall we say, having fun a bit, a con, auto-destroying of what it promised, suicidal, *evil.* (One might want to call by such a term, whether in its Baudelairean sense or beyond, as Derrida deploys in *mal d'archive*, a machinal order of cognition whose engines guarantee a passive triage of its own and the erasure of innumerable species.)

It would not be one blindness among others from which "insights" are mounted but a sort of *blind* of blinds. It turns against the current ideologeme of the "human" as if from a different justice—as one might, today more obviously, on behalf of terrestrial "life."[24] Thus there is a strange *moral* force to de Man's auto-dismantlings, his disappearance into inarticulation which has been left unattended. It makes Derridean ethics, turned back toward an ethics of *the other* (being), a bit dissembling, even unethical—at all events, rhetorically strategic.

As they might say in Brooklyn: Just what part of *defacement* don't you understand?

Might one ask, with discrete frankness (for the academic professions, where a certain cloying tribalism and hesitancy to give up investments rules), what *our* "toxic assets" are in terms of referential rituals, pious repetitions, postures of empty and costless solidarity, hoarding discursive capital, and so on? And whether they involve, *entre nous*, certain predilections that have been machinally programmed for the *nous*, the "we"? To speak *entre nous*, as I have pretended, might that not point not to what is between ourselves, like gossip, but what is or is not between various *nous* and *we's* as such? Now, you can open your eyes, which I earlier asked you to shut. We can return to the "real" now, to the relief of wakefulness. After all, the economy is in the hands of Tim Geithner, and "deconstruction" lies in the most competent hands—friends. Which still leaves us the question of what to do with de Man's *remains*. This de Man has no natural "friends," we might say, nothing to please anyone: the "sublime" inverts a banality; face is not given; the "human" does not, strictly, exist; the very machines that produce communal faith, ecotechnics, cannot but formalize the suicidal acceleration the latter would oppose; "modernity" does not occur; the disjuncture between discourse and event is permanent; the hermeneutic "relapse" defends an interiorized churchliness yet is itself destructive and criminalized by what it enforces allegiance to; death is a "linguistic complication," to be thought accordingly, "organicism" the touch-stone of ideology; "life" is an after-life (that is, a semio-mimetic effect); "history" is not temporal; empiricism is an idealization; what is termed *praxis* cloaks an aestheticization; "ideology" as an aesthetic effect binds Left and Right into structural and referential proximity; "hope" and "weak messianism" are relapses, and so on.

## 12

But all of this assumes "we" are not in an academic environment but—and this is what permeates me from what I called my dream—in a now permanent and invisible (and irreversible) position in relation to cultural participation and resistance something akin to a permanent and anaesthetized *war* from which no cognitive practice is removed.[25] All of our habits of participation in the relative benefits of the corporate feudal trance are, relatively but inevitably, criminalized. Why would this today name, ineluctably, a war—whose premise is, as Benjamin remarked, that it is lost in advance—within the technogenesis of reference, perception, mnemonics? Such a war of and over inscriptions is caricatured in the militarization of telemarketing.

One can go back, for a moment, and speculate on the residue in this narrative of "the war"—that is, first, of the "so-called world war" (Derrida), which defaced de Man's brand by a return of archival events defined by *it*. And one could try to identify more closely what, in fact, was Paul de Man's other war—what mobilized this writing. With hermeneutics, with "deconstruction," with what it most resisted perhaps, "theory." I leave aside, out of discretion, the entirely inappropriate *response* of (non)defense to that polemical trap at the time (by Derrida, despite himself, and others). De Man will navigate labyrinths of error and mnemonic mutilation for which, as in Nietzsche, the discourse of "truth" communally defined would partake of chiasmically structured lies of power without exit. One can see why no one wants to go *that* far, until you have no choice maybe, which certain scans of coming decades might conclude.

When regimes of reference expand to a criminalized and suicidal totality (in which aesthetic ideology is most entrancing, telecratic, without apparent exit), a certain resistance goes hyper. From this angle, de Man did not signal an anti-human drift, or one dehumanized as such; he posited the undoing of an arti-ficed variant of "human" normativity which itself would appear, at the heart of hermeneutic assumptions, machinal and suicidally complicitous. It is the same logic by which Benjamin, decrying the fascist "enemy," does not name Nazism but a cognitive and archival practice of passive reference, *historicism*. This sug-gests a different condition of war than the premise of a "so-called world war" fought over mere domination, territory and eugenics. One does not really see this last historial drive (eugenics) today as a uniquely fascist position conquered and set aside for the flourishing of Western market democracies so much as transferred to the latter and a different time-scale. The *eugenics scheme* had not been erased so much as itself "democratized" by replacing the decideratum of one conquering race with that of the eventual separation of global *wealth* as the desideratum—or the megawealth being separated out today from the planetary. It would seem *that* "war" never ended with Western democracy destroying its fascist other. Rather, the suppressed fascist logics would be merely absorbed by a then to be global "humanity" at war with terrestrial life, with the so-called non-human, with "life" itself.[26]

So, where then is this *war* today—between de Man and Derrida, between Derrida and himself, between America and its suicidal accelerations, between what we call humans and the preconditions of "life as we *knew* it" or what were local norms for a few score years? What mutates within the definition of "*the* war," the 20th century human on human variety (imperial, colonial, racist, territorial, genocidal, of and with a human "enemy" other), when it moves from a fratricidal model to a totalized horizon (as species) against itself, its out-side, its many supposed "others" in an invisible and horizonless zone of active and carbon-driven backloops? De Man's youthful contamination by the lan-guage of power and murder—in the context of what would emerge as the Holocaust—might appear in this regard a rare tutelage.

What I would propose, here, is only to extract three algorithms of sorts that, each found in the essay on Benjamin called "Conclusions," de Man's last, can be mobilized differently today before the areferentials of an era of climate change. These will be: *the relapse*, *irreversibility*, and *the inhuman*.

## 13

One could submit several hypotheses using "de Man" as the name of a critical anomaly and a *destructive* metric today:

- That "de Man" represents a negatively empowered non-site in the arc of theory that returns as a toxic asset not in the post-theory "present" (the theoretical clime seeking sustainability of signature investments) but before what we will call "21st century horizons" that have revealed a rupture in 20th century epistemological premises broadly;

- That when Derrida situates de Man with "nuclear waste" outside the "ecosystem" he deposits him in and with the one domain he himself would also turn from—that of climate change, the ecographic and zoomorphic configuration before which the "human" can today appear in an inertial, accelerating aporia, or suicidal form;
- That in this, de Man conjures a metric of "irreversibility"—from a zone of mnemotechnics which, properly *inhuman*, would not be unrelated to non-human zones of life-forms and dynamic processes (DNA, *abiosemiosis*);
- That de Man formulates a pre-emptively suicidal war machine perhaps more suited to 21st century problematics than the social and historical urgencies of the 1990s, before horizons that are now broadly *post-binarized*;
- That what de Man calls the "relapse" appears to define and organize cognitive channels in the late anthropocene present, and that it becomes the former, itself a machinal and disembodied reflex constitutive of the phantom of the home or tribal "we," that could itself now be identified with what calls itself "the human"—not a species or even an idea but a machinal producer of semantic proprietizations, faux interiorization, hyperconsumption;
- That such a relapse can be traced within critical idioms today that deem themselves, chronologically and otherwise, "after theory": retro-organicisms and returns to phenomenology, the soft anthropo-colonialism of the "animal," various collectives to come, embodiments, the selective fetishization of one "Derrida" at the expense of another;
- That the 21st century horizons may require *asubjectal* modes of thought before an unusable "materiality" in which disappearance, dispossession, and inhospitality are thought outside of redemption narratives;
- That there was here, in a way one may want to erase, a "materialist" thinking of *anoikos*, an *aterra*, or an an-ecological textualization of the human effect not as one that extends itself to commune with "the otherness of the other," thus propping up the index of a Self, but situated within an inhuman process ("*a* process") of which the inescapable linguistic trace is not what separates the former out from abiotic matrices that are called the biosphere but what instead is permeable with the latter in mnemotechnics and the pre-letteral, before any era of the Book (or monotheism) were in place; one whose non-negotiable premise is an "epistemological critique of tropes," which is to say the politics of cognition itself, before which the metaphor "man" is impossible to conceive within the turn-styles of sovereignty—not because *he* is gone beyond, become post-human or hits the singularity button to get out of mortality, but because "he" never existed as a definitional;

In what has been advertised as a *post-ideological* era the flavours of ideology do not retire. Rather, they proliferate in zombie fashion, miming where they assume or remember themselves to have been. The left is famously disconsolate; deconstruction is in its auto-immune mourning phase; the era of "democracy" is a palpable anachronism covering telecratic corporatism; "new organicisms" sprout; and a conscious *disjuncture* stands as a constant hum between public discourse and the reals of continued planetary existence. One has the option to identify against the mechanisms that have produced this totalitization or blind—which is not the same as being against "humanity" altogether. Rather, one could speak of an irreversible "critique," destructive necessarily, of the current techno-genesis of ideation—from a position preceding conceptual formation, face, value, anthropism, "voice," *and* object, as naturalized contracts. From this perspective, the "human" as a hermeneutic artifice is unable to intervene in the hypermutation of rogue Capital, today, because it has no other site to stand apart from it; because its feeding structure is related—even if, like "environmentalism" or "the" ecological, it serves that maelstrom by thinking it stands apart, in a relapse whose structure (an abstraction) is in fact that thing.

Which is why the story of de Man's abjection doubles as an *American* fable.

## Pastoral

> If the word man is a conceptual figure grafted upon a blind metaphor, then the referential status of the discourse about man is bound to be curiously ambivalent. It claims to refer to an entity (man), but this entity turns out to be the substitution of a definition for what was only a hypothetical knowledge, an epistemological metaphor substituting certitude for ignorance on the basis of an assumed resemblance between passion and perception, fear and size, inside and outside.
>
> (Paul de Man, "Textual Allegories")

In the question and answer session following de Man's final lecture, on Benjamin, we encounter the following exchange. At issue is what is meant by the "inhuman" in his talk, originally referenced to Benjamin's notion of language in "The Task of the Translator":

NEIL HERTZ:   ... At the same time, the word "inhuman" keeps pulling in the direction of the mysterious. You no? [laughter] Not for you? ...

DE MAN:   ... The 'inhuman,' however, is not some kind of mystery, or some kind of secret [. ... ] *since there is, in a very radical sense, no such thing as the human.* If one speaks of the inhuman, the fundamental non-human character of language, one speaks of the *fundamental non-definition of the human* as such, since the word human doesn't correspond to anything like that. So by extension, any ... but let's not go that far—I'm now ahead of the statement. ...

(96, my italics)

One would like, of course, to intervene, tell de Man he is welcome to get "ahead of his statement" at the point where he breaks it all off. "So by extension, any ... "—yeah, ok, and? Why not "go that far"?

I've been fascinated by this remark. A variation of this broken off elaboration might be toyed with, from today's perspective, that of a 21st century in which, as opposed to its predecessor, material entities (commodities, oil, gold, soybeans, rice) appear broadly more "political" than persons. So let me try, not to finish the sentence broken off, but nonetheless ... If "in a very radical sense, there is no such thing as the human" as a definitional then the *inhuman* does not exist, of course, as a mystery or a beyond of the human—not, say, as an otherness of the other (human), or "nature." It is there, it is, and then there is the effect of the "human" as phantom definitional (a technic of closing off), as a cognitively militant metaphor covering a non-site, forged in cognitive declamation; a plug which, to feed this void, must consume to produce the effect of interiority (semantics); a non-definitional, the name of a programmed interpretive "relapse," *Oikos*, "self," *nature*, history. What "the human" is definitely not is a subject or subject effect, a conferred citizenship of various guilds of "we," the description of the animal-man, or one historical flavour of man, such as the corporate simulacra of Enlightenment man or even the last man of current telecracies. In each case one has assumed a "human" as premise to begin with, however modified. It is from there, in our recent habits, one extends oneself to a variety-pack of "others," while remaining, because of that contractual logic, somehow the more oneself.[27]

One here sets aside the rhetoric of the *post*-human altogether, of course, since there had been no "human" as such to begin with—and the former becomes a bulwark to keep the latter in circulation. The "human" was meant to connote an intention-endowed sentient being and one in fact wired to the tribe, nation, the home, property, consumption, *interiorization*. It is not accidental that the term "post-human" has migrated from the term's early Nietzschean inflections to the future synbiotic preservation of an individual against death—the present extended forever with a synthetic body. But the implications of de Man's little remark here bleed on, or ooze.

The inhuman is not merely "non-human," since it is other than man altogether and does not exist primarily in reference to him. But then it could not, since in a "radical sense" there is "no such thing." One has shifted from one reading of Protagoras ("Man is the metros ... ") to a very different one without leaving the text ("'Man' is an effect of an inhuman metrics"). One might want to translate the materiality in question, one of inscriptions (*hypomnemata*), into something like mnemo-technics for the moment.[28] Such would seep as if down through the preletteral mark or interval, down to chemical process and DNA coding, traverses life-*forms* of organic and inorganic process (global heating, chemical balance virtually). That is, again, the disclosure that signs are not added onto the *bios*, but rather that the latter emerges with and from mnemo-semiotic process and formalizations.[29]

Such a premise has a more than metaphorical accord with what is articulating itself in the sciences as *biosemiosis*—though with the caveat that both *bios* (with its Aristotelian-Agambian aura) and *semiosis* (with its 20th century extensions as a base) be subject to elementary or routine deconstructions in which the hypostasization of "life" or "sign" are redistributed in relation to *abiotic* violence, a telemorphosis or *abiotelemorphosis* …

What Hertz is curious about in de Man's talk is this reminder that in Benjamin language is not human and, consequently, the "human" as a referential does not exist "as such." Banal enough. Yet much resides in the premise that it does "exist," is a given, or did in a certain very definable way, which is guaranteed by certain credit reserves or *we's*, enforced by laws, intermittent genocides and wars. Discourses on *sovereignty* or those on extending the human toward some discrete or projected *other* to commune with or recognize—the long commodified trope of "the other" or an "otherness of the other" (which runs from all identity critique to animal studies and eco-romanticism)—coil here, massed within diverse regimes of sustainability.[30] Each of the latter wants to retain its mutual funds while extending, sustaining, its position. Each shares a programmatic relapse, a cognitive default or automatism which formal structure itself (independent of any content) offers the sole referent of the term "human."[31] This would be independent of any referent or ideologeme, much as this cognitive reflex would imply a constitutive analytic of *ressentiment*. One cannot commune with *a human other* (or non-human animal "subject"), as if the latter were enabled by a friendly extension of an empathic self of the (non-existent) human it presumes to begin with. One shifts to a pre-phenomenal non-site, tracks a "materiality" that cannot be used or identified, not allied with the random alone, itself viscous, *Khora*-like, of a *plasticity* in the sense probed by Malabou or that of an oil plume which, to take form, requires to drape itself about another form, contaminate it, miming an ink pool without any face whatsoever yet nonetheless the recycled source of "light," the very premise of hyperindustrial modernity, the accelerations of a late technic era that could never be defined, from without, as "Capitalism" alone. Capitalism, rather, transports this artificed and backlooping accord into the vortices of financialization where the meme of "man" (or, currently, the corporation as legal "citizen") finds itself fully and properly disembodied.[32]

The "inhuman," this is mysterious, says the human (in this case, Neil Hertz), who according to this template himself does not exist. But today there is some context as the background shifts from 20th century to 21st century referentials and the problematics of extinction posed by "climate change."[33]

A *language* that is inhuman, that is of course not *organicist*, that cannot be intentionally structured, and that is not temporal should not be closed off just for referencing what cannot be closed off—or for turning to a point at which personification is not yet contracted or forged. It defaces without supplanting "human" exceptionalism, even the premise that the human simply has language and other life forms do not. Does such a perspective err by comparing "us" to mammals without our form of social language, rather than mark the import of mnemotechnics across all "life" forms and, as it were, scanning in reverse the singularities of our own ("rhetoric")? Our languages operate on mimetic assumptions that produce and commodify reference, fabricate Selves, whereas mnemo-semiotic life-forms appear to mime their inscriptions forward *physically* (cell-formation, photosynthesis, atelic "evolution"). The rainforest or coral reefs are charged with lethal mimicries and camouflage between shape-shifting organisms (metamorphoses, chemical defense, organ mutations). In this sense alone there is no reason to restrict this use of "language" to an inhuman agency which is, nonetheless, only for humans (who, moreover, definitionally do not exist). One could, conceivably, retire the term "human" as name in this sense without any loss—as a meme it is as contingent and appropriated as would be "American," or a Yankees fan, or being issued an identity card. It does not refer to humanity but to a mechanism itself of cognitive relapse—what is shared, invested in, a formal structure regardless of semantic content, and one that remains a radical threat to "life."

The "relapse" is thus not one tactic among others. It is not chosen but para-machinal, then self-feeding. It is not any more or less *innocent* than an insect, say a wasp, that appropriates another "living" body to create an auto-nourishing womb for its eggs. (I am thinking, here, of the curious anecdote Derrida inserts into "The Typewriter Ribbon," that of prehistorical insects caught in the act of coupling and preserved in amber, like the critical duel staged in that episode.) At every discursive juncture in which a transcendental, tribal, onto-materialist, empiricist, "communal" truth is hypostasized, it consolidates or notarizes in advance whatever referent is claimed as its lead. It is militarized, seeks the homogeneity that de Man's sentence on "nature" and "deconstruction" finds interchangeably generated. De Man's scan of "ideology" might better be referenced as an analytic of ideationology itself (it is hard otherwise to translate "epistemological critique of tropes"). What the term "language" implies is not just an inhuman agency from which to scan back at the "human's" techno-genesis (the position, say, of what de Man calls irony). Again, this is the obverse of what Jameson labeled, misappropriating Nietzsche, "the prison-house of language," as if that were a formal abyss that keeps the formalist from reference and the hurtful real of History. What would be in question is the prison-house of *reference* as that is generated, bounded, policed and proprietized. That is, the aberrant fashion in which reference is generated, codified, symbolically assumed, rendered objects of faith, made a *mise en abyme* by referencing itself as natural. Could one overshoot here and switch the "ethical" lever the other way, and view this discrimination as a war—"Paul de Man's *other* war," similar to Benjamin's—before a passive holocaust to come?

Now, let us hypothesize this defaced position: imagine having an ear for these seeming truths at all moments in the most refined vibrations. Is not the remark about the "inhuman" on the one hand rather plain and unremarkable today, and yet also an Archimedean point to orient to outside of a totalizing phenomenal or referential regime? De Man accounts for the experience of "irreversibility" here. Irreversible implies a position from which the militarized machine of recuperative traits breaks the circuit. That is, it cannot get back from here to there, toward humanisms and historicisms and naturalisms, which are themselves "linguistic complications." It brackets ideology not because it is superior to any in insight but because ideation or conceptualization formalizes itself here and, sharing similar structures, triggers an alert. It arrives with the glue of cognitive moralisms and builds a reserve account and value. The premise of "aesthetic ideology" is itself damning, neither innocent nor descriptive. The latter arrives as an artifice and anchors itself to an organicist façade. It could be said to take over the artifice "man," which continues to circulate as a fiat currency. It critiques not this or that ideology in the name of another, but counters the invariable theologization by which such emerge – hence the always suspicious similitude between so called left and right, not only in corporate politics but in contracted epistemographies, theotropes, contracts of reference. Such would perhaps only apppear tolerable if one had been forcibly displaced from a human on human history or model before another. One would think the word materiality were itself the very worst term in this apparatus, since, as a referent of reference, it would be the alibi of each (pragmatism, empiricism) and its own cancellation (theisms).

## Anecographies

> This movement [is] a kind of permanent exile if you wish, but it is not really an exile, for there is no homeland, nothing from which one has been exiled.
>
> Paul de Man, "Conclusions" (de Man 1986)

The pulse of toxicity, here, remains undispersed—or perhaps, like BP's oil dispersants that place the plume outside visibility beneath the surface, discretely doubled. Where does it next turn up? What form does the irradiation take from such a position? I have wondered whether to add this note out of discretion, but since we are speaking still *entre nous*, it is too signal a symptom to leave untouched.

I return to the sentence we have not gotten out of, that in which *nature* appears as a self-deconstructing logic redoubled fallaciously, its appearance of homogeneity the after-effect of a *re-totalization*. The sentence also marks by proxy a sort of site—that of a misreading of nature in "Romanticism"—out of which a thousand ideological ships would be, in de Man's sense, launched. "Nature." It displaces this preoriginary dissonance before a formalization (or naturalization-effect) which, instantly yet conversely, "deconstruction" itself shares. Yet, the sentence separates itself from the premise of "deconstruction" as if the latter found its limit in this Moebius-like redoubling and retotalizing of itself at once. That is to say, as the advance ghost of its auto-immune phase.

The sentence accounts in advance for differential readings of itself, from which it detaches in turn, folding in alternating referentials and shifting antecedents before injecting its toxins: that "nature" had all along been the name of a *process* that was in advance entirely self-deconstructing (and, semiotically considered, destroying); alternately, that a practice of "deconstruction" requiring a prior metaphysical template or period *to deconstruct* is similarly caught, may appear naturalized in its redoubling, pre-assimilated; or … but it can not stop rewriting itself, like an affront to a grammar which it inhabits like an excuse.

This operation can be condensed. One of the implications of this sentence (and one may hear the word, now, in its juridical echo, as being sentenced to a Sisyphian labour) is that it discretely assumes a foreclosure of the ecological and the *oikos* ("home"). This is a logic which we hear articulated specifically in the Benjamin lecture from which the remarks on the inhuman proceed: "for there is no homeland, nothing from which one has been exiled." Just as one might juxtapose with a little manipulation Derrida's hospitality to de Manian inhospitality, so one finds the premises of what might be called an *anecologics*. The hole in Derrida's script, the one he produced as the "late Derrida" who would not address "climate change," seems indexed to a sliding prohibition. That is, of an afigural zone he left de Man partitioned in, but also due, perhaps, to the lack of any (apparent) inscriptions in the archive itself from which to depart, or read. Yet here a certain discretion, as I said, is due. It is not as if one could make de Man "green," who begins the sentence in question with the entire artefaction of "nature" itself—its anarchism. What would be entailed if a de Manian vector were applied to the "ecological" man—including what is called "environmentalism"? That is, to the very repository of wandering or homeless aesthetic ideologies that wish to gather, today, in a hopeful or helpfully resistant site—yet whose perpetual organicist "relapse" unwittingly accelerates the self-cancelling arc of hypermodernity or hypercapital entering the 21st century broadly?

The *eco-catastrophic* imaginary today arrives, I suggested, not as a discourse of *crisis* at all, which as such would be appropriable and subject to apocalyptic triggers and tropes, but a sort of Archimedian point of reference outside of what we might call, in what is not even a slight stretch, machinal "anthropism." That is to say, it does not arrive as a discourse of "crisis," or as an invitation to apocalyptics or the trained avoidance of apocalyptics. It has nothing to do with apocalyptics or its deconstruction, is indifferent to both.[34] It implies, however, not a dispossession from the *metaphorics* of the home, from hospitality, and from commodified reference regimes, but a disclosure that the first were never there as such to begin with. The eco-catastrophic can be *used*, as Zizek does (2009), to pivot a sort of green Stalinism as the only possible response (thus, having declared such a moment a "zero degree" affair, sneaking back in the communist redemption of a 20th century project). It can also be used to authorize a destructive scan, of sorts, of the ways in which critical ideologies, ecocritical precepts, and cultural consumption have been *tropologically* programmed. You will understand in a moment why, here, I speak of a certain discretion as well.

Timothy Morton has recently opened a sort of war machine—in *Ecology without Nature* (2007) and related writings—against what he terms the figural premises and epistemological relapses in contemporary critical menus that cluster together in the concepts of systems theory, animal studies, new media, embodiment and what he terms, in general, *the ecomimetic*: "Ecocriticism is too enmeshed in the ideology that churns out stereotypical ideas of nature to be of any use. Indeed, ecocriticism is barely distinguishable from the nature writing that is its object." (13)

But the same *critique* will apply in differential registers to a more general "revised organicism" (191) of diverse brands of "after theory" today (systems theory, animal studies, embodiment, multitude studies, and so on). Morton indexes the default to a broad misreading of Romanticism, or its "nature," which plays a central if unwitting cognitive role in the blind of eco-catastrophic acceleration. For one thing, the phantom of interiority it ceaselessly would produce parallels insatiable eating. He finds what one could adduce as an array of *aesthetic ideologies* in the figure of *the ecological*—and its machinally replicating trope ("the fake otherness of ecomimesis" (169)). That is, where a certain anthropomorphic relapse perpetually engineers itself, what entraps the unsuspecting (systems theory, animal studies). This conceptual program is textured by a compulsion to naturalize reference, to expropriate, to consume, to attempt to *interiorize*, to eat. In the dissolution of any subject-object model Morton uses the phrase "a sentient being" rather than the name man. Morton inverts the ban on what he calls "theory" as absolute self questioning (*"environment is theory"* (75)), demands a "close reading" apparatus that includes a sort of China-syndrome meltdown toward RNA, and dissolves the tropes of subject or man itself into a situated descriptive: "sentient beings suffering under catastrophic environmental conditions" (12).

Morton could be said to write as easily of "ecology" without *the ecological*, understood not only as the final reserve of aesthetic ideology but a certain metaphorical accord that has become zombied by consuming its futures, life, as its destructive trajectory. This project, he defines in faux gothic mode as "*dark* ecology." What would be dark would be outside any tropologies of "light," stripped of redemption or personification, materially banal, "the poisoned mud" (202), entirely aware of the acceleration. More interesting for our purposes is what one would not want to call attention to, except in whispers, and with considerable discretion. That would be that the volume follows—in the most remote style possible and without any indexing, or acknowledgement—a serial and recognizably "de Manian" itinerary. Speaking from a vantage point properly indifferent to proper names, he ticks off the theoretical heritage of the present as properly kitsch. And if Morton were consciously following a de Manian agenda, in the least likely style and as a sort of unrecognizable "critical kitsch" (155), he would be right to delete the proper name "de Man" entirely, since it could only get in the way of a readership. The name itself appears neither in the index nor the preface in which he tells how he wants to be read and what his influences are. He identifies these as a respectable hybrid of Derrida (who nonetheless appears quite generic when invoked, and minimally) and of Marx (in a pop inverted and primarily displaced way, where consumption absorbs production). This would be its *front*—much as Adorno or Benjamin ("a theorist with whom ecocritique could engage productively" (161)) are invoked as particularly serviceable names to attach to this broader problematic today. The traces of de Man are all but coded and egregious, flashing up in the endorsement of "theory" as putting a totality into question, a totalization of the "aesthetic," an insistence on "close reading" (despite the formal absence of that), the targeting of "new organicisms," a pretextualization of "nature," the historical default of modernity in a misreading of Romanticism, a targeting of otherness merchandizing today (forms of embodiment, the animal, "systems theory," eco-criticism, and so on). What is remarkable is not that de Man would be an effaced template for Morton's work, or that the proper name itself is carefully deleted for the latter to do its work. It is that this work and transposition should occur, today, as targeted at the ecographic and ecological blind as the central station of aesthetic ideology—and that the latter, more or less, appears as a key factor in the ecocatastrophic itself.

Morton's war against the ecomimetic is against the manner in which mimesis itself is mistaken for reference in constructing a faux interiority, the home, which is militarized (against itself). If there is one practice that mobilizes the blind drive of human hyperconsumption, it is a tropological pathology riddled throughout cultural and "critical" idioms (and not just "ecocriticism"). There is nothing "uncanny" about this exposure of the *oikos*, since the latter is not violated or desanctified but is exposed as never having been there as such. This enigmatic compulsion engines a hyperconsumption of the earth ("Romantic environmentalism is a flavor of modern consumerist ideology" (172)). It is the aesthetic ideology of the "ecomimetic" that epistemographically engines its own disappearance. Thus Morton performs arcade-like drive-bys ("Systems theory is holism without the sticky wetness, a cybernetic version of the ecological imaginary. ... it merely updates Romanticism for an age of cybernetics" (103)). He reverses the *donnée* and trend that one has moved away from mere text to the world, which he finds only shows the "beautiful soul" projecting an access to his real, unmediated, only to then paint that world in the most entrenched metaphorics possible ("The beautiful soul is ecological subjectivity" (121)). This gothically self-caricatured "dark ecology" without redemption or transcendance genially includes the upbeat reminder that, well, *we* are still in the game and still game-changers potentially. That is, at least, if we could purge ourselves of the *ecomimetic* referential sickness. The latter, by this analysis, programs "us" in apparently suicidal modes (eating oneself out of house and home).

Logically, Morton can only proceed further into a literalization of this "inhuman" language, understood now with reference to the micrological orders precedent to letteration or sound. This other materiality finds a template in the domains of recombinant RNA and cellular production in the Darwinian imaginary purged of teleologies. Thus, in the chiastically titled "Ecology as Text, Text as Ecology": "An algorhythm is a script—a text—that automates a function, or functions, and in this case the script is encoded directly into matter. The matter-information boundary is permeable." (Morton 2010, 4–5) This *permeability* is only assumed if one begins from a linguistic premise to which the "human" is an effect different than but among other mnemotechnic orders that cannot be closed off.

At issue, on the contrary, is a too inescapable textuality embedded in advance of and traversing "life" forms, of which the linguistic "human" is a situated, if virulent, centre. It is an inverse tendril of what, as said, is in a sense today gestured at in the trope of *biosemiosis*: "There is no way rigidly to separate the biosphere and the non-biosphere. If the Earth had no magnetic field, for instance, life forms would be sizzled by solar winds" (9). This licenses less an *abiosemiosis* than a "calligraphy as biology" (15). The domain of a proto-mimetics of inscriptions (in the example of RNA) persists as an organic and *atelic technogenesis*: "Just as textuality smears the text-context boundary into aporia, if not oblivion, so the genomics version of ecological interrelatedness requires us to drop the organism-environment duality" (8). Differently, the random of genetic *pings* ciphered into cell-generation and reactive mutation echoes inversely with the algorithms of computerized market trading that "increasingly describes the entire financial system" today, the programs like *Lexicon* that digest innumerable articles and data on stocks, condense instantaneously, and make *decisions*—bypassing the human trader's tardiness of narrative, symbolic interpretation, fear.[35]

Morton's war with *ecomimesis*, a trope which itself supplants the vagueness of "anthropomorphosis," occurs at least in the name of a limitless auto-deconstruction: "Far from needing filling out with some positive 'thing' such as 'nature' or the ecofeminist / Lovelockian image of Gaia, this negative awareness is just what we need" (84). What we call the "human" is a discrete reference not to a living species but by and as a shared cognitive or linguistic reflex. It is a hermeneutic reflex indifferent to content itself, a *structure* in effect, in which what is affirmed as the home, as semantic propriety, as "we," is the most machinal of effects. Thus the "new organicism is possibly even stranger than the old one. In the new organicisim, 'emergent' formal organization—compared with the growth of flowers or the spread of clouds—depends upon the operation of some essentially algorhythmic process." (2007, 191).

## Currency Wars

> "We may no longer be hearing too much about relevance," de Man wrote in the late 1970s, "but we keep hearing a great deal about reference." In the subsequent decades, though, relevance proved more compelling than reference. Although … relevance may seem to have been more fantasy than fact, it's a fact that feminism, queer theory, critical race theory, and cultural studies continue to transform the way teachers and students view themselves and the world. But it is also the case that irrelevance, however irritating, is not necessarily an unproductive condition.
>
> Bill Brown, "All Thumbs" (Brown 2004, 452)

I return to my opening scan. That is, of how a sort of becoming-nuclear-waste occurs. Derrida begins in "Biodegradables" by fighting off and caricaturing this gesture by those attacking de Man in *Critical Inquiry*. This gesture of exclusion will later be taken up and discretely enacted by Derrida, under a different logic, in "The Typewriter Ribbon."

In the last named text Derrida performs an odd sort of *contretemps*, as Andrzej Warminski recently reminds us with an intricate examination of its stakes and warring manoeuvres titled "Machinal Effects" (2009). Warminski recalls the unusual scene, in which Derrida, having accepted to address de Man's much-delayed publication of work of "materiality" (*Aesthetic Ideology*), chose to all but ignore that and rather to return to the scene of the crime between the two. That is, to go back to Rousseau, and to have the final word, as Warminski puts it, as regards the text from which de Man's critique of *Grammatology* issued. He would instead settle scores with de Man, and in the process take back the word "deconstruction," all of this while managing to avoid the question of de Man's "materiality" almost to the end. After taking over a hundred pages winding through the first task, including a remarkable detour within a detour on two prehistoric insects frozen in amber, he turns to the latter and what we are given is a quick application with the *X without X* formula to the term (that formula had become a sort of Derridean *App* by that point). De Man's use of the term will be interpreted as "a materiality without matter," at once illuminated and diverted into the Derridean reserve of open-to-the-future regulations ("weak messianism").

Warminski focuses on what is nonetheless difficult to give a name to, a divergence between them, since neither Derrida nor de Man were to have openly named or addressed "it" after an initial exchange of letters following de Man's critique of *Grammatology*. There was something between the two—Warminski calls it "the disagreement or the divergence" (1072)—which they could not bring themselves to address but which they could not stop, nonetheless, referencing everything to. Warminski himself defers explaining the "divergence" to another occasion, and prefers to call it simply, well, "it," keeping the prohibition he finds the two enacting ("it's not this divergence that interests me here—perhaps I will have an opportunity to talk about it again another time—but rather what Derrida says about it—or, better, what he does with it" (1074)). Derrida cannot quite finalize his strategy, ensure he has the final word, and Warminski allows the problem to formalize itself as another machinal effect of Rousseau's purloined ribbon. This "it" or "divergence," which is the only thing that matters here, will have to be passed over in a way. "It" will also be deferred in Warminski's closing to another sort of "it." That is, that at issue beneath all of this after all will be, for Derrida, how to pardon the "unpardonable"—and that too is being talked around, gestured to, as if confessed to by not being confessed by de Man, and so on. *It* will become the only possible referent, as if replacing the first "it," though what is meant as "unpardonable" by Derrida may have a different referent than that of the wartime journalism (for instance, the critique of *Grammatology* he, Derrida, cannot stop going back to).[36] Warminski walks into a sort of primal scene which he cannot take his eyes off yet also wants to walk around. Like Obodiac's discrete assurances that de Man's repeated erasure of the word "deconstruction" in "Textual Allegories" does not reflect his engagement with Derrida, something emerges that is more lethal, perhaps, than deconstructive family lore wants to digest.

What Warminski identifies, as alluded to above, is where Derrida performs the discrete ritual of taking the word "deconstruction" back from de Man:

> one of the things that "Typewriter Ribbon" also does is to repeat, in a certain sense, Rousseau's theft. That is, Derrida steals back what had been taken from him, from his own text, in the first place. This would include de Man's appropriation of the term "deconstruction" first of all, as well as "dissemination," and the critical wielding of Austin's performative.
>
> (1088)

This taking back of a word as one's property is itself something of a trap and shows Derrida in a peculiar mode. He had mourned (and incorporated) de Man without success; he had defended (and undefended) de Man without success; here, he will erase de Man without success. In so far as one cannot take back what had been given back or cancelled in advance, the instinct to purge here positions him uncomfortably. Derrida would be left in the rather unde-constructive posture of maintaining the purity of "deconstruction," or essentially forging a new genealogy for the term henceforth, with de Man erased, backdated as necessary. This logic is sticky, viscous. It tars Derrida in assuming the posture of house-cleaning, of purifying, expunging, of a retrieval of the originary—thereby enacting one point of de Man's originary critique of him. Derrida would be simulating the position of the law.[37] At issue beneath this episode is not only the name "de Man," or the wounds he inflicted in and to "deconstruction" (essentially, in fact, suiciding it for itself as a gift), but what-ever the latter's "materiality" invoked. Derrida, of course, had every reason to eschew "de Man," who not only began by wishing to cancel Derridean deconstruction (if the text *deconstructs itself*, what exactly does the deconstructor "deconstruct," and so on?), but circled back after death to sabotage the brand. And yet what emerges is something other than a love dance of annihilations. Derrida, rather than engage de Man's "materiality," returned to remove this critique of himself from the books—as a bank might wish to do with its *toxic assets*.

The description Derrida gives of de Man's "materiality" should be retraced however. First, the characterization accords with the logics he deploys else-where of *khora* ("not something sensible or intelligible")—which may tell us that it is in the essay of that name, in fact, that Derrida's most relevant com-mentary on de Man occurs, though the latter's name is never evoked.[38] But one notices, almost too quickly, that in the phrase a "materiality without matter" an appropriation is under way:

> The materiality in question – and one must gauge the importance of this irony or paradox – is not a thing, it is not *something* sensible or intel-ligible; it is not even the matter of the body. As it is not something, as it is nothing and yet it works, *cela oeuvre*, this nothing therefore operates, it forces, but as a force of resistance. It resists both beautiful form and matter as substantial and organic totality. This is one of the reasons that de Man

never says, it seems to me, *matter*, but *materiality*. Assuming the risk of this formula, although de Man does not do so himself, I would say that it is a materiality without matter.

(Derrida 2002, 151)

Derrida does not explicate de Man's "materiality" so much as divert it toward the *spectral* circuitry which he himself would like to keep open—one which maintains the rhetoric of the *to come*. In turn, one could say that the formulation involves a sleight of hand, in so far as de Man's term suggests rather a sort of *matter without "materiality"* if the latter term retains any conceptual or binary form at all. Its asemic zone is ineradicably of the material world, an outside without interiority, perhaps "nucleic" or granular or preletteral, at the unintelligible point of non-contact between the technics of memory and the anorganic. ... Derrida both renames and defaces what "resists" here by softening it up for his own alternative appropriation of Benjamin. It might now be merged, if it were at all relevant or useful (it would not be) with *weak messianism*, openness to the future (by curtailing its address), hospitality, the "democracy to come." Among the more astute remarks on this dilemma in the contemporary context is Claire Colebrook's characterization of a *destructive* "materialism" that cannot be either purged or effaced:

> Materialism would be an annihilating and rhetorical gesture, destructive of any matter that would function as a stabilising and recognisable organised body from which human actions would supposedly proceed. The putatively materialist Derrida of a naturalised life along with the Derrida of an ethics of the labouring polity would be extinguished by a conceptualisation of matter that refused to accommodate our attachments to the figures of humanity. But a certain Deleuze of materialism would also meet his end here, precisely because a Deleuze coupled with radical materialism would be a Deleuze of micropolitics. This radical materialism would address matters that exceed living systems; but would also be mindful of concepts and radical ideality.
>
> (Colebrook 2011)

De Man's "materiality" would then not be susceptible to the *X without X* shell-game and cannot be marked even as a non-word. It falls for de Man, perhaps, into a set of words withdrawn from trope altogether, *not susceptible of deconstruction*. In the unpublished manuscript "Textual Allegories" we find: "'Self' and 'society' are mere figures susceptible to being deconstructed. The same is true, of course, of such simplifying conceptual labels that pretend to distinguish between political, ethical, or even epistemological *texts*. ... The same applies to less superstructural—and hence perhaps less obviously, though no less actually ideologized—metaphors such as "man" or "self" or "love". This is not true of such terms as *praxis* or *figure* or *text* (are they categories?), which are truly ineluctable in their manifestation, despite (or because of) their falsehood." (De Man 2009)

Derrida's processing of a de Manian "materiality without matter" is part of his suppression of de Man's having staged, experienced, marked, and departed from the death of "deconstruction" *productively*—alternatively, in advance, and then again after death. As in the sentence on "nature," it would also curtail any fetishization of legacy or corporate formalization as a "fallacious re-totalization" to be defaced. There is in this poisoned gift a certain politics of *friendship*. Derrida would have every reason to resent the trap de Man set for him yet that would not exclude something like a bad conscience (to himself)—having placed himself in opposition not with his constructed "de Man," but with a certain Derrida that might have sided with the latter's place (an "early" Derrida, say).[39] In turn, de Man might all along have been reading what he saw as most "irreversibly" at stake in the early Derrida—rhetorically distilled.

Derrida backs away. He had every reason to hate this loop. It gave him nothing back, it attacked him from behind and sabotaged him from after-death, it poisoned the brand—it was time to sacrifice it, were it sacrificeable. But here we see something like the revenge of the *homo sacer* position.

Derrida reflects in "Biodegradables" on another possibility. That is, that de Man had anticipated a post-mortem release of his scandalous journalism. He does not go on to suggest from what perspective he thinks de Man might have done so. For instance, sabotage as a gift of Nietzschean *friendship*? A time-bomb that would go off later would also be a challenge for Derrida to exceed the termination of a "deconstruction" that could be formalized, pretended to as a canonical legacy, lose its destroying import or "irreversibility." Such a move would be rather Zen, perhaps as practiced by Poe, on de Man's part—and, necessarily, toxic. One who would suicide the proper name did not stand to lose anything not discounted in advance; the other had become hostage to the narrative of his creation, which he required to survive. This accounts, in Derrida, not for the cryptic Hebraicism that is forever sought but a mimic trace of the Christianity that would fascinate him as much as it scandalized. Derrida, in "The Typewriter Ribbon," found himself machinally performing the inevitable, a self-immunizing ritual that takes into itself the purging gesture of his earlier antagonists. It is the departure point for what can seem a moment of bad faith in the "late Derrida's" artefaction. I have speculated elsewhere on what a Derrida who had lived for another decade or so might have written in turning toward the aporia of climate change (Cohen 2010). I have wondered whether he did not occasionally get bored performing the "late Derrida," once crafted and wired to it, or tend to phone it in a bit, or be subtly contaminated by the closed circle of buffers, dependents, servicers, friends, and translators who would urge on or enable the strategy. Derrida's decision to insulate himself from a certain *Nietzschean* strand within his work by purging "de Man" involved, again, a turn against another possible or deferred "Derrida"—and he soured at that ghost, not of a de Man who may have trapped Derrida in some way, but a choice tainted by an oversubtle calculation of survival.

What one could say, however, is that Derrida's most consequent reading of de Man would occur in an essay in which the latter's name does not appear, is not cited, and has no overt index—and yet where the "materiality of inscription" as a proactive and pre-phenomenal site (or non-site) is conjured, engaged, as at where the memory programs would as if be set, erased, or given place. That is, an agency "radically rebellious against anthropomorphism" which Derrida solicits—in a departure from the political, ethical, and religious agendas—as *khora*:

> And yet, "khora" seems never to let itself be reached or touched, much less broached, and above all not exhausted by these types of tropological or interpretative translation. One cannot even say that it furnishes them with the support of a stable substratum or substance. *Khora* is not a subject. It is not the subject. Nor the support [*subjectile*]. The hermeneutic types cannot inform, they cannot give form to khora except to the extent that, inaccessible, impassive, "amorphous" (*amorphon*, 51a) and still a virgin, with a virginity that is *radically rebellious against anthropomorphism*, it seems to receive these types and give place to them.
>
> (Derrida 1993, 95 [my italics])

With all the impossibilities of this conjuration, mediated by a half personified non-figure, what is implied is the most "political" domain conceivable—what precedes epistemologies and cognitive regimes. Today these are hyperliteralized in pragmatic if caricatured fashion as various softwares, telemarketing circuits, genetic engineerings. And one could assume when a program of reference launched from *khora* had become totalized and suicidal—as it had for what Benjamin called "fascism"—the question arrives of a pharmacological intervention, destruction, dispersement of what had seemed the "material inscriptions" as if in place. De Man, who wished like Benjamin's so-called "materialistic historiography" to displace such a chimera at its phantom source (to stay within this *mythos*), thought he had experienced an "irreversibility," at least, from which this spell might not be returned to. What Derrida fought off in his "de Man" was not just a damaged name, or a version of "early" Derrida he wished to rebrand, but the possibility that de Man's negativity, "radically rebellious against anthropomorphism," irreversibly so, would be an inevitable supplement to his scriptive legacy, would have to return in the afterlife that is "life."

All of this can be anachronized today from a point in time at which the "biodegradable" has shifted from a metaphorical zone to a literal one which, in turn, rereads the negotiations. In a recent consideration of the *dead de Man's* transformation within Derrida, Tze-Yin Teo notes: "Derrida's straw-man distinction here and his suspicion of the violence of the biodegradable ... seem to take place on a common presupposition separating the 'living organicity' of the event from the mechanistic forces (textual or biodegrading) seeking to rend its singularity apart." (Teo 2010, 102). But behind these is Derrida's reluctance to address a question of "materiality" associated with de Man. This unconfigurable and unusable *(a)materiality* that assigns to de Man a figural status linked to ecological waste is not only conflated with ex-anthropics, the (in)organic, oil, insects, and something that resists every communal and anthropic model of the *bios* itself. Teo repositions it as a weapon interrupting a suicidal acceleration of holocaust proportions, regarding "responsibility" to the unborn:

> Whereas biodegradability seemed at first, by necessity and definition, to be assimilable and unassimilable at the same time, if it is now thought of as the force of a materiality that has lost its very matter, then the issue lies not in assimilation, but its potential for *usure* and deterioration—biodegradation without bios. Moreover, then, not only does it not commit violence to the victims of trauma, it may in fact function as the ethical and responsible mode of resistance in itself—a disseminating force that can even, it seems, relate and equate the insect to the comedy of human incest, or give rise to alternate spaces of responsible discussion.
>
> (105)

The anecdote of the prehistorical "insects" caught in amber—a frozen archive unto itself—occurs as an interlude.[40] The "insect," outside mammalian temporality to say nothing of history, non-biodegradable in its own archive (amber), is allied to the typographical error—yet which spins off, in this zone, in association with his de Man. We may add this premammalian exoskeletal insect to the ex-ecoskeletal figures by which "de Man" was fossilized.

Teo takes advantage of the term *biodegradables* to mark an intervention: "perhaps Derrida did not know that (even) if waste is non-biodegradable, the next most responsible thing to do is to put it to other use." (95) Teo transposes this nuclear waste, redeploys it, re-oriented in the face of the present's indifference to countless virtual generations of the unborn. In so doing she reverses the ethical posture of "de Man" who, rather than rhetorically tainted by the last century's iconic genocide, posits an indigestible resistance to cognitive totalizations that passively incur a future one of unthinkable proportions: "Oddly (or aptly) enough, then, biodegradation without bios can be a responsible force of materiality tracing the contours of a living space for the future unborn." (105) *It* does so for breaking with the anthropic or biocentric circuit, the same model as that of a faux sustainability of a faux "eco" system, often telecratically managed as "public space" today. And it does so, with no credit, by dispossessing the metaphorics of the home, by an "irreversibility" that exceeds the hermeneutic relapse as cognitive reflex (and effacement), by positioning the inhuman in advance of the enphantoming of a "human" that had never existed as a definitional—that is, reversing the cultural extension toward otherness, toward the "otherness of the other," in various sub-categories, that defined the supposedly ethical preoccupations of the 1990s.

What this unpacks is not another reversal of position. Here "materiality" is not of language in any singular sense (English, Russian) but any possible *mnemotechnics*—including the pre-letteral mark outside of any era of the Book, or the "inhuman" outside any speciesization of *man*.[41] This "responsible force of materiality" would trace "the contours of a living space for the future unborn." It repositions what was called "de Man" against a foreclosure abetted, if not steam-rolled, by the epistemographic and referential blinds of historicism, culturalism, empiricism, phenomenology, and so on. Contrary to the invectives of "fascist" that Derrida had to parry, the import of Derrida's "de Man" purged from humanist discourse (itself now collaborationist as much as historicism was nihilist) challenges a 21st century passive holocaust to come (it is implied) wherein countless generations would be robbed, cut-off, despoiled of legacy, resources, by the rapacious "present" of today. One has moved from mythographies of a last world war, a contamination by its rhetorical horrors, to a resistance to a totalization that implies mass extinction events. It was never a simple issue of which side one was on (liberal democracy vs. fascist, free market vs. communist, both), since the totality of the subsequent "global" era would only make normative and accelerate that war with itself, with the earth, with other life-forms, with its "self." Incest, *insects*, indeed—frozen *in flagrante* in transparent amber like, in a sense, the two "Ds" stuck in the amber of this text, frozen in time at their point of initializing non-contact. To a degree Derrida speculates on himself arrested in this amber, once viscous, adopting the male position to de Man's pre-emptive defacement, calling back his property in a break up, trying to legislate a purge and even doctor the nominal birth certificates—a hurt love, not taking in the enigma of the feminized position, viscous, plastic, *as if* "literary." Yet within the equivocations at work here is the instability of an aberrant reversal: that the Derrida who would proceed from this point, and precisely that on the "political," would be literary, and that the "materiality" here lost as a non-figure, or its hostility to "anthropomorphism," involved an irreversible excess.

## (Academic) Resource Wars—a Satyr play in no acts

> Look at the headlines and you'll see what I mean. Populations are exploding. The environment is stressed to the max. Massive climate changes, whether natural or manmade, are accelerating. Disasters are hitting with alarming regularity. We're witnessing one giant global game of "survival," operating under the same dynamic you see after a hurricane, flood, or earthquake. Every person and every nation is clamouring to get their piece of the natural resource pie. They're desperate for fuel. They absolutely MUST have water. And for ultimate security, they rush to gold and silver. Not surprisingly, as inevitably occurs in any disaster zone, that means these natural resources – the building blocks of lives and societies – are getting *more valuable*.
>
> Sean Brodrick, "America's Next Crisis is Dead Ahead," *Money and Markets* (2010)

Naturally enough, there is a question today of how to play (as the market says) natural resources or commodities—in and out of finances. This includes the academic arena: the UK slashing of Humanities support, the defunding of the public universities, the corporate allocation of resources. It is increasingly clear the "Humanities" has mysteriously failed to market itself well in this environment. I would not give that defense, here, but do find it curious that (to conclude the above analysis) the minimalist, viscous, unusable, mnemotechnic, prephenomenal, conceit of de Manian "materiality" might, in all common sense, offer a robust explanation and, at the same time, a site of acute resistance to the perspectival interests of the education industry to come (finance, science). This is particularly valuable to imagine in relation to the public university—and it returns to where the non-figure itself remains, again in its way, the true disclosure of what American pragmatism might have entailed as a cognitive orientation.

One can see why Derrida wished to circumvent de Man's "materiality." It is not only that he considered the word toxic, the very signature of metaphysics, and must have first sniffed at de Man's deployment of it. He may or may not have reflected that the choice, which seemed radically innocuous, was taken in the face of Derrida's dismissal. And perhaps he calculated there was nothing to gain from it at all, the timing was not right, the referentials would not be recognized, the *aporias* it released were not, perhaps, manageable, and impeded the sort of identification process that a community could engage and feel ennobled by. Moreover, it did not lead to a spectrology. With the economic crash the phantom of ecological recuperation in politics was effectively nullified, were that not already accomplished with Bush's war on terror distraction, and one passes from the first reactive modes to a post-"tipping point" regard in other ways. With this the neo-feudal corporate order consolidates itself, security apparatuses consolidate, long term economic and geographical triage accelerates. These pressures operate too within the university's *resources*.

A New York State University announces in 2010 it has decided to close language-centered Humanities programs before chronic budget slashing, a situation echoed everywhere (the UK's withdrawal of all funding for the Humanities, California's department and salary slashes). Unable to have mounted an explication or defense of the "Humanities" before the sciences and finance interests in the last decades, when it had time and some leisure to do so, *we* are of course shocked—just shocked—to find the long expected occurring. A huge rally of signatures from all over testifies that this was to be opposed on all counts, that it signifies an end of high culture (if not the Humanities) as such: it is to be rolled back, or else. ... The gesture of resistance is worth reading, however, as it might be heard from without, even as the pieces are slipping into place for the corporate-feudal order of the future university (BP reportedly now determines what the Gulf university scientists can report and study). As Tea Party types arrive with no interest in public university funding, and the nation's education system is falling, and a movement forms rejecting the high price or need of these degrees for the indebted young, this much we know: we can't give up language programs (in translation), acknowledge the eclipse of European language studies, or that the Humanities as crafted by post-war ideology on 19th century theo-philological models themselves bogus ("*the* Humanities"?) might, perhaps, have been long zombied for a reason. What interests me, though, is less the gesture of wanting to restore, hold in place, retain, give up nothing, even as millions lose jobs in the emerging feudal economy or undergraduates enter a world in which Mandarin might be thought an imperative. While the 1970's order of comparative linguistic studies (which de Man was a core viral of) gives way, without the Euro-directed cold war premise remaining, it will be sustained in private universities for a time. What is more interesting is what or how public universities mount or continue a "Humanities" study that is not, increasingly, seen as a preparatory service for corporate centres of the university (the sciences)? It is here strangely, on the most pragmatic level, that the technical premise de Man departed from raises a question.

It is not often academics get to rebel in righteous indignation, and it is a great bonding moment—but the fact is we are not going back to the 20th century accord, any more than the "West" is atop the political and economic hill. It is Europe and America that are juggling bankruptcy, as the economics of American universities—or *public* universities—is disarticulated.

It might be more in keeping with this disarticulation to refrain from solidarity by English departments with language programs and, instead, request that "English" itself be dissolved in order to leave this model entirely and reconfigure in a way that acknowledges vast changes in global and local realities.[42]

In the public university it seems the question is not that posed today—of unfairly amputated programs themselves—but what those imply: in the university in question, that is a concession of abandonment of the research university model in the Humanities, or its pretence, and the re-orientation to the future financial anchors of such an entity, the sciences. Things die, institutions end. But the question of a public university supported by corporate interests (there, the castle is nanoscience) represents an interesting opportunity: to reconceive a "Humanities" entity that can explain its import in relation to finance, the sciences—preserving the traditions it takes with it in relation to the new court of corporate universities in a survival mode. That is, a public university defunded by those who do not see its need or purpose in the economy—or the need of "higher" education for a swathe of population, when the real "higher" education is in the private great universities. The ante has been upped—beyond that of a Euro-centred model that has been, after a great run, decentred.[43]

Is the reaction I described by the humanities community again symptomatic of the denial if not denegation that courses through America—which itself seems about to give way to a succession of impacts with a "materiality" it cannot cognitively ingest? The alternative would be, rather than try to recuperate an unworkable educational contract or even definition (*the Humanities* as artificed from the 1970's), like restoring a lethal Wall Street regime with counterfeit trillions for a time, to pre-emptively dissolve that (take "English," too). Such would allow an ex-Humanities entity to "go under" and reconfigure itself in partnering with the sciences and business interest not based on department fiefdoms, language models, the ghost of Euro-culture, and the inevitability of a service relation to the latter that discards the research interests of these imponderably rich traditions and reading practices. This residue, on innumerable levels, of the era of the Book would allow itself to reconfigure the post-disciplinary knowledge formations and a post-culturalist *paideia*. Such might be reconfigured around something as simple and misleading as the phrase *'Textual' Systems*, a figure that could as readily bridge the universe of finance and cellular "life" systems (the binding thread being marking systems, mnemonic, programming).[44] It would not be textualist in the sense once misleadingly conferred or caricatured, as if that were separate from the world of reference itself, since it would not discriminate initially between systems of inscription that pervade the life sciences and financial algorithms. All the ideological investments famous in the humanities—from the so-called political to the crypto-theological and back (which is not far)—would take place, but would also be *marked*, too, as conceptualized systems among others, like the comparative religions approach, only focused on how various fields of reference and power organize themselves within these resistances.

The "materiality" I have been addressing, the focus on the politics of differential reference systems, the ability to turn across registers divided by old definitional guardrails more apt for 19th century impasses, the gathering of diverse interpretive agendas in relation to what both marks and precedes letteration, the passage into the shared "commons" of other materialities, the situatedness in and of the inhuman, the always possible auto-critique of "aesthetic ideology" or organicist epistemographies drawing into the field of discussion the mutation of resource and biosystems together with the iconographies of the 20th century "social"—these tranches would be always possible to jointly index in a period in which reference itself is under translation.

What is interesting is that just such a reconfiguration would be commonly oriented, or must, in relation to a shared tele-figure of "materiality" that threads these knowledge orders and mnemonic systems, and contests each. It would assume what may be called *telemorphosis* itself—and the association of language, concept, phenomenalization, "ideology," and teletechnologies with the negative transformations of a suicidal epistemology. Such an aggressively minimalist agenda need not pre-assume any semantic core (shared values, Western tradition, cold war fictions). It is in a sense amusing that such a commonsense orientation might, in outline, describe what certain bare elements of a *de Manian* pedagogy might be in its most serviceable level: that is, where the "textual" systems that enwrap the earth generating power formations and absorbing life-forms involve a vaster study of mnemonics and cognitive differentiation. Since a moralistic and referentially enfaithed left came to define the point of such study as bound to imaginary politics and politically correct attestations (which served key purposes before being commodified and assimilated), it had lost more and more purchase on any political eventuations, and may be thought to have been the perfect unwitting accompaniment with a side of cultural studies for the "Bush" years. One would argue that the sciences, though, should not have too much smug *Schadenfreude*. Vouchsafed grant money at the price of becoming mere technicians for corporate interests, they are cut off from political and pop discourse just as effectively (climate change science).[45]

One can see the recoil—but, at the present juncture, insisting on the restoration of a cherished status quo has something unreflective about it. This becomes the more fascinating as this zombie struggle, this relapse, occurs before calculations that are altering the biosphere, seeding resource wars, promising inundated coasts, and spinning global finance off any recognizable path in a frenzy of temporal cannibalization (consumed futures, zombied presents). This seeps out daily, and has become a numbing cognitive accompaniment, as histories appear calculable against geological markers, and the "after theory" generation appears, if anything, drawn back to stealth organicist models—at times, pre-critical ones. Is there a counter-genealogy to this rather exitless or aporetic "present" and, in the minor domain of cultural and linguistic theorization, was it sealed with the erasure of its one relentless counter-point: Paul de Man? All of which is not to say, as I have insisted, that this backward glance into an alternative genealogy of the "present," a distinctly spellbound present, is in any way a movement designed to "save" or recirculate or deploy "Paul de Man's legacy." It is only to suggest that those who will have to invent an unrecognizable model in the next horizons that practices an asubjectal mode, will find a resource in a 20th century anomaly.

The problem of *inscriptions* is that of cognitive technologies and geological time. An example of such inscription would be the calendar. It presumes a zero point of departure (and forgetting), in this case a gift from Rome, yet in practice is little different than advocates of intelligent design marking a moment of creation itself. One would tip over innumerable cognitive regimes were one to in general practice daily date one's taxes or birthday or semesters to geological time (say, 5,200,372,011 years?) or even to the "anthropocene" clock. "2011" marks itself—or will be marked from backglances to come—as the rough date when the irreversibility of extreme global warming would be publicly conceded, the sixth mass extinction event calculated, the "anthropocene era" naming itself as if from without. *Geoengineering* has become the quiet fallback discussion (as has begun at Cancun, since, at least, it can generate new industries).[46]

The reason why this is an "American" fable is that there has always been a way of reading de Man that would clarify the rhetorical meme of an American *pragmatism*. That is, of a *pragma* heard and understood as it was by the Greeks, as thing and letter, the precise inversion of the sort of narcissistic façade that makes of that term a sort of "opportunism" or conning today. One could file this episode then under a dossier to come on the American hallucinology during the period, or hinge-decade, in which the negative destinies of terrestrial life stretching forward aeons had been passively determined. There is a certain clarification involved in this irreversible passage, since it suspends the regressive rhetoric of a "crisis" and its faux recuperative desires to evade, deny, defer, appropriate, sustain, mitigate or redeem. There is something ineluctably positive about that clarification from the point of view of this irreversibility. The allegory of auto-betrayal of *the abjected de Man* returns as the counter-pole to the profounder auto-betrayal of America more broadly—of and by an

"America" which, perhaps, as a definitional, never existed "as such." De Man's unusable "materiality" may be read as mere common-sense. If perception and action are premised on memory programs, and these are constituted necessarily by trace mechanisms, and the former has itself entered something like a totalized trance itself become suicidal and auto-accelerative, then the only appropriate intervention is not to repeat the mimetic *données* of "the political" that maintain a disabling metaphorical and referential alliance with that stream, but to assault the non-site at which these had been as if installed, what are consigned the apposite name of a "materiality of inscriptions." It is interesting that de Man was never read as what in some senses he was, apart from the media surrounding "deconstruction." That is, read through the lens of one as if executing the micrological premises, stripped of rhetorical pathos or messianic postures, of Benjamin's "*materialistic* historiography"—that is, again, of a Benjamin who de Man almost always avoided addressing and would not write directly on until his very last lecture (and this, in a "lecture" delivered only from notes). A Benjamin who, he once quipped, was "an overrated writer." One can also see why that has not occurred, since it would have taken away the *Benjamins* most sought and invested in, as occurs in "Conclusions" itself.

I have suggested that one can up the stakes a bit by reading the abjection of de Man also as a viral fable of American self-betrayal on autopilot—that is to say, a fable also diagnosing a hyperperiod of telecratic capture, financial despoilment, consumer intoxication, imperial decline, and so on, in what increasingly appears to have been a losing planetary wager (5 percent of global population, 25 percent of its energy consumption, general stupor). According to this deep-sea perspective, in its fashion, the *abjection of de Man* had involved a suppression of the originary implication of American *pragmatism* itself. That is, before it devolved into the slick opportunism of self-invention, and well before Rorty and his heirs' convenient appropriations. Such a de Manian *pragmatism*, which could be extracted with little effort from Emerson, re-initializes the original Greek *pragma* itself (as thing and letter). American *pragmatism* was to have been the index of a detheologization of the world through an exploration and evasion of tropological seduction, the resetting of "man" as a responsibly sentient cognitive force "free" from old world cultural indexes. That is, to speak in now archaic terms, something that does not result in but departs from an epistemological critique of reference without reserve or reserves.

# 3   The calculus of individual worth

## Claire Colebrook

De Man was making it up, faking it, knowingly misleading – driven by Theory's *parti pris,* by prejudice, to get a stock response. Nowhere in his essay does Benjamin say the task of the translator is impossible – only that it is very hard (at best it can only be like an interlinear version of the Bible, but it can be done in this fashion). And such mistaking on Theory-driven grounds is typical of Paul de Man.

(Cunningham 2002, 92)

Assuming there is a Yale mafia, then surely there must be a resident Godfather. One is forced to finger Paul de Man, who exhibits qualities that may earn him the role of Don Paolo, *capo di tutti capi.*

(Lentricchia 1981, 283)

## The cost of theory

Today is possibly not the day for theory. It may have been possible once – or at least we might have been lured into a certain luxury – to believe that theorizing was not a violent indulgence occurring at the expense of practice. Those days seem to be over. We are not facing local or delimited crises that demand some reflection on an otherwise healthy polity. For many, there is no longer any politics: either circumstances of environmental and financial catastrophe are so intense that we have abandoned urbane reflection and adopted a state of emergency (necessary to avert chaos)[1] *or* the sense of a state of emergency has been used to reduce what *ought* to be a political and deliberative life to a system of bureaucratic management that has closed down any sense that our system of government and law originally emerges from practice and decision.[2] The world we live in today is ambivalent in its post-theoretical malaise (Elliot and Attridge 2010). We are post-theory in a desirable sense, for we feel threats to human and organic life far too intensely: these threats demand more than reflection and distanced scrutiny. But the condition of the post-theoretical is also deemed to be lamentable; whereas we might once have argued that denying theory was really a way of asserting the universality of one's own theory (and therefore one's own politics) – because we all know that perception and experience are 'theory laden' – experience is now flat, deemed to be devoid of sense, 'life-world' or framing.[3] In part, Paul de Man is blamed for this sense of theory as *mere* theory, a sense that ought to be overcome (it is argued) by grounding theory in politics, which (in turn) would be a genuine sense of radical history:

> For de Man, representation could only ever be self-representation, and its ironic component could only ever be an aspect of individual consciousness, or personality. In political terms, this is the basis of a certain kind of 'democracy', identified as that which underpins the bourgeois individualism of the so-called 'free' democracies, paradigmatically America. But the political question of representation is potentially more complex than this, especially if we shift form the de Manic position which is founded on the centrality of homogeneous self-identity towards a position based more on the heterogeneity of alterity.
>
> (Docherty 1996, 132)

The idea of de Man as a paradigmatically American individualist (however ironic) is just what this essay seeks to contend. If Docherty appeals to a better mode of deconstruction, liberated from 'de Manic' isolationism, he is typical of a generally proclaimed turn to a more properly historical and actively political theory. We live, it would seem, in an age of the bio-political where life is regarded as so much matter to be managed and maximized. What is lost is both *the political* (or a critical sense of the world deliberated with the distance of theory) and the conditions in which such a theoretical polity might be regained (Eagleton 2004, 87). De Man's supposed role in depoliticizing literature, in turning it into a mode of individualism, privation and even a 'Final Solution' is symptomatic in at least two senses; de Man represents a past of high theory that turns in upon itself and that now (we are told) needs to be opened to politics, and de Man is constantly invoked as an evil from the past in order to secure a more proper, more human future. But for the grace of good politics we might all one day become de Man. De Man is used to define a certain risk of privation, of reading turning in upon itself. Eagleton's 'guide' to literary theory places de Man in a line of increasingly amputated reading, moving further and further away from a reality that Eagleton would (eventually) aim to save from the laziness of postmodernism:

> For de Man, as for his colleague, Hillis Miller, literature does not need to be deconstructed by the critic: it can be shown to deconstruct itself, and moreover is actually 'about' this very operation. The textual operations of the Yale critics differ from the poetic ambivalence of New Criticism. Reading is not a matter of fusing two different but determinate meanings, as it was for the New Critics; it is a matter of being caught on the hop between two meanings which can neither be reconciled nor refused. Literary criticism thus becomes an ironic,[4] uneasy business, an unsettling

venture into the inner void of the text which lays bare the illusoriness of meaning, the impossibility of truth and the deceitful guiles of all discourse. In another sense, however, such Anglo-American deconstruction is no more than the return of the old New Critical formalism. Indeed, it returns in intensified form, because whereas for New Criticism the poem did in some indirect way discourse about extra-poetic reality, literature for the deconstructionists testifies to the impossibility of languages ever doing more than talk about its own failure, like some barroom bore.

(Eagleton 2008, 126)

Imagine what the contrary to this assertion would be: literature does not deconstruct itself, for it attaches to a reality that is not at all ambiguous from the literary point of view. There is a reality, and it is political; it is found in work – real work, not literary work. And we *know* this because a guide to theory tells us so. We might ask whether secure knowledge (or what we can grasp without getting caught up in the messiness of reading) is really today in such short supply. In an era where there is no shortage of information – when data regarding climate change, world poverty and illicit financial practice is readily available, and yet where denial occurs alongside the detailing of certain facts – would we not benefit from *reading* in a manner that confronted a certain paralysis, a certain tendency to take the text simply for what it is, as a clear and comforting assertion that 'we' all know who 'we' are and what 'we' mean? What is left of theory tends now to be coterminous with what is left of the 'Left,' and for both these remnants there is a quite clear answer to this question of whether we might not be better off *without* secure knowledge. The answer is a firm and defiant 'no.' Reading today is largely defined *against* theory. There is no shortage of diagnoses of how theory lost its way in textualism and can now be returned to the body, life, affect, ethics, animality or living systems (Moore and Kosut 2010; Fraser, Kember and Lury 2006; Clough and Halley 2007; Davis and Womack 2001; Gottschall and Wilson 2005; Moretti 2005). (I name a series of trends and turns that have proclaimed their distance and redemption from poststructuralist imprisonments in language.) Far from confronting the inability of life as such to appear in its obvious and self-evident good sense and moral certainty, literary criticism has produced a series of new foundationalisms that restore literature, away from theory, and back to living systems (with the 'living' increasingly being established through a regressive reading of Darwin). The current dominant in theory takes the form of a return to Darwinian life (despite Darwin's radicalism[5]), and it does so often as an explicit cure for the ills of de Manian deconstruction:

In Paul de Man's critical theory, as in the defense of de Man constructed by Derrida and seconded by Jameson, pro-Nazi commentaries on the Jewish problem in Europe during World War II would appear as undecidable textual events, but to the people who died in the showers the death camps were neither textual nor undecidable. ...

Every reader has his or her own structure of beliefs or values, but the text itself is not amorphous. If the reader has even the most minimal competence – if the reader can read at all and is not literally illiterate – the determinate structure of meaning in a text exercises a stimulating and constraining influence. *That is why we read texts.*

(Carroll 1995, 92)

De Man has a certain journalistic worth, as a figure typical of theory's blindness to politics (Lehmann 1991); but the real symptom of de Man is evident within theory itself, for theory after de Man is ever more insistent on its practical task and properly engaged nature: 'Politically, deconstruction translates into that passive kind of conservatism called quietism; it thereby plays into the hands of established power. Deconstruction is conservatism by default – in Paul de Man it teaches the many ways to say that there is nothing to be done' (Lentricchia 1985, 51). Other forms of deconstruction might pretend to be ethical and political but de Man's anti-political politics – his reduction of everything to private and sub-jective reading – has been asserted quite boldly by those in the upper echelons of the literary critical industry. Valentine Cunningham, for example, uses de Man as an example of Theory as 'Final Solution' (Cunningham 2002, 1) and as an assertion, by way of negation, of anything outside reading, of the subjective:

this isn't simply a matter of following the tricky logics of deconstruction, and reading negatives as positives – recognizing that the human subject was really present in and through all of its negativizing by Theorists, like saying that Jews were really being granted their due cultural importance by being featured in Paul de Man's anti-Semitic articles (a common deconstruc-tionist move) ... Though there is something in such a mode of approach-ing and seeing through Theory's great negativity about the old human contract of reading. The intrusive presence of the Theorist, for example, insisting on staging herself as a reader, pushily shoving himself into the forefront of the scene of reading, was of course a declaration of human identity, of the necessity of the human subject in the reading act and of human contact with the interpreted text.

(Cunningham 2002, 143)

De Man is at once, therefore, the intrusive theorist who might be identified as committing the 'common move' of mentioning a term and thereby releasing oneself from any attack on one's failure to address cultural importance; at the same time, de Man is someone who shows the importance (despite himself) of 'human contact.' Let's pause and examine the 'logic' of Professor Cunningham: there is a fault in passing from mentioning a term to affirming the term. The 'chance' example would be someone who said that an anti-Semite (such as de Man) affirms Judaism, just by mentioning a term. Now, did *anyone* say this? Did anyone ever claim that de Man's work asserted the due cultural importance of Jews, precisely by being anti-Semitic? Never mind: Cunningham, while speaking about the corruption of truth, creates a quick analogy or figure (Theory as 'Final solution', *like* someone who *would say* … ). Cunningham's quick association cannot be argued *against*, because it isn't asserted. David Lewis (1979) has referred to this as 'scorekeeping' in conversation; if a term circulates without explicit notice or comment, then assertion is beside the point; it counts as a move that remains in play unless returned to and challenged explicitly. The aftermath of theory is just such a fog of vaguely associated smears, and is akin to so-called forms of political 'debate' that lament the fall of political intellect but do so by short-circuits in thinking (by *not* reading, by knowing – in advance – the common moves, the negativities, and the 'necessity' of the human subject). Theory, of the de Man style, would paralyse or slow down such easy and glib identities, and would be worth practicing in just those domains that his work would seem – by being about reading – to exclude. Glen Beck (of USA's Fox news) recently associated universities with mind-control, and Beck did so all in the name of saving the *real* America.[6] Like Cunningham, there is an attack on supposed confusion. The attack takes aim at threatening figures – universities, theory, de Man – who have questioned 'our' (surely self-evident) moral foundation.

The riposte to such hysteria should not be to assert de Man's genuine morality, nor the real security of deconstruction, but to say that such warring confusion is not an accident: reading, like ethics, is only possible because one must decide, and one must decide because there is no indisputable law or meaning available outside the labour of reading. Further, there cannot be a separation between good theory – grounded in politics and publicity – and bad theory, closed in on itself and self-interested. Indeed, it was de Man, more than any other thinker, who did not allow himself the comforts of such a divide. Michel Foucault also noted that whereas pre-modernity could possess a morality, or normative code, modernity was now solely 'ethical': not able to assert this or that norm but only capable of normalizing a properly human (lawful) reason against 'mad' (ungrounding) and inhuman unreason (Foucault 2009). Rather than battling on the terrain of decisions, modernity has grounded ethics on some proper underlying form of good sense. Some (many, in fact) might say that it was this failure to think morally that allowed de Man to fall into the traps of anti-Semitism. But is it not more likely that the scar in de Man's work – the blind mention of certain anti-Semitic motifs – resulted from a moment of residual ideology and *not* from his ruthless and abyssal mode of interrogation? Such a de Manian mode of reading and rhetorical attentiveness would not only preclude the simple opposition of *anti*-Semitism (relying on a bounded national identity and relatively unified political grouping); it would also operate as a force in today's smug moralism that rests securely in an opposition between real commitment and supposedly irresponsible and indecisive theory.

## On not reading de Man

In an age of threatened global catastrophe, whether that be through resource depletion, viral terrorism, panic or financial meltdown, it makes no sense to turn back to the Athenian polity or bourgeois public sphere dreamed of by the Enlightenment; nor is it adequate to simply assert the proper 'human contact' of life. But this refusal of nostalgia and rejection of a certain mode of narrativizing history raises the problem of how one might proceed in the absence of a model of good life. What ought to be prescribed to inoculate 'us' (we humans) against the looming disaster of a life that no longer has the time to practise theory as such nor possesses the meaningful frameworks that might produce a theoretically engaged politics? I will leave aside those (supposedly philosophical or critical minds) who have said that the answer lies in religion or scripture (Cottingham 2005; Eagleton 2007, and 2009, 293).[7] Two other paths have been offered: one hope is that praxis itself becomes and replaces theory, with living and loving labour creating *for itself* a political and communicative network that would replace any top-down sovereignty or separate public sphere: 'The primary decision created by the multitude is really the decision to create a new race or, rather, a new humanity. When love is perceived politically, then, this creation of a new humanity is the ultimate act of love' (Hardt and Negri 2005, 356). (In popular parlance this would be the dream of a new civility, an engagement in deliberative democracy enabled in part by new media, new technologies and the less pernicious webs of globalism.) Alternatively, one aims to think some transcendence or break with *the system,* so that the political would not so much be theoretical distance – would not be academia, political science or literary criticism reading the rhetoric of political relations – but would be the thought of the genesis of politics. What if we could imagine, once again, not an already constituted system of laws suitable for a thinking humanity, but the human potentiality of politics as such? This has been the path taken by Agamben, and others, who have appealed to the figure of St Paul whose positing of the universal is radically contrasted with the already constituted and communicable terms of the polity (Agamben 2005b; Zizek 2003). The widespread use of two concepts – affect and potentiality – testifies to a post-theoretical or post-linguistic attempt to think of politics not as the negotiation of speaking humans within their already actualized world, but as the thought of the emergence of the human. What if we could confront humanity at those points where politics is *not actualized* – the death camps or even the hedonism of modernity? It is when humanity is *not* speaking in common that the potentiality for speech is disclosed. And it is here also that one recognizes a pure, bare or proto-politics of affect: despite post-theoretical attempts to avoid literalism and naïve materialism, it is now affect, or the potentiality to be perceived, that grounds all further social, political and ecological relations. Before an actualized language or law there is an affective response, a web of relations or an ecology *from which* something like the system of lived politics emerges.

How might de Man be located in this world that is at once 'after theory' and yet (barely) prior to a depleted and catastrophic future? If received wisdom is taken as a guide, de Man would typify the symptom against which a good potential future might be defined. De Man was, after all, a dehistoricizing depoliticizing textualist, the figure in 'theory' who exemplified a narrowness of linguisticism and aestheticism.[8] The present, by contrast, would have reformed deconstruction by an ethical turn away from play and text towards the future, the other and democracy,[9] and would have returned deconstruction either to nature (Roden 2006) or to the embodied mind of evolution and biology (Spolsky 2002). Beyond deconstruction, or returning to nature and life, we would have recovered the pre-linguistic event of affect, subjective decision or politics. Reading de Man today we can perhaps open up a genealogy of this future we have set for ourselves. It seems that theory has turned towards an intense focus on the genesis of politics and language, *not* assuming that politics or affective life could be reduced to, or mediated by, language. But what if our sense of the present as having overcome an evil and pernicious theoretical past that was overly textualist relied upon a structural occlusion of de Man's mode of argument? What if our confidence in the life of the future depended on *not* reading the style of problems that were posed by de Man? Let us at least entertain this suggestion for now: the current turn to genesis, affect, life and the emergence of political man from living systems is a reaction formation. It is precisely at that point of history when 'man' is at his most narcissistically self-enclosed that he affirms – ever more shrilly and redemptively – that he is ecological (always already connected and open to a world that he feels affectively, lives politically and experiences in common).

## The body politic

The problem of the transition from individual to polity, from individual to collective, from biological to social body – this problem is *the* question of political theory. After all, it is common to cite the beginnings of modern politics as occurring when the political body is no longer transcendent (as some norm or model imposed on worldly life) but immanent: the polity occurs as the assembling of individuals, either for the sake of mutual protection against a default and natural hostility (Hobbes) or because of some idea of a humanity that would maximize itself in some mode of general will (Rousseau) (Dumont 1986). Some of today's most often quoted and celebrated authors affirm this positive transition to modernity. Michael Hardt and Antonio Negri's *Empire* and its sequels see the present as an opportunity for creative immanence whereby the polity is nothing more than the communicative relations among labouring bodies (not an imposed model), and where bodies are nothing more than the fruitful encounters they bear to other living humans: 'homo homo, humanity squared' (Hardt and Negri 2000) – such is the joyous modern organicism that will insist that there is no whole that transcends or governs relations from outside, and no distinct parts or individuals outside the constantly self-forming and creative political whole. The current vogue for the work of Hannah Arendt can at least in part be explained by her criticism of the threats of Platonic political models (which for Arendt consisted in both the imposition of norms and the appeal to a higher logic, both of which would be outside the coming into common of political discussion). For Arendt the fall into Platonism (or transcendent logics) can be overcome by the retrieval of a creative and immanent 'speaking in common' (Arendt 1978). Giorgio Agamben also laments the degree to which 'the political' has become disengaged from its 'practical' (that is, active, world-disclosing and formative) origin; a once active, collective and productive generation of creativity from praxis has – in both totalitarianism *and* hedonism –become nothing more than the management of biological bodies subjected to normalizing rules, rather than deliberated norms (Agamben 1998). Agamben's criticism of Foucault was that while Foucault had done much to understand and expose contemporary biopolitics (or the modern reduction of relations among bodies to the managerial and pseudoscientific control of healthy populations), Foucault had failed to examine the genesis of sovereignty. How, Agamben asks, can we today ask the question of the emergence of the political body? How can we retrieve a sense of the polity or of law that would *once again* – as in Ancient Greece – be mindful of man's capacity to create a political world for himself, a polity that does not inevitably follow from natural being, and that can be disclosed as much when it is *not present* (death camps, totalitarianism, bureaucracy, late capitalism) as when it is actualized? Foucault was, of course, trying to ask quite different questions, aiming to shift the nature of politic problems away from the question of how 'life' becomes subjected to an external power. Indeed, Foucault questioned the very notion of the concept of 'life' and sought to examine language *not* as the means through which man makes sense of himself but as something that possessed its own *inhuman* force. In a manner that was similar to de Man's attempt to see any theory of *the* political or *the* genesis of the body politic as covering over quite particular and intricate rhetorical moves that require analysis, Foucault sought to avoid a general political paradigm in favour of complex and multiple genealogies. Gilles Deleuze, commenting on the significance of Foucault's criticisms of 'life, labour and language' as organizing figures of modernity suggested that only if language were freed from man, and only if life were freed from the figure of the organism could thought approach a future (Deleuze 1988).

Agamben's critique of Foucault, along with his retrieval of bare life and the problem of sovereignty are symptomatic of the same present that can also not assimilate de Man's probing analyses of the false problems of sovereignty, law and 'the' political. Foucault's entire project was, in its radical historical mode, critical of any notion of man who would then have a history; it would make no sense to write a history of the genesis of the political precisely because historicizing modes of political thinking were bound up with the very concept of 'life' that marked modernity (Foucault 1970). That is, a specific figure of history – whereby man is political because he must form a collective world for himself and then become increasingly reflective as history progresses – is irreducibly modern. (Here, Foucault repeats a motif also noted by de Man: modernity has been defined as the increasingly self-conscious awareness of our historical mediation. This is a dialectical understanding of modernity that de Man finds in Gadamer, and that Foucault finds in phenomenology and Marxism; both de

Man and Foucault reject this highly moral twinning of man with a disclosive history in which conditions of mediation are progressively brought to presence.) The mode of knowledge by which one studies the emergence of man as a biological being whose nature requires an evolving political history presupposes a highly normative figure of *life*. Man is an animal whose natural being requires the supplement of history and political formation; man only knows himself as the effect of that ground, never grasps himself transparently, but only by reading the effects of history. For Foucault this highly normalizing style of thinking could not be overcome by aiming for a deeper history or more profound and critical concept of man; what would be required would be an uncoupling of the concepts of history and life. History, as long as it is understood as the unfolding of man as a natural being into a political formation that allows him to read and master himself, must always occlude an ultimate moralism. Life, human life, is *properly* deemed to be that which maximizes and realizes itself through ongoing and productive self-formation. Man becomes the readable sign of a life that is at once a hidden ground but also a continuous foundation.

To insist that today we ought to revisit and reform the transition from individual to political collective is more often than not to assume that man is a properly, naturally and morally political animal – a being whose nature it is to live in common and to find himself only through a good form of dynamic and historical (growing/progressive) development and realization. This idea dominates what remains of high theory – such that even those theorists whose work is defined against all forms of naturalism, nostalgia or the proper nevertheless insist on the singularity of the subject. Alain Badiou (2009) focuses on 'the subject' as point of decision subtracted from actual political systems; Hardt and Negri put forward the idea of the self-making multitude; Zizek insists on the revolutionary break, while Agamben insists on returning to the praxis from which the political world is generated. More important, though, is the way a logic of retrieval and redemption marks the popular political landscape. Left movements for political localism and right movements against 'big government' both aim to revive an authentic and lived relation to political process. The very idea of a *human science*, of studying man as a natural being whose collective and political formations are at once grounded in biology (yet also ways of transforming and disclosing that biology) operates well beyond the disciplines and discourses that were Foucault's objects of criticism. (And it was precisely against that falsely interdisciplinary image of the social sciences that de Man set the task of *literary criticism* [de Man 1967]). The thriving disciplines of evolutionary psychology and cognitive archaeology today take the emergence of language, music, sociality, altruism and economic rationales as objects of study, presupposing man as an animal whose history is at once empirical – to do with specific and contingent events – and transcendental (always affected from certain imperatives of life to maximize and flourish as it goes through time) (Dunbar 1996; Mithen 2005; Hauser 2005). More significant, though, is the extent to which the normalizing, moralizing and humanizing concept of *history as the development of collective complexity from bounded individuality to self-organizing whole* inflects other contemporary discourses, such as literary history and political historical critique. Here, the work of de Man, even more than that of Foucault, can be read via a symptomatology. That is, just as one can see the incorporation of Foucault by theories of discourse (Macdonnell 1986) and the social sciences as an appropriative mis-reading that testifies to the essential difficulty of his work, so we can also regard de Man's consignment to the historical dustbin of 'high theory' as the symptom of resistance.

If Foucault's work remained unreadable, often being used to justify a historicism rather than rethink the very concept of history, then the (non-) assimilation of de Man is similarly revealing, and can perhaps best be read and re-read today through the problem of the relation between individual and collective. First, this problem is also a problem of the literary and its proper historical relations. If deconstruction was judged to have been an era of irresponsibly aestheticist, self-enclosed, depoliticizing and formalist high theory, then de Man would seem to be the prime culprit. But before we examine this apparently literary problem, we can consider the defining modern political problem of the emergence of the polity, and all the moralisms that accompany its formulation. I have already looked briefly at the ways in which contemporary theory presupposes a proper genesis of the good polity, a self-conscious transition from the individual who is (or ought to be) nothing more than the active and productive relations that bind him to a self-realizing political whole. But the same applies to popular discourses regarding the fall from a good self-making, self-productive and self-conscious polity. The figuration of the evil of capitalism takes both literary critical and political-economic forms. In its literary mode, capitalism allows objects to become detached from their growing origin; no longer speaking or intentional, they become frozen, detached, formal, aesthetic – no longer *political* (or of the polity) they are reified and deadened. It was in this respect that de Man's supposed formalism and aestheticism, or deconstruction in general, were deemed to be complicit with a regressive conservatism. Only a properly political and active historicism can restore literary texts to their life. The criticism of de Man as a critic concerned with enclosed 'play' or consciousness is only possible because it is assumed that texts have a life or context that can be read, restored, revivified and that can, in turn, enable the present to become aware of its own political being. A certain figure of the economy is at work in this axiology: texts are parts of a whole, not systems unto themselves, and ought to be located within the broader life of which they are a fragment. There is a single system or context, however complex and dynamic. To forget the productive and generative context of the literary object is – in a manner analogous to political conservatism – to forget the genesis of relations. One way of overcoming de Man's (or deconstruction's) textual self-enclosure has been through historicism or political consciousness. Here, again, it might be worthwhile to couple de Man not with Derrida (who could be read as a more ethical philosopher leaving the play of the text for the messianic thought of the future), but with Deleuze and Guattari. Deleuze, writing on Leibniz, argues that there is not *a* world of relations within which identities are situated, but that each point in the cosmos opens out its own infinite (Deleuze 1986, 71). Deleuze and Deleuze and Guattari's notion that 'relations are external to terms' is an anti-organicism: there is not a system in general that gives each individual its identity, such that each being could be understood as an aspect or expression of a system. An individual (or text) does not possess intrinsic relations, but can be read or actualized through multiple registers. This means that there is not a relativism of truth, but a truth of the relative: one needs to examine the multiple ways in which relations, systems or series of lines are figured (Deleuze 1986, 21). In their book on Kafka they argue that it is when the text is at its most cramped – seemingly cut off from relations – that one can begin to think the ways in which texts *do not have a context or an already existing system of relations within which they can be located* (Deleuze and Guattari 1986, 17). What such a textual or differential logic insists upon is that individuals are neither self-sufficient wholes from which relations emerge, nor aspects of a single system. In the beginning is the differential.

## Individual economies

One of the most strident and unquestionable criticisms of the present has focused on the eclipse of the political individual by the corporation. The 2008 global financial crisis led to a constant denunciation of the parasitic and self-serving Wall Street by a (supposedly) more practical and authentic main street. The distinction between main street and Wall Street is a distinction between real politics – the domain of working, voting, living bodies that are both productive and living in common – and parasitic networks of finance. The highly moral focus on the secondary, parasitic and *unproductive* self-serving nature of business has a long history, and a highly theological rhetoric. Interest, speculation, finance for its own sake: all these 'practices' are deemed to be pernicious precisely because they are detached from praxis, or the production of bodies, by bodies, for the sake of a body's furtherance and extension. In the 2008 crisis the long-standing moral critique of a parasitic and life-denying usury was inflected with a different tone. The global financial crisis was widely deemed to be the result not merely of old-style speculation, in which one anticipated that objects, goods or resources in the present *would be* valued more highly in the future – a mode of speculation that in nineteenth-century literature was associated with an inhuman disregard for present needs and a voracious desire for future profit. The newer forms of economic activity, such as hedge funds, credit default swaps, sub-prime mortgages, futures and derivatives take on a different slant from older modes of future-predictive speculation. There has always been an anti-capitalist rhetoric of speculation where money begets money in a groundless manner, ranging from Christian prohibitions on usury to contemporary distinctions between a good and fruitful investment versus an evil and parasitic monetarism (Bayer 1999). Such suspicions of speculation as a form of self-enclosure or systemic blindness are in line with Freud's remark that speculative philosophy was in many ways a form of paranoia, an extreme tendency to create an all-inclusive commanding system for the present and all futurity (Freud 1991). Financial speculation, in its older sense of betting on an increased value of equities in the future, is similarly paranoid, relying as it does on an assumption that the speculator sees beyond the present and will be able to map the future course of values. (Deleuze and Guattari also describe pre-capitalist despotism as a form of paranoia, the subordination of all relations among differentials to a single point [Deleuze and Guattari 2004, 76]).

Current anxieties regarding the increasingly autonomous and life-denying nature of corporations and the finance sector both extend a traditional depiction of speculation as the detachment of economic relations from their living and practical origin *and* a quite distinct mode of criticism that is now directed at the doubly parasitic – and one might say psychotic – nature of speculation. Hedge funds, futures and derivatives – as the very notion of 'hedging one's bets' implies – allow for profit from failure. If a bet on the future fails one can profit from what was (initially) a mode of protection against the risks and contingency of the future. Rather than only being a way of insuring oneself against the failure of bets on the future, derivatives can now profit from non-realization. If old style speculation required some vision (and possibly manipulation) of future markets, the recent global financial crises rely less on predicting and mapping future growth than *psychotically* closing off all sense or imagination of the future. The betting relies on non-realization, non-production, failure or absence of outcomes. This, in turn, intensifies the capacity to mark, even further, a distinction between living bodies (with needs, located in a presence of praxis) and parasitic institutions, now detached not only from present demands and real production but from demand and production in general. What appears is a system unto itself, closed off from life and imagination, closed off from *history* or the anticipation of the future for the sake of the present, and the saving of the present for a more fruitful future. It would seem to make sense, today more than ever, to reassert the distinction between individual and living bodies capable of politics – of gathering in common to deliberate strategies and outcomes – and systems that operate as a law unto themselves without any regard for life or relations outside those of exchange for its own sake.

This need to distinguish individuals from corporations was rearticulated in the alarmingly quiet response to the January 2010 US Supreme Court decision, following the first amendment, to grant corporations the same rights as individuals when it came to political speech. The history of this decision is, in part, grounded in both race and property, or race as the capacity for humans to become property. Corporations have long used the fourteenth, fifth and fourth amendments to claim equality of status before the law, equal rights to speech and equal protection from intrusion. The fourteenth amendment was intended to annihilate any capacity for individuals to be treated as property and to be granted the same rights as all other humans. From its inception, though, the amendment was repeatedly invoked by business and industry to claim equal rights for corporate and human bodies (Bakan 2004; Hartmann 2002). This is so much the case that not only have corporations now been thoroughly anthropomorphized, such that they can be granted equal status and bodies *and* rights to speech, the very concept of the living human body itself appears to be threatened. One might mention here – in addition to the motif of the increasing mechanization of human life with encroaching industrialism – an argument that is dominant in late theory regarding the importance of the body, the lived body, materiality or processes of embodied recognition that would 'cure' the overly linguistic inflections of late theory. There would be agreement or convergence between those very few who expressed horror with the US supreme court's 2010 decision to grant corporations the same rights as individuals to speech, and those who would insist on the political importance of the lived body. Legally one requires the distinction between practical, living and labouring individuals and ongoing systems such as corporations precisely because the latter do not have a spatio-temporal or mortal limit (Bakan 2004). So just as contemporary theory laments a loss of *the* political and aims to think the genesis of bodies and bodies politics *from life* so popular movements against corporations aim to reground systems on living bodies, production and praxis.

What is presupposed is a moral distinction between the living active productive body and the secondary parasitic corporate body; this in turn yields the opposition between good living deliberated polities and unbounded, sprawling, parasitic systems. Finally, this pertains to how we might negotiate an ethics, or counter-ethics, of the future: we might regard man or humanity as having been deflected from his proper ecological affinities by alienating systems of corporatism, *or* we might – after de Man – see the supposedly accidental corporate deviation as structural to the very possibility of something like a body. If this were so then the human would be a pacifying lure of propriety and origin that was enabled by, and continues to enable, what might better be referred to as *inhuman*. The inhuman is not the posthuman; it is not some recognition of the limits of the concept of humanity that might be overcome or ameliorated by recognizing forces outside 'man' (Hayles 1999). The *inhuman* in de Man's sense is what he aligns with language or linguistic forces, and it is here that we strike the strange status of his work. On the one hand, he accords a seemingly humanist, literary or even cognitive priority to the linguistic, as though he had not yet realized the biological, ecological, genetic, pre-linguistic, micro-political or material forces from which language emerges. If this were so then de Man would be a curious historical oddity, a reactive extension of New Criticism's isolation of the text from contexts, force and history. On the other hand, de Man aligns this seemingly linguistic foundation with a violent and contingent history – not a linear, narrative or natural history, but an unreadable rupture – and insists on language's status as *inhuman*. The inhuman, then, would have been strangely figured as human. Indeed, we might say that what appears as the figure of 'man' – the speaking animal of politics and progressive history – is not only made possible by inhuman forces, such as the material inscriptions or tracing mechanisms that allow for something like the illusion of a stable body that maintains itself through time. There would also be something of an uncanny or

doubling relation between human and inhuman: all those predicates that supposedly single out 'the human' – speech, political formations, historical self-
consciousness – are also those that render any identity impossible or unreadable.
But this then allows us to make a remark regarding life in general. The figure
of the organism, or the bounded, individuated and auto-poetic whole, is at
once necessary – for any attempt to think *nature as such* or life in its pure state
will always be the effect of having deconstructed *figured* life. 'Nature' is that
which recedes, which we can read as having been there – unreadable – in order
to yield the readable figure or lure.

In terms of political theory this means that de Man will perhaps be the theorist
of the twenty-first century, for he was always mindful of the extent to which
the deference, reverence and debt we owe to the nature from which we
emerge is a linguistic machine that will always enclose us in a consuming and
annihilating blind. At first this might appear to offer nothing but a paralyzing,
life-denying, nihilist retreat from politics. But de Man's quite specific reflections
on the genesis of the body politic suggest something more complex. The figure
of the collective body of humanity masks an essential piracy or brigandry.
Confronting the unreadability of those 'birth pangs' or the 'double rapport' that
operates between the figure of the political body and the forces that can only
be read *ex post facto* precludes any nostalgic politics of the individual, the polity
or life. It does, however, open a genealogy of the future: there is no proper or
natural trajectory of life or man, for any figure of the proper belies the
forces from which it emerges. As a consequence we are confronted with the
question *not* of sustaining, maintaining and protecting life, but of reading
the unreadable figures of life that have done so much violence to what appears
as 'the living.'

For de Man this unnatural operation of the figure of nature was already at
work in the writings of Rousseau and Benjamin, both of whom were critical of
easy typifications of a supposedly natural body politic. And yet it is the property
and propriety of life and the body that has come to the fore not only in recent
theory but also in contemporary political debate. Whereas de Man not only
demonstrates the double unreadability of affect (at once utterly singular, and yet
banal in its generality),[10] the concept of affect has done much to domesticate
popular and theoretical politics. Discontent, ill feeling, sentiment, sensitivity,
emotion and affect: all these terms are now championed as ways in which the
'linguistic' prejudices of an earlier era of high theory might be overcome.[11]
And yet two points need to be noted. By linguistic, de Man referred to inhuman forces, impersonal relations and machinic systems that could not be
reduced to speech or already actualized matter. Further, de Man regarded affect
or life neither as foundation nor as linguistically constituted actuality, but as a
violent, monstrous and receding force that could neither be read nor reduced
to the figures we have of it. Instead, what he suggested was an interminable
and abyssal politics of (mis)reading: we cannot but produce figures of a good
life, nature or affect that would precede constituted systems, and yet any
attempt to arrive at this proper origin would always already be contaminated

(*and enabled*) by the seemingly secondary system that is being critically nego-
tiated. If theory were to offer anything to concrete political problems it would
not be by leading the way towards a neurally-based, embodied or realist
foundation, but by shifting the style of problems from the readability to the
unreadability of affect.

In his essay on Rousseau's general will de Man writes of a 'double rapport'
whereby the force of a public system of law must have the generality of a
grammar in order to be lived as law and *not* subject to, or corrupted by, the
vagaries of affect; and yet the individual passions that this system would supposedly belie are lived through the figure of the body politic in a narcissistic
mode, 'each' individual taking the figure of the collective or image of 'man' as
*really* himself (1976, 665). That is, the 'real' – or that which must be lived as
necessary for figures yet masked by figures – is also necessarily and *improperly*
appropriated by each individual as the sign of his own universal worth. There is
a transcendental substitution, piracy or stealth in the figure of the individual's
productive transition from singular to universal. Every individual who lives
their privacy as a good mode or example of the public good is essentially a
brigand, living the immediacy of affect as the universality of the good: privacy
is piracy. He ostensibly lives his life as an exemplary citizen, and yet privately –
affectively – feels himself to be the exceptional singular individual expressed by
the general will:

> There can be no text without grammar: the logic of grammar generates
> texts only in the absence of referential meaning, but every text generates a
> referent that subverts the grammatical principle to which it owed its con-
> stitution. What remains hidden in the everyday use of language, the fun-
> damental incompatibility between grammar and meaning, becomes explicit
> when the linguistic structures are stated, as is the case here, in political
> terms. The preceding passage makes clear that the incompatibility between
> the elaboration of the law and its application (or justice) can only be
> bridged by an act of deceit. "S'approprier en secret ce mot *chacun*" is to
> steal from the text the very meaning to which, according to this text, we
> are not entitled, the particular I which destroys its generality; hence the
> deceitful, covert gesture "en secret," in the foolish hope that the theft will
> go unnoticed. Justice is unjust ...
>
> (de Man 1976, 669)

In the manuscript on Benjamin de Man will extend this 'double rapport': the
general will is not an expression of individuals, for individuals are effects of a
general system, even if that system is always the consequence of inhuman violence, pains, destructions and appropriations that are lived as proper. They are
lived figurally or meaningfully, as expressions *of* a proper life. It is the task of
criticism – which is also a task of impossible translation – to display the non-
passage or non-relation of the double rapport, or what de Man also refers to as
the two rhetorical registers of grammar and meaning, or (in the notes on

Benjamin) as the divide between translation and original, or between criticism or philosophy and some supposedly faithful and mimetic doubling. Translation, criticism or philosophy appear to be secondary or derived, to be distanced from some prior foundation or proper source: and yet, what they all disclose is a certain impossible non-identity at the outset. The originary, individual and fecund natural first object is *nothing other than* a proliferating source of non-coincidence. Or, in political terms: the individual who is supposedly belied by alienating law (and who would therefore provide the ground for a return to good law) is nothing outside the systemic violations of his supposed natural good will; he is an effect of this supposition.

This is not to say that one throws one's hat in the ring with corporatism and capitalism, that there is nothing outside system and relations. On the contrary, de Man's insistence on 'double rapport,' 'translation' or the two registers of rhetoric focuses on a necessarily impossible non-relation. A text at once demands to be read – it generates a prior meaning, ground, nature, or subject of which it is the expression – but also remains *unreadable*. Any prior nature of which the text would be deemed to be an effect, can in turn be read as an effect of text; the *real, original and proper nature* is always receding and yet always promised, always exposed as an effect of destroying the priority of law and system, and yet never available outside system.

We can conclude by noting four consequences of de Man's destructive deconstruction:

1  Individuals as bearers of property with rights and laws are effects of a constituted system. The rhetorical perspective – which allows one to examine *how* reference occurs – shows one side of the law as acting among individuals and their property (law considered from the point of view of the individual). At the public level – disclosed in international conflict *or* when the law has to confront its own limits – one regards the law not as operating on individuals but as a system without reference. This impersonal, inhuman and machine-like register is that of 'pure grammar' and it is *this* mode that is historical: it is historical *not* because it ties events into a narrative sequence, for it is history that is constitutively covered over in the linear, causal and progressive appearance of an expressive life that unfolds through time.

2  Individuals are not only effects of law; they cannot be reduced to being nothing more than parts of a whole. The individual – through a process of metalepsis – regards his body as the proper referent of the law. The political body that historically (or non-teleologically) is a violent grammar without reference, is from another point of view – that of meaning or narrative – the proper reference or life that is always effected from any deconstruction of political actuality.

3  Politics, or the strange bind between individual and state, or living body and corporate body, is also the necessary and unreadable problem of relation between constative and performative. There are always two rhetorical registers,

not only the performative distribution of forces that creates a relation among seemingly stable terms, not only the grammatical, empty or translating dimension. There is always the figural lure of reference and narrative.

4   There are two sides of sovereignty: the body of the state, which is static or public and general, and the body of active law that appears whenever the state relates to or imposes itself upon the individuals it defines. This second dissolving force of sovereignty is active and historical; it is at once the expression of law and its destruction.

These four political dimensions are articulated through the impossible task of translation in de Man's reading of Benjamin, and the ways in which Benjamin has not been (and cannot be) read. If we think that texts refer to or express referents, that each sign has a body, then this is only because we are not reading the text's creation of the prior ground to which it would be secondary. Translation occurs from text to text, grammar to grammar, and in so doing it exposes a general and inhuman process of ungrounding or violence that is covered over in the figures of the natural body or of organic life. The nature that would precede and undergird texts is not fragmented *by textuality*; it is from textuality *as fragmented* that some nature is revealed and that would be in excess of relations among already given parts. It is from fragmentation that one might imagine a whole: not a whole that coheres, but something like fractal fragmenting. All the attempts to bring systems into line and coherence cannot but produce some other (missing, receding) system.

## De Man on Benjamin

Some of the working concepts in de Man's text on Benjamin – when translated into the context of the present – seem to indicate an uncanny prescience, as though this notorious persona from 1980s high theory and 'textualism' had metamorphosed into a twenty-first century thinker of the future. Reading de Man again today might prompt us to reverse the received wisdom regarding deconstruction and politics. Perhaps it is not the case that deconstruction began as a playful nihilistic textualism and then rediscovered its properly political vocation by side-lining de Man and incorporating Levinas. Consider these de Man motifs in turn: first is the concept of *afterlife* (followed by, and intertwined with, the *inhuman* and the radicalized conception of *text*.) The translation of a text is not a faithful progeny of a living ancestor but a persistently obstinate repetition of an already dead original. The original is dead precisely because it does not speak; no translation can bring it to life, because the mobility and activation of the translation is required by the rigidly inert and frozen original. (A comparison with de Man's essay on Rousseau and the text of law would look to this same opposition between stasis and life; it is the very *identity* or fixed form of the original text that both requires some activation or application that would differ from the first text, and that also therefore discloses that the first text is canonical, lawful or fixed precisely because it is empty, frozen, not yet applied, general and therefore silent and inactive.)

Second, the concept of the inhuman refers not only to those 'originally' fragmented, dispersed or machinic tendencies through which 'man' or the subject comes into being as an identified individual, for what is more important to note is that *there is no human.* This is not to say that humans are subjected to, or mediated by, a textual condition; that would be far too narrow a concept of text. For de Man 'text' is not just some a priori, systemic condition that then enables the distribution and relations of individuals, as though individuals could be seen as effects of a textual process. Such an account would still be too linear, too much like a narrative that describes the transition from condition to con-ditioned. More than any other thinker de Man problematized the motif of man as the animal who by virtue of speech and culture knows himself only as he is individuated linguistically and culturally. On the contrary, the supposed human is fundamentally a 'non-definition.' If one accepts the word 'human' as it functions, as the ground from which texts, speech and language would grow, or as – in the essay on Rousseau – the private, bounded, individual from which the articulation of laws and rights would follow, then this word becomes (through its own speculative structure) *unreadable.* The notion of text, in line with this deconstruction of the human, is neither a condition – such that we are all effects of text – nor a product, such that text follows from or expresses humanity or nature. Any text has two sides, or allows for two rhetorical regis-ters: a text is at once that which, *as readable,* possesses a stability, systematicity or formality that allows for its repetition and reactivation from context to context. A text offers itself for translation, or (if it is a legal text) for activation and interpretation. A text is therefore frozen, canonical, authoritative, machinic, grammatical or *public.* In that respect it is also, for de Man, contingent and historical. It does not express or follow on from any nature, and it occurs not as the consequence of a mappable sequence of entailed events but as a disturbance or violent rupture, a 'birth pang' or suffering. De Man contrasts the speculative side of the individual, a force that returns to, views, and gathers itself – a stable and bounded whole – with the historical contingency of law and texts. The latter are fragmentations or found dispersals, contingent machines that create relations and relative stabilities *from which* one might imagine a prior nature or human ground. But if text is this contingent, public, historical, disarticulating force that distributes a field *partes extra partes,* it is also that which seems to demand reading, activation, individuation or meaning – a reference or grounding of that machine in some point of ownness or 'mineness' (*Meinung*).

So if de Man is a thinker who privileged text this was not because of some linguistic idealism whereby either the world was constructed through, or by, language or whereby there was only 'a' system or relations with individuals as effects of that system. De Man was neither a social constructivist nor a systems theorist, and this may well be why he stressed the 'inhuman, dehumanized language of linguistics.' The human is a one-sided, narrative, private and figural concept, suggesting either a ground from which language, history and speech unfold *or* a defined, normative and system-defined effect of social and political systems. For this reason de Man does not want to explain the human by looking at man's relation to language, nor explain language by accounting for its genesis from either humanity or organic life.

By stressing *inhumanity* and textuality de Man did not just give a different name to the condition through which 'we' come into being; he destroyed the logic and linearity of conditions. Or, we might say, the logic of *life*: growth, production, fruition, survival and nature. These expressive concepts are unreadable precisely because the supposed nature that would act as ground or origin can always be exposed as a figural effect of some system, and that conditioning system in turn comes into being as a result of a reading or critique that only results in more text to be read. Text faces in two impossible, conflicting directions: back to the origin of which it would be the effect or expression, and forwards to the general, public, shared and repeatable systems that it renders futural or promissory.

Finally: in addition to the importance of afterlife and the inhuman (both of which would render problematic any linear narrative of nature and its expressions, for both would be dispersed by history as a violent and fragmenting process), de Man also stresses the concept of *survival*. But the mode of survival is not one of coherence, nor of propriety, nor of the poetic (if the latter refers to a direct and almost sacred act of naming). Survival occurs by way of destruction, fragmentation, disarticulation, and de-canonization. A text can only live on through a repetition that releases its frozen, seemingly closed, poetic or sacred unity. The poetic text becomes prosaic, no longer a privileged, authoritative, canonized origin, but the errancy or secondariness of an afterlife that undoes or destroys any prior unity.

## Inconclusion

We can return to the present to rethink the scandal of the 2010 supreme court decision (in *Citizens United* v *Federal Election Committee*) to grant corporations the same rights as individuals under the fourteenth amendment (the same fourteenth amendment that was originally framed to grant any body born in the USA equal rights before the law – including ex-slaves – and that is now being criticized in 2010 for enabling those born in the US to non-citizens to be accorded the same legal rights.) Before the 2010 decision there was already some anti-corporation critique and scandal regarding the amendment's relation to corporations. The famous 1886 *Santa Clara* v *Southern Pacific Railroad* decision that sets the precedent for treating corporations as political bodies with the right to equal status before the law, was, according to one narrative, itself the victim, subject or 'original' that suffered an accident of translation (Hartmann 2002). From the earliest days of the articulation of the fourteenth amendment, railroad corporations had sought to use the law to relieve their tax burden. The Santa Clara case that granted the railroads the right not to be taxed on certain areas did indeed mention the amendment, and also decided in favour of the railroad, but the decision in favour of the railroad was on the basis of another issue entirely – the inclusion of fences in the taxed area under dispute. The received history, possibly a result of journalistic transcription, was that Santa Clara decided that corporations were, for the purposes of the fourteenth amendment, individuals. When this same status was revisited in 2010, this time in relation to the right to political campaigning and the spending of moneys, the same criticism that was aired against earlier grantings of rights to corporations was repeated: individuals and corporations differ ontologically, practically and politically. Ontologically, an individual is a finite living body, whereas corporations are indefinite and renewing. This leads to practical consequences, including liability – for an individual has rights coupled with duties, whereas corporations can operate with limited liability and are able to act and manage without a direct tie to ownership. Indeed, an individual is defined, properly, through property; he is a subject capable of labouring upon and possessing material (and landed) property because he submits to the same law as his neighbour, whereas corporations often act not within the law of the land but in relation to, or in competition with, other lands, states and laws. Corporations are not defined as property-owning individuals before the law, but themselves have a force or network that can take on the law.

Politically, then, this problem of the relation between individuals and corporations opens up a new concept of politics. From the point of view of the individual, which is the point of view of meaning, narrative and nature, politics is a coming together – as polity – to decide in common or in general. The individual point of view is referential, always regarding relations as expressions or signs of a prior whole. From the point of view of generality, the public, or the corporation, politics is a dynamic system of forces that is as much destructive as it is creative. This register is what de Man refers to as materiality – but by referring to systemic dispersal, difference, or grammar as materiality, the aporia of reference opens up: one can only use the notion of materiality as a refer-ential weapon, a way of referring that destroys reference. The term 'acts' para-doxically and destructively. Paradoxically, because to say that what we think of as referential (as having some prior ground in nature or being) as actually being material (or fragmented, dispersed, *not* substantive) is to give a destructive power to materiality. Material politics would not only destroy the standard illusions of the polity, the state of nature, the general will, or the individual, but also anything deemed to be originally unifying or unified. Materiality works destructively. Destructive: because politics in this sense – in the sense of law, grammar, text or (in de Man's essay on Rousseau) the sovereign – can only act if it does not respect the individuality of the individual, if it does not attend to the purity of the present but acts as if from any point in time whatever. *That* violence done to the narrative of the present is, for de Man, history and text. History is neither natural nor organic, neither narrative nor human. So text should not be seen as a general system of relations through which life or meaning comes into formation. Text is, in de Man's essay on Rousseau (in a manner akin to the term 'translation' in his notes on Benjamin), a mode of 'double rapport'. Text effects or distributes relations among relatively stable identities (or individuals). In the Benjamin lecture text takes the form of a suffering or birth pang, a rupture that marks out what appears to be a human nature that could be gathered together to form a whole, but that – upon examination or any mode of activation or translation – gives 'us' nothing more than disarticulation or an afterlife and survival that is merely the lingering on of death.

One thing is clear, both in following de Man's provocation *and* in aiming to read the relation today among individuals, corporations and the constitution: one cannot appeal to the individual or the natural living body as the origin of relations (relations that would supposedly then become detached and fragmented by corporations and misreadings of the constitutional text). To counter the obscene uses of the US constitution by corporations who appeal to their rights as individual bodies by invoking a *proper* reading of this original text *makes too much sense*. One installs oneself within a narrative of sovereignty (or the genesis of the good polity from the founding fathers' spirit), rather than competing on a textual or material domain that would refuse the grounding concept of the man of good reason (the man of good reason whom 'we' would all claim to be in 'our' relation to 'our' constitution). Is it any wonder that both sides of the political spectrum, left and right, talk of the theft of America? (Thiel 2009; Freddoso 2008; O'Leary 2009). But what if America, like any nation, were constitutively – as an effected narrative whole – an essentially criminal body, necessarily masking its textual non-origin as a natural body?

The individual is an effect of relations, constituted as a property-owning subject (with a specular capacity to turn back and reflect upon himself). He can become a political person in relation to other members of the polity only because of a prior text that at once disarticulates and binds. The narrative that one should return Wall Street to the values of main street, or that one should vanquish the former in favour of the deliberative and constitutional spirit of the latter can only come into being because something like an economic, systems or material distribution has always already occurred. To regard *money* as the perversion of speech and politics forecloses the recognition that speech and social relations are always already monetary; the I-thou relation occurs through a system of values and differences that no human can own, author or command. Why, though, if we accept that there is no original purity to the subject – if the subject is already an effect of something like corporation (or a dispersal of forces across a field capable of reactivation beyond its point of emergence) – should we not then accept a pragmatic or tactical defense of the individual? (This was Richard Rorty's [1989] liberal notion of irony: as an individual I recognize the pure convention of one's vocabularies, and yet behave publically as though one were committed to the system that makes our conversations possible.) Yes, corporations and individuals are both constituted through monetary systems of exchange and property/propriety, but an individual is a limited, finite and accountable body, unlike the diffuse and improper network of the corporation. Surely some functional notion of the individual as a legal and liable limit would serve us well?

But here is the problem: the appeal to the individual as living body, owner of his own self, master of his own speech and liable for his own expenditure and risk, begins by assuming a constituted body and set of relations and forecloses any thought of the radical history and contingency of constitution in its broadest sense. Before there is the actual text of *the* constitution – this sacred text that arises from and protects *the* individual and that therefore can be deemed to possess a living spirit to which we might appeal – there is already constitution, already a text or system through which individuals come together politically as surviving humans with a narrative history, a sense of property/ propriety, and an investment in a surviving State. This means that granting the same rights to all individuals (to see them all as owners of themselves) defines humanity according to self-ownership, to the capacity to spend and invest in one's own manner, thereby creating a closed system of expenditure and return upon oneself. It follows that the good polity would be a similar such natural self-regulating body, spending in order to maintain itself, limiting its circulation of force so that no profligate, endless, reckless or nihilistic expenditure would destroy its own borders. Any monetary body would need to be internalized and bounded; banks and corporations ought to be systems within the sovereign nation state, not ungrounded forces unto themselves capable of destroying the very (speaking, breathing, working) life from which they arose.

Two points need to be made in conclusion, one theoretical the other practical. The point of view of theory, or of detachment from located points of view, yields new questions and problems regarding constituting texts. Before the fourteenth, first or fifth amendments, before the property owning individual whom the constitution would express and defend, there is not a self-evident truth but the blindness of forces. This composition and dispersal of force requires attention and judgement, not nostalgia. We should not be asking how to return force to the individual but rather look at the figures, lures and narratives that take the blind chaos of affect and render it (putatively) readable. Second, practically, the war between corporations and individuals – as currently articulated – creates a moral landscape that has decided in advance the propriety nature of the political subject. This not only defines selves through a speculative self-ownership, blindly privileging the working, self-defining, auto-poetic subject – the same subject whose survival and mastery has allowed both a corporate ethic of maximizing production and interest *and* an anti-corporate ethic that would privilege a constitution that has – not accidentally – been translated to defend the rights of the corporate body. That is, both individuals and corporations are possible only because of the 'double rapport' or inhuman history that might be referred to broadly as constitutionality, or that de Man referred to with the twin terms of meaning and grammar, or State and sovereign. There is at one and the same time some constituted system of individuation, allowing for various bodies to relate to each other *speculatively* (or with some already given sense of the whole and temporality within which actions and promises take place); and there is also a process of constitution that becomes evident when the political body enters into relation with other bodies, such as markets, corporations and other polities. It is precisely when politics appears to be corrupted by, or stolen by, corporations that one might think again not of the proper body politic opposed to money and inhuman forces but the contingently violent or violently contingent 'pangs' that give birth to any body – corporate, political or individual. This is contingent or linguistic, if we take 'linguistic' to refer to processes that are not expressive of nature, are not bounded by living self-reflecting organic wholes and are active rather than static. What sort of politics might this yield?

What would result would not be a politics of the polity (a negotiation of the polity on the basis of, expressed by and for individuals), but a politics of *polemos* where the individual is already the result of exchange, force, war, violence and an inhuman afterlife. The threats of corporate thieving, piracy and brigandry would bring to the fore a transcendental piracy or appropriation that occurs with the very figure of the individual. Certainly the fourteenth amendment that would include all races within the law is at once an act of expansion – allowing non-whites equality before the system of justice – *and* capture, defining individuals as ideally property-owning, labouring subjects of speech. If corporations are forms of unlimited rapacity with limited liability and a lack of concern for any future outside their own afterlife (which is not that of bodily flourishing but merely that of survival, or perpetuation) then they are possible only because of what de Man refers to as the inhuman. This 'inhuman' is what is occluded and foreclosed by the non-definition of the human: it is because we have the figure of the private individual – a speculative, productive, labouring, working, self-furthering individual who operates by *not* reading the forces from which he is composed – that we remain incapable of a politics that does more than yearn nostalgically for a return to the living body of the individual.

When we look at the rhetoric that defines the edges of politics today – whether that be the climate change rhetoric concerned with adaptation, survival, mitigation and cap and trade *or* the rhetoric of global humanity that will ideally have no force beyond its own immanent and auto-poetic self-making – the destruction of humanity can be viewed as a positive and affirmative event. The rapacity that is now evidenced by the findings of climate change science cannot be seen as a late accident that has befallen an otherwise benevolent humanity. For man, as individual, is precisely defined as a figure of self-ownership, appropriation and survival, with the environment always being that which *environs* or surrounds a proper body. The rhetoric of globalism, whether that be the high capitalist ethos of bringing the *developing* world into line with one narrative trajectory of empowerment and mastery or the seemingly opposed theory of the multitude as one self-loving self-constituting political body, presupposes a life of natural self-governing bodies. Today, more than ever, should be the time to question whether any body possesses a self-evident right to its own existence. Rather than oppose the integrity of the natural body to the inhuman forces of calculation, it would be better to acknowledge that the processes of calculation – weighing individuals against corporations, human survival against cost to the planet – are still human, all too human, not yet able to face the impossible task of reading forces or matters that are not those of bodies.

# Notes

## Introduction

1 Kirby Dick, Amy Ziering dir. *Derrida* (2002).
2 As already noted, the work of Walter Benjamin has received increased attention recently through the work of Giorgio Agamben, whose theorization of the concept of *bare life* has enabled 'theory' to look away from language as some closed inescapable system towards both the emergence or genesis of language *and* to those historical moments when 'man' is deprived of speech and is therefore exposed as a being with the potentiality *to speak*. Agamben's theory of sovereignty, life, speech and 'man' is defined, by Agamben himself, *against* deconstruction (Agamben 2005, 64), even though de Man's text on Benjamin deals precisely with these concerns (and in a highly radical manner that is certainly not unquestioningly 'textualist').

## 1 Paul de Man at work: In these bad days, what good is an archive?

1 See de Man 1973; http://dspace1.nacs.uci.edu/xmlui/handle/10575/1092. Accessed March 23, 2011. This is reproduced by kind permission of Patricia de Man. I am extremely grateful for that permission.
2 "Theotropic Allegory" was initially sent by email attachment both in facsimile and transcript to all the participants of the conference on "Property, Sovereignty, and the Theotropic: Paul de Man's Political Archive," held at the University of California at Irvine, 24–25 April 2009, at which an initial version of part of this present essay was read. I am grateful for having had the opportunity to present a preliminary paper at that conference. The first part of the section of this chapter on de Man's Benjamin essay was presented, at the invitation of Professor Kyoo Lee, at the Graduate Center of the City University of New York, on 21 March 2011. I am grateful for this opportunity and for the helpful and perspicuous discussion that followed. That discussion and my own return to both Benjamin and de Man in preparation for the event has led me to add a few sentences to what I say here. I have been led to try again to read Benjamin's essay for myself, to see what I think it really says.
3 See http://www.google.com/search?client=safari&rls=en&q=Mad+Magazine&ie=UTF-8 &oe=UTF-8. Accessed March 21, 2011.
4 Jacques Derrida, in *Specters of Marx*, discusses Marx on Stirner at some length, focusing in one place on three of the pages I also cite (Marx and Engels 1976, 157–59). See Derrida 1993, 201–37; Derrida 1994, 125–48.

## 2 Toxic assets: de Man's remains and the ecocatastrophic imaginary: (an American fable)

1 This inquiry is indebted to the efforts of Martin McQuillan and Erin Obodiac to re-examine the "de Man archive" through, initially, the recirculation of an unpublished

manuscript from 1972—transcribed by Erin Obodiac – and submitting that to discussion with the aim of re-examining its contemporaneity or otherwise today. I will allude to the occasion itself below, but they can consider this a delayed response to the invitation to that inquiry (which I was unable to attend).

2　The 2004 U.S. Department of Defense report on Climate Change (Townsend and Harris 2004)—issued and suppressed during the Bush wars – was notable for its split realities. It evoked comments like: "you've got a President who says global warming is a hoax, and across the Potomac river you've got a Pentagon preparing for climate wars." One might conclude the "Bush" people *knew* all about the latter, and that the denial itself was only confirmation of it: that denial would be not only Big Oil driven (obviously), but a decision of long term disinformation for what had become irreversible and the tending of which would only wreck the economy, political control, and the strategy of split wealth respeciezation it anticipates. The German military's recent report makes that plain, anticipating the Peak oil upheaval (Tencer 2010), makes similar points. What the DoD laid out was that climate change was a massively greater threat to "homeland security" than any war on terror (then sucking up all referential attentions). It laid out a rich menu of disaster scenarios according to calculations of resource and response, devolving to a state of ceaseless resource wars, megadrought, mass migrations, and "population culling."

3　A recent account in the *New York Times* (Gillis 2010) of the $CO_2$ readings from Hawaii finds them being called "shocking" by one scientist. Jeffrey Sachs observes of this: "Fossil fuel emissions, they say, are like a runaway train, hurtling the world's citizens toward a stone wall—a carbon dioxide level that, over time, will cause profound changes. ... The risks include melting ice sheets, rising seas, more droughts and heat waves, more flash floods, worse storms, extinction of many plants and animals, depletion of sea life and—perhaps most important—difficulty in producing an adequate supply of food."

4　It would be insufficient to use some phrase like "climate change" as more than a place holder to mark this domain, since the phrase is not meant meteorologically nor can be taken in isolation, itself redundant and merged with other corridors instantly (carbon and oil narratives, "capitalism" in its mutations, biomorphic events without local metrics). I deploy it—a redundant pairing of terms—as it applies, as well, to the mutation of perceptual, cognitive, and conceptual premises. What is "material" about climate change cannot be understood in the manner in which materiality as a philosophical conceit has been binarized, dialecticized, in essence, humanized.

5　The general topographies of narrative justice in relation to "the other" or the "otherness of the other" (human, subaltern, animal, eventually one should work one's way down to microbes) saturated the close of 20th century preoccupations. Derrida deployed these as convenient, even where contradicting his own earlier work (for instance, on Levinas). But it may be that "the other" as a term has proven a costly figure, an endlessly commodifiable meme that can never deliver what it promises (communion) and gives way before what cannot be packaged by that term today.

6　De Man's remarks on irreversibility emerge in the final lectures with a certain insistence, and he remarks in "Kant and Schiller" (de Man 1996, 132): "Well, the topic that has emerged and which I didn't deliberately want to—or which I didn't even know about, in a sense—has been this problem of the question of reversibility, of the reversibility of models which I have been developing on the basis of texts. And this is linked to the question of reversibility, linked to the question of historicity. ... This was not a deliberate theme. It has emerged of itself ... and is therefore more interesting than any other to me." He elaborates: "That process ... is irreversible. That goes in that direction and you cannot get back from the one to the one before ... It will always be reinscribed with a cognitive system, it will always be *recuperated*, it will relapse, so to speak, by a sort of reinscription of the performative in a tropological system of cognition again. That relapse, however, is not the same as a reversal" (133). Kevin Newmark makes the case that it was a strategic editorial error *not* to have published the "Messenger Lectures" as an independent volume—a texture of arguments that devolve from and reference one another in a limit exploration—rather than scatter some among different volumes (Newmark 2009). Given the various interruptions to follow, and the arguably inefficient title "Aesthetic Ideology" given the long delayed volume that would include most of these, one could infer that certain strands at work within this "set" itself deferred an integrated encounter or reading—for instance, the category of the "irreversible."

7  Timothy Clark observes in "Derangements of Scale": "His *On Hospitality* (2000) argues how the supposedly inviolable interiority of the home is already de-constituted, turned inside-out, by its multiple embeddings in public space, the state, the telephone line, monitored emails etc., yet there is residual idealism in Derrida's exclusive attention to systems of law and communication. The focus on the moment of decision in individual consciousness and its pathos (its ordeal of undecidablity etc.) seems narrow and inadequate in a context in which things have now become overwhelmingly more political than people ( ... ) Thus 'On hospitality' mentions TV, email and internet but not the central heating system, cooking appliances, washing machine or car (or, for that matter, the institution of private property itself, despite its crucial connection to Derrida's topic of personal sovereignty)" (Clark 2011). David Wood, in a different vein, presses this perceived lack differently: "What is clear from these kinds of interventions, however, is just how limited ( ... ) is the role to be played by the 'messianicity without messianism', and 'democracy-to-come' in their refined versions, versions which abjure 'the future' in favor of a universal immanent structure of experience" (Wood 2006, 292).

8  Martin Hägglund's *Radical Atheism—Derrida and the Time of Life* (2008) tracks the remarkably viral if not systemic recuperations and relapses that Derrida's most imminent commentators bring to their integrations of Derrida's innovations in ethics, religion and "the political" in particular. What Hägglund describes as a systemic relapse and broad return to theotropisms among many of his foremost commentators (the list is soberingly inclusive), in the mode of exegesis, appears to shadow the production of a "late Derrida," a tag Derrida eschewed but did not dispel, since it described a corpus repeatedly turned toward problematics of hospitality, the ethics of undecidability, the prosthetics of faith (or religion), "the political" in various contemporary configurations. What remains scandalous is that a 21st century book need be written to remind *Derrideans* that Derrida is not theistic but what can one say? To rely on the phrase "radical atheism" itself speaks volumes, perhaps, and somehow would appear irrelevant and desultory if even applied to, say, de Man—for whom no theistic/atheistic imaginary is in question. The limits of Hägglund's divigations emerge only in the wake of its negative restoration of sorts (a return to the formulation of early Derrida, and the logics of the non-present present). One is, that while Derrida generated these recuperations, and sometimes indulged them, he was not unaware—which implies, properly, that he had embarked on a rhetorical venture ("late Derrida") that exploited the dialectics of hospitality to enter the mainstream arteries of humanist (academic) thought, albeit as a Trojan horse strategy over time. A strategy of embedding, seduction, and survival. The second is, that the Derrida who he retains at the end can only be reduced to some fairly pragmatic and minimalist dicta—remaining in a circuit that, looking back, does not yet resituate the question in the contexts of "climate change" or its absence in Derrida's work. The argument takes another form or symptom, that of placing in check a "retheologization" of late Derrida with a corresponding call (as in Hägglund) to recentralize the early, ex-anthropic column of his work, in a new materiality: "The later Derrida's tendency to project the aporia into a messianic future risks depriving history of its own aporetic force—wherein the future is already being invented here and now—and turning it into little more than a passive, undetermined and provisional place-holder. This theological turn must be consigned to deconstruction's past if the historical present it describes is to gain inventive or transformative power and the radical future it affirms is to open. In the twilight of Derrida's idols, we might be able to glimpse a new future for deconstruction" (Bradley 2006, 38).

9 The text of "The Typewriter Ribbon" cited is that appearing in *Without Alibi* (Derrida 2002). This is a revision of the version first published in *Material Events* (Cohen et al. 2001).

10 I refer to Erin Obodiac's transcription of de Man's unpublished manuscript, "Textual Allegories," reported as "written as a single continuous text around 1972–73 while de Man was in Zürich," parts of which were to appear in *Allegories of Readings*. The occasion itself was titled: "Property, Sovereignty, and the Theotropic: Paul de Man's Political Archive," 24–25 April 2009, UCI. Part of the invitation focused on how the terms "sovereignty" and "theotropic" circulate in today's "post-theoretical" environs: "this aspect of de Man's work should be revisited today in a 'post-theoretical' landscape concerned with political theology, occupied with the transformation of the western model of sovereignty, and faced with the apparent collapse of the capitalist global contract." My remarks below are indebted to both McQuillan and Obodiac. A volume of proceedings will appear as *The Political Archive of Paul de Man*, edited by Martin McQuillan and Erin Obodiac (Edinburgh: Edinburgh University Press, 2011).

11 A recent collection attempting to resuscitate or fill this lack, *The Legacies of Paul de Man,* edited by Marc Redfield (2007), suggests how little also has evolved in the decades since de Man's "purge" (Derrida's term). The return in this volume to arguments, rehearsals, polemics, and reading styles of de Man—despite some brilliant contemporary extensions – has the feel of a delayed *Festschrift*, compensatory, at times testimonial, which might have occurred a decade ago or more. And what if de Man's were the style, specifically, that rejected the formalization of "legacy" as such?

12 The following notes were originally written for the symposium referenced above hosted by Martin McQuillan and Erin Obodiac, which I was unable to attend but retained the occasion of as a point of departure.

13 This sentence appears, minus a hyphen, in the chapter "Promises (Social Contract)" in *Allegories of Reading* (de Man 1979, 249).

14 Derrida's death spawned an ensemble of able and often admirable critical scion given over to talking about "ethics," about "religion," to exegetical commentary, to recuperation and stitching back, to almost outbiddings of mourning and friendship shaded into a quiet stupor of orthodox and policing networks, to writing for one another, to its auto-immune phase. One might look less for feral names than viral symptoms, as if this were not a factor of personalities quite, but a collective viral, flitting here and there, particularly with those who confuse contact with Derrida with his text (a somewhat different "Derrida"). Of these symptoms, beware when an essay finds itself reminiscing about "Jacques," locating his origin in Husserl, naturalizing the text, pleading ethics and "negative theology," loving hospitality, or (should one stop?) invoking Cixous as a celebrity substitute.

15 One would of course hear de Man's "materiality" as a technological and micrological refinement of Benjamin's "materialistic historiography," conceived as a praxis of intervention in inscriptions themselves. Thus Zizek in "Nature and its Discontents" (2008), 67–68, proposes a *Benjaminian* model of interactive temporalities prefaced by a complete assumption of the "catastrophe" premised on Jean-Pierre Dupuy's *Pour un catastrophisme éclairé*. In fact, Zizek only fakes adopting Dupuy's model of affirming the catastrophic, since it invoked as a hedge to get out of the present's aporia, fingers crossed in the same way as "zero-point" circles back. But in fact the literal demands of Dupuy's calculus, would lead to de Man's Benjamin, in whom "hope" must be extinguished to have any *chance* not to relapse to the very propertied-semantic formations that accelerate the self-cancelling vortex (for Benjamin, *historicism*). This parallels why, in the last decades, left and right thought have had the same effect on the geo-political trance—none.

16 James O' Rourke summarizes the double inversion by which Gasché helps clarify deconstruction in the "strict" sense by "foreclosing" de Man and neutering "deconstruction" (as "respectable" philosophy)—while pleading the opposite, effectively formalizing from within what those without wanted, more or less, to be told. Derrida could not but find this useful at the time, more as propaganda than orthotics: "The most

familiar account of the history of deconstruction in America is probably the one that describes the domestication of the radical force of Derrida's work as deconstruction was transformed, primarily by de Man and his Yale colleagues, into a method of literary criticism. ... [T]he presumption remains of a binary opposition between what is potentially valuable, radical and authentically Derridean about deconstruction and its use as technique of literary criticism. This belief ... depends upon an unexamined foreclosure of de Man's argument. ... The decline of de Man's critical fortunes has coincided with an increasing visibility accorded to the work of Rodolphe Gasché, whose chastisement of deconstructive literary critics for their supposed 'miscromprehension of deconstruction in the strict sense' (186, 3) has helped to justify the marginalizing of deconstructive literary criticism at the same time that Gasché has provided a more respectable public face for deconstruction as an advanced form of philosophy (O'Rourke 1997, 49–50).

17 This "present" disjuncture permits Chris Hedges to describe American democracy today as an "inverted totalitarianism" before which any "resistance" must be reconfigured without the prospect of intervention, go fugitive, and consider survival beyond a coming era of overwhelming human violence (this, after all, is what "climate change" implies), see Chris Hedges, "We Stand on the Cusp of one of Humanity's Most Dangerous Moments" Alternet.org, 18 March 2010: *http://www.alternet.org/story/146005/*, consulted 25 March 2010, 3.11 p.m. On "democracy" as engine of cultural consumer suicide, see Arundhati Roy, "Is there life after democracy?" *Dawn.com.* 5 July 2009: http://www.dawn.com/wps/wcm/connect/dawn-content-library/dawn/news/world/ 06-is-there-life-after-democracy-rs-07/, consulted 7 January, 2010, 4.03 p.m.

18 As it did, classically, in New Orleans after Katrina—where the curtain was lifted for several days on the protocols of civilized "modernity," disposable underclasses triaged, the erasure of coast-lines rehearsed, the histories of oil and the early Americas drawn back by what contemporary theory has difficulty conceptualizing, a force without sovereignty, the regression to vigilantism and the suspension of "law" disclosed, and so on.

19 There is a quip among systems theorists – looking down on the hamster wheels of critical theory past as a domain surpassed by descriptive scientisms – that (as I have heard) Gaia "doesn't give a shit" about the signifier. This is curious, not only because "Gaia" herself is one—that is, an organicist trope and, of course, goddess—but since whatever is implied by "anthropogenetic" climate change emerges from the memory programs and perceptual grids, conceits of "nature" that define that effect itself, telecratic trances. One might speak rather of a *telemorphosis*—which the figure of the anthropogenic both signals and holds in place, as if it, still, could at least claim sovereignty over its own disappearance still.

20 One must be tempted to cipher this suiciding logic in de Man by a biographeme—that of his discovery, as a young man, of the hanging body of his suicided mother. Perhaps the "ruthless" undoing of the artificed Self by its own textualized premises is an endless reading itself of the "mother's" choice. But one would then want to hear the figurality of "mother" as, in fact, a *khora*-like non-site, prephenomenal, amaternal, inorganic.

21 One is mindful of a sentence from "Textual Allegories" that will appear in *Allegories of Reading* : "the 'outside' in the sentence just quoted is not the outside *of* a corresponding 'inside'. In the mode of pure sensation, everything is 'outside' everything else; there are nothing but outside differences and no in-tegration is possible" (de Man 1979, 223).

22 Christopher D. Morris, in *The Figure of the Road: Deconstructive Studies in Humanities Disciplines* (2006), argues that the "late Derrida" is a counter-valent response to the negative example of Paul de Man's abjection and its effect on American "deconstruction."

23 The question will be how to deconstruct the conceit of "semiotics" and "information" so that it is not metaphoric: "Biosemiotics can be defined as the science of signs in living systems. A principal and distinctive characteristic of semiotic biology lies in the understanding that in living, entities do not interact like mechanical bodies, but rather as messages, the pieces of text. This means that the whole determinism is of another type. ... The phenomena of recognition, memory, categorization, mimicry, learning,

communication are thus among those of interest for biosemiotic research, together with the analysis of the application of the tools and notions of semiotics (text, translation, interpretation, semiosis, types of sign, meaning) in the biological realm" (Kull 1999: 386). In a recent popular review Charbei El-Hani references the "importance of going beyond metaphor" (Else 2010).

24　In this regard, Zizek remarks of the cultural Left—in reference to eco-catastrophic exigencies it appears muted before—that it, or the culture, partakes of a way of generating the "visible" which has been itself the guarantor of what is invisible to it: "what has to remain invisible so that the visible may be visible" (Zizek 2009, 101).

25　This is not what is called, today, the need for a war against, say, global heating, the insight that a collective must rally against an anthropomorphic enemy (itself ultimately) or that the figure of "climate change" is accompanied necessarily by a rhetoric of *crisis*— what shades into a conservational moralism ("green") or a derealization and denial. Thus the phantom call here and there for a "mobilization" against an enemy (we need a new Churchill, and so on) is set against the inverse "adaptation apartheid" of social and neo-speciest orders: "What is significant about the apparatuses of security and securitisation managing the climate crisis is that their risk logics come increasingly to bifurcate populations in 'adaptation apartheid': splitting populations between the climate exposed and the climate insulated, between the ecologically 'at risk' and the ecologically risk capable; between, ultimately, the dwellers of the ever burgeoning slums of the planet's mega cities and the 'Earth's first-class passengers' ensconced in 'green and gated oases'" (Dibley and Neilson 2010, 50).

26　Bin Laden had, before death, shifted the rhetorical cause of his Jihad from Islamic ideology to a simpler, broader premise of assaulting the engine of climate catastrophe, global warming, and so on, in the wake of the Pakistan floods. See "Bin Laden blames US for global warming," 10 January 2010:
http://news.bbc.co.uk/2/hi/south_asia/8487030.stm, consulted 3 July 2009, 6.05 p.m.

27　David L. Clark: "A disturbing and freakishly counterintuitive notion, this: that language is not human. ... For de Man the 'residual' or 'material' linguistic functioning which makes the concept of subjectivity as a concept available to thought radically exceeds the subject, remaining other than and irreducible to it. Moreover, the perilous surety of human being is achieved only by turning away from the inconceivable blankness of this linguistic materiality, a turning—or 'troping,' he would say—which enables the mind to 'shelter itself from self-erasure'. ... " (Clark 1990, 770).

28　The conceit of a "materiality of inscription" has a certain correlation to what Bernard Stiegler proposes be thought as *hypomnemata* (drawing on Plato), the technological premises or mnemotechnics of perceptual and conceptual organizations, "the organization of the inorganic" (Stiegler 2006).

29　All are generated from inscriptions, like Kurzweil's synthetic bacteria which was announced as the first artificing of life by man, in which cells were even inscribed with random signatures (website addresses of the scientists) to confirm the implanted authorship within the cell. The example might make a discrete illustration of an afterlife that imagines itself as "life" (immediacy, nature, present)—since it is invariably "linguistic," technic, artefacted, and so on.

30　Johanna Zylinska, "Bioethics Otherwise, or, How to Live with Machines, Humans, and Other Animals," examines how "animal studies" has entrapped itself to an anthropo-colonialist (and regressive) posture—an extension of human pseudo-empathics onto mostly mammalian pets, a premier relapse formation. Today's animal studies display recurrent focus on their empathic relations to subordinate pet mammals (cats, dogs, horses), a discourse that waivers between an extended anthropism and a soft humanism reappropriation (however much it indexes itself to misreadings of Derrida). It implies that, rather than projecting outward identification with favourite domesticated mammals ("being undone by pet love") one must begin to read backwards from outside that territorialization (attributing subjectivities to animals from humans who may not have them either): microbes, insects, and so on, back toward the human construct: "what happens if this animal is not just a dog, a cat or a horse from the family of befriended or domestic animals, but rather a parasite, bacteria or fungus?" (Zylinska 2011). A recent example of how a sort of dissimulated regression is constitutive of "animal *studies*" is Cary Wolfe's "Cognitive Science, Deconstruction, and (Post)Humanist (Non)Humans," *Oxford Literary Review*, 29:1, 103–25, where one is given a critical review of animal theorists as if pivoting around a Derrida citation. Wolfe bases his address on explaining to readers that "language" matters, an echolalic offering from 1980s deconstruction emerging in a time-warp, and concludes that while he doesn't know if he is or is not a post-human, we must approach with "humility" the thought of so many animalian subjects, with their own "otherness," and so on. One of the spectacles of the "post-theory" moment is how, through proper sophistication, one ends in pre-theoretical conservatisms.

31  For de Man, *this* is the product of a machinal operation in the sausage factory of communal meaning formation—and the production, one might say, of the "human" as a stabilizing center. Thus the hermeneutic relapse which de Man probes appears a cognitive artifice and reaction formation that could be said to define human consciousness (or identity) to itself, ignoring the fiction involved in such a theotropic designation. Such a machinal relapse is reflexively at work in proprietary formations such as in "after-theory" today – recuperative naturalizations, pre-critical returns (e.g. to phenomenology)—or the reflex to keep the old "Wall St." afloat as long as possible, but equally in *ecological* thought generally. That is: in the terms of sustainability (of the system that, nonetheless, produced the "crisis," like the old premises of economic growth), the new figure of mitigation, various Gaia-esque personifications, the "Green," not to mention the ciphers presented by "Copenhagen" or "Cancun." Such a refold fuels not only the acceleration of a feudal-corporate order but an eco-catastrophism which it thinks itself as countering.

32  Derrida activates this link that wends from oil and waste, through carbon (ribbons), through ink as an unmanageable and liquid agency: "And when one makes ink flow, figuratively or not, one can also figure that one causes to flow or lets flow all that which, by spilling itself this way, can invade or fertilise some cloth or tissue" (1989, 122).

33  De Man's address is as reduced and void of Nietzschean pathos as his *materiality* is void of Benjamin's revolutionary declamations and appropriations of Kaballah or Marx: a theory without future, a resistance to "theory" itself.

34  The language of *crisis* associable with ecological catastrophe is readily appropriated and unnecessary. Since it always poses itself as a juncture in transformation, it captures the "subjectivities" it suffuses: "To invoke the notion of crisis is to construct a particular injunction to judgement and action that establishes in itself the imperative for redressing that crisis. In crisis, as it is popularly noted, we find ourselves in a moment of danger and opportunity. Unsurprisingly, much of the current discourse on climate change oscillates between these two poles: most dramatically, between imminent catastrophe and the prospect of renewal; between unimaginable humanitarian disaster and the promise of a green-tech revolution" (Dibley and Neilson 2010, 144).

35  Salmon and Stokes (2010): "*Lexicon* has helped automate the process of reading the news, drawing insight from it, and using that information to buy or sell a stock. The machines aren't there just to crunch numbers anymore; they're now making the decisions. ... That increasingly describes the entire financial system." This disincorporated corporatization attaches itself, in monopolist capture, to Goldman Sachs' or Morgan Stanley's "perfect" trading quarters: "If, as James Howard Kunstler asserts, the US stock market has become 'a robot combat arena where algorithms battle for supremacy of the feedback loops,' Goldman Sachs must control the 'Supreme Combat Robot.' " (Fry, 2010).

36  What "it" would reference might be reduced to de Man's formula that the "text deconstructs itself"—or, by extension, the implications of the sentence on "nature" cited several times above. From the outset, to say the text deconstructs itself in the face of *Grammatology* is to say: if it does, then what is it that deconstruction deconstructs

exactly—not the canonical author Rousseau (as you pretend), and not "metaphysics" (since it would never have existed as such)?

37  Having unearthed this "divergence" which is given no content, Warminski tends to find an autobiographical nod toward monstrous affiliations, and allows it to emerge as a singular and insistent referent (very un-de Manian that). And yet, just this reading was responsible for Derrida's fall into the rhetorical trap that had been, with the dead de Man's co-operation, set for him from the start: "it is in fact what Derrida's 'Typewriter Ribbon' is all 'about,' as one says, or rather it's what his text does, or would do: namely, to perform an act of impossible forgiveness for the unforgivable" (Warminski 2009, 1086).

38  David L. Clark discriminates between Derrida's use of *khora* and de Man's appeal to a radical senselessness in "the materiality" of the sign itself: "where Derrida and Kristeva exuberantly affirm the prephenomenal 'notions' of différance and the chora for their power to liberate thinking from the metaphysics of presence, de Man attends to the materiality of the sign, stressing the hidden threat that its radical senselessness inescapably poses for reading, for cognition, and for what is reassuringly familiar about the fundamentally humane (or 'phenomenal') space that is constituted by language" (Clark 1990, 770).

39  I leave it to others to unpack or not a fortuitous anecdote. But when chatting while walking east on 10th Street in Manhattan to catch him a cab, Derrida turned to talk of de Man and remarked, without seeming context, that it was "unpardonable" for him, himself, to have used the term "unpardonable" in that connection.

40  Derrida excavates the scene in which de Man critiqued Derrida upon first taking up the word "deconstruction," and narrates a typographical error he had to correct in the proofs of *Grammatology* itself, in which the word "incest" had become "insect"—a mere shift of "c" and "s," which Derrida (on reflection) corrected, restituting "incest." Yet this segue recurs, later, in the remarkable anecdote of prehistorial insects preserved for aeons in honey amber. Teo has an ingenious commentary on this.

41  Again, Teo: "Indeed, the tangentially complementary nature of these two exchanges is strongly hinted at by the title of 'Typewriter Ribbon: Limited Ink (2)', where Derrida reads de Man's *Allegories of Reading* 'underscoring *materiality* in place, so to speak, of *matter*, then insisting on *thought of materiality*, or even *material thought of materiality*, in place, if I may put it this way, of *materialist* thought, even with quotation marks'" (Teo 2010, 80).

42  The term "English" itself is a nod to the old worship of British culture at its infancy and hardly defines the mix of styles, talents, data-streams and virtual objects of study today. The accelerations of publishing and sheer data makes the definition of periods and genres increasingly implausible. In trying to justify its existence elsewhere, "Comparative Literature" went to generate "global literature," an anthology approach to tutelary global inclusion in English books (global English then being its shared lingua in fact), as at a tasting buffet.

43  Given the iconic dimensions of the program closings, one could expect the elder states-men of the "profession" to enter the breach with a robust defense or articulation of the necessity of the Humanities as such, and the contrarian Stanley Fish attempts just this in a widely read piece in the *New York Times* in which he uses the event as a trigger or watermark, titling its first part "The Crisis of the Humanities Officially Arrives" (Fish 2010) and the sequel "Crisis in the Humanities II" (one notes said "crisis" is already repeating itself). What is remarkable is that, after various twisting and recitations, Fish seems to have absolutely no "defense" of the Humanities as constituted except one that caricatures his colleagues even more as narcissists—a classic passive aggressive move. Needless to say, this evoked some dismay among the troops. Joshua Landy, responding at once in *Arcade*, notes: "The President of SUNY Albany has just decided to close its programs in French, Italian, Classics, Russian, and Drama. Here's a great idea: let's tell him he did the right thing! Yes, that's just what Stanley Fish decided to do, in his much-forwarded *New York Times blog post*. He writes—I kid you not—that humanistic study serves only one end: allowing professors of literature to eat. 'I have always had trouble,' he says, 'believing in the high-minded case for a core curriculum—that it preserves and

transmits the best that has been thought and said—but I believe fully in the core curriculum as a device of employment for me and my fellow humanists.' Is this supposed to help? Let's put it this way: if the most prominent humanists are publicly proclaiming their belief in the utter uselessness of what they do, what reason could a cash-strapped administrator possibly have for not shutting down their departments?" (Landy 2010).

44 That one could also use appellations like *Mnemotechnic Regimes* reminds us why de Man found such words possible to replace "deconstruction" when applied to a self-deconstructive textuality interchangeable, in Rousseau, with "nature."

45 Mark C. Taylor uniquely seems to respond to the new economics – in which the value of the degree at all is being seriously questioned in tandem with a corporate decision against public higher education as we knew it (the demographics cannot absorb and will not need this lower income variant of "higher education"). Taylor, in columns titled "End of the University as we know it" (Taylor 2009) and "Academic Bankruptcy" (Taylor 2010), he pragmatically argues for a reconfiguration of disciplinary as well as inter-institutional resources before the institutions are simply disarticulated in a model that cannot survive (about which it remains in denial).

46 "2011" will perhaps mark a hinge-date from which a new or mass acceleration of resource expropriation will be unleashed, with the flowering logics of resource wars (peak oil breakdown, 2011 food shortfalls), since with each anticipated depletion survival competitions will overwhelm the logic of preserves (the Arctic). The conclusion of the Cancun UN conference on climate change to follow the collapse of Copenhagen finalized a global inability to prioritize any "future" peril over competitive economic pressures. As even loose carbon goals were well under those nominally resistant to a minimal "tipping point" the UK and Americans began finally to address geo-engineering— which can make money, at least, of the evolving circumstances, the recognition that can be capitalized (Hanley 2010). The new normal of implicit acceptance of "irreversible" climate change has fully entered the value zones of financialization. In a column announcing mere advice on commodities, the light is shined on "Biotech genius" Michael Murphy for enunciating a positive attitude to all this—a long-time perspective— on the supposition that "the carrying capacity of the earth is much lower than the current population" and "population die-off" is inevitable. Replacing the focus on alternative energies, which cannot work in time, Murphy shifts to what continuing populations in isolation will need for health management, future diseases, and so on (Farrell 2010).

## 3 The calculus of individual worth

1 The key reference here would be James Lovelock (2009) whose warnings of ecological catastrophe led him to suggest radical and decisive actions that would no longer be those of the nation or polity deliberating the maintenance of its collective well-being, but an intervention in, and surpassing of, national politics in order to save and maintain the greater value of the earth and its ecology. For a critique of this position see Smith 2009.

2 Giorgio Agamben's criticism of the state of exception, whereby the polity suspends or reinscribes the limit of law, refers to a modern biopolitics in which politics has lost its active world-disclosive potential; rather than politics, we are subjected to management (Agamben 2005).

3 'The successful institutionalization of theory, of Modernism and Marxism has stymied the radical pretensions of their movements and philosophies. What is worse, theory and Marxism have become, doubtless despite themselves, complicit with the institutional imposition of limits upon their revolutionary credentials. Here, I am proposing that postmodernism and postmarxism are called on to 'wake' theory and Marxism to a proper vigilance against theory's own inherent tendency to conservatism' (Docherty 1996, 1). 'De Man's fundamental manoeuvre is similar to Derrida's in the attack on the metaphysics of presence; for what de Man does is to empty out the supposed presence of an

empirical and social history onto the endless self-representations of a consciousness' (Docherty 1996, 123).

4 De Man did not allow literary criticism to be ironic *simpliciter*; irony was at once necessary – insofar as reading does not give us immediate secure reference – and impossible, because there is always reading, always the relapse into seeing the text as the faithful double of its prior and properly expressive ground. And to prove this point we have the figure of de Man himself, easily and readily identified, before reading.

5 For a more nuanced and future-oriented approach to Darwin see Grosz 2004.

6 http://www.glennbeck.com/content/articles/article/198/45073/

7 In a televised public debate on 27 November 2010 the former British prime minister Tony Blair argued, against Christopher Hitchens, that a world without religion would be devoid of moral foundation. This provides a salutary reminder that de Man's critique (and insistence on the persistence) of theocracy possesses more than a historical interest.

8 'If narcissism is selfhood at the price of flexibility and play, this discourse of the radically decentred subject teaches play at the cost of selfhood. ... But something else happens as well in this radical dissociation and abstraction of mourning from lived experience. By turning death into a purely linguistic operation, de Man precludes the possibility of distinguishing one victim from any other. Furthermore, the historical victim – the victim of this or that moral shortcoming or failure in the realm of empirical decisions and politics is overshadowed here by an impersonal and apathetic "dismemberment" at the violent hands of the signifier; to be a victim of history is, in the end, to be a victim of a "purely ... linguistic complication"' (Santer 1993, 29).

9 'Perhaps the most complex and productive effect of the de Man affair was on the work of Derrida. Painful though it was, the controversy seems actually to have stimulated Derrida not only to expand and deepen a meditation on ethics that was, as we have seen, present in his work from the beginning, but to move his general critique in a new direction, his formidable style becoming in the process much more flexible and accessible' (Harpham 1995, 390).

10 'The affective code is unreadable, which is equivalent to stating that it is not, or not merely, a code' (de Man 1976, 672).

11 For a highly insightful critique of this opposition between the linguistic frame of post-structuralism and the concept of affect see Hemmings 2005.

# Works cited

Agamben, Giorgio. 2000. *Means Without End: Notes on Politics*. Trans. Vincenzo Binetti and Cesare Casarino. Minneapolis: University of Minnesota Press.

——1998. *Homo Sacer: Sovereign Power and Bare Life*. Trans. Daniel Heller-Roazen. Stanford: Stanford University Press.

——2000. "The Face." *Means without Ends: Notes on Politics*, 91–102.

——2005a. *State of Exception*. Trans. Kevin Attell. Chicago: University of Chicago Press.

——2005b. *The Time that Remains: A Commentary on the Letter to the Romans*. Trans. Patricia Dailey. Stanford: Stanford University Press, 2005b, and http://www.thelondongraduateschool.co.uk/events/new-texts-by-paul-de-man/

Arendt, Hannah. 1978. *The Life of the Mind*. New York: Harcourt Brace Jovanovich.

Badiou, Alain. 2009. *Theory of the Subject*. Alain Badiou. Trans. Bruno Bosteels. London: Continuum.

Bakan, Joel. 2004. *The Corporation: The Pathological Pursuit of Profit and Power*. New York: Free Press.

Bayer, Richard. 1999. *Capitalism and Christianity: The Possibility of Christian Personalism*. Georgetown University Press.

Benjamin, Walter. 1996. *Selected Writings, Volume 1, 1913–1926*. Ed. Marcus Bullock and Michael W. Jennings. Cambridge: The Belknap Press of Harvard University Press: 236–53.

——1969a. "Die Aufgabe des Übersetzers." In *Illuminationen: Ausgewählte Schriften*. Frankfurt am Main: Suhrkamp. 56–69.

——1969b. "The Task of the Translator." In *Illuminations*. Trans. and Intro. Hannah Arendt. New York: Schocken Books. 69–82.

Bradley, Arthur. 2006. "Derrida's God: A Genealogy of the Theological Turn." *Paragraph* 29. 3: 21–42.

Brodrick, Sean Broderick. 2010. "*America's Next Crisis is Dead Ahead.*" http://finance.moneyandmarkets.com/reports/CPH/0652/a06520.php?s=g446&e=4047107

Brown, Bill. 2004. "All Thumbs." *Critical Inquiry* 30.2: 452–57.

Burke, Kenneth. 1945. *A Grammar of Motives*. New York: Prentice-Hall.

Carroll, Joseph. 1995. *Evolution and Literary Theory*. Minneapolis: University of Missouri Press.

Churchland, Paul. M. 1988. *Matter and Consciousness: A Contemporary Introduction to the Philosophy of Mind*. Cambridge: MIT Press.

Clark, Timothy. 2008. "Toward a Deconstructive Environmental Criticism." *Oxford Literary Review* 30.1: 44–68.

——2010. "Some Climate Change Ironies: Deconstruction, Environmental Politics and the Closure of Ecocriticism." *Oxford Literary Review*, 32.1: 131–49.

——2011. "Derangements of Scale." *Telemorphosis: Theory in an Era of Climate Change, volume 1.*

Clough, Patricia Ticineto and Jean Halley. 2007. *The Affective Turn: Theorizing the Social.* Durham: Duke University Press.

Cohen, Tom, Barbara Cohen, J. Hillis Miller, and Andrzej Warminski. 2001. (Eds.) *Material Events, Paul de Man and the Afterlife of Theory.* Minneapolis: University of Minnesota Press.

Cohen, Tom. 2010. "The Geomorphic Fold: Anapocalyptics, Changing Climes and 'Late' Deconstruction." *The Oxford Literary Review* 32.1, 71–78.

Cohen, Tom. ed. 2011. *Telemorphosis: Theory in the Era of Climate Change, volume 1.* OHP Press.

Colebrook, Claire. 2011. "Matter without Bodies." *Derrida Today.* 4.1: 1–20.

Cottingham, John. 2005. *The Spiritual Dimension: Religion, Philosophy, and Human Value.* Cambridge: Cambridge University Press.

Cunningham, Valentine. 2002. *Reading After Theory.* Oxford: Blackwell.

de Man, Paul. 1996. *Aesthetic Ideology.* Ed. Andrzej Warminski. Minneapolis: University of Minnesota Press.

——1979. *Allegories of Reading: Figural Language in Rousseau, Nietzsche, Rilke, and Proust.* New Haven: Yale University Press.

——1983a. *Blindness and Insight: Essays in the Rhetoric of Contemporary Criticism.* 2nd ed. Introduction by Wlad Godzich. Minneapolis: University of Minnesota Press.

——1967. 'The Crisis of Contemporary Criticism.' *Arion.* 6.1: 38–57.

——1976. 'Political Allegory in Rousseau.' *Critical Inquiry* 2.4: 649–75.

——1983b. Notes for his lecture on "The Task of the Translator," available in this present book both in facsimile and in Claire Colebrook's transcription.

——1984. *The Rhetoric of Romanticism.* New York: Columbia University Press.

——1986. *The Resistance to Theory.* Minneapolis: University of Minnesota Press.

——2009. "Textual Allegories by Paul de Man." Manuscript transcription by Erin Obodiac. UCIspace @ the Libraries, 2010. http://dspace1.nacs.uci.edu/xmlui/handle/10575/1092 (Accessed February 6, 2011)

——1973. "'Theotropic Allegory.' In "Rousseau." MS. Box 9, Folders 1–4. Paul de Man Papers. MS-C004. Special Collections and Archives. Critical Theory Archive. The University of California, Irvine, Libraries, Irvine, California. http://dspace1.nacs.uci.edu/xmlui/handle/10575/1092 (Accessed February 6, 2011). This URL gives access both to the facsimile and to the transcript by Erin Obodiac (de Man 2010) of "Theotropic Allegory."

de Landa, Manuel. 2005. *Intensive Science and Virtual Philosophy.* London: Continuum.

Deleuze, Gilles and Félix Guattari. 1986. *Kafka: Toward a Minor Literature.* Trans. Dana Polan. Minneapolis: University of Minnesota Press.

——2004. *Anti-Oedipus: Capitalism and Schizophrenia.* Trans. Robert Hurley, Mark Seem, and Helen R. Lane. London: Continuum.

Deleuze, Gilles. 1988. *Foucault.* Trans. Seán Hand. Minneapolis: University of Minnesota Press.

——2006. *The Fold: Leibniz and the Baroque.* Trans. Tom Conley. London: Continuum.

Derrida, Jacques. 1996. *Archive Fever.* Trans. Eric Prenowitz. Chicago: University of Chicago Press.

——1989. "Biodegradables: Seven Diary Fragments." *Critical Inquiry* 15, 812–73.

——1992. 'Force of Law: The 'Mystical Foundation of Authority.' In *Deconstruction and the Possibility of Justice.* Ed. Drucilla Cornell, Michel Rosenfeld and David Gray Carlson. London: Routledge.

——1993. "Khôra." T. Dutoit. *On the Name.* Stanford: Stanford University Press, 89–130.

——2000. *Le toucher, Jean-Luc Nancy.* Paris: Galilée.

——1988. "Like the Sound of the Sea Deep within a Shell: Paul de Man's War." *Critical Inquiry* 14: 590–652.

——2001. *L'Université sans condition*. Paris: Galilée.

——1995. *Mal d'archive*. Paris: Galilée.

——2005. *On Touching—Jean-Luc Nancy*. Trans. Christine Irizarry. Stanford: Stanford University Press.

——1994. *Specters of Marx: The State of the Debt, the Work of Mourning, and the New International*. Trans. Peggy Kamuf. Intro. Bernd Magnus and Stephen Cullenberg. New York and London: Routledge.

——1993. *Spectres de Marx: L'État de la dette, le travail de deuil et la nouvelle Internationale*. Paris: Galilée.

——2002. "The Typewriter Ribbon: Limited Ink (2)." *Without Alibi*. Ed. and trans. Peggy Kamuf. Stanford: Stanford University Press. 71–160.

——2002. "The University Without Condition." *Without Alibi*. 202–37.

Dibley, Ben and Brett Neilson. 2010. "Climate Crisis and the Actuarial Imaginary: The War on Global Warming." *New Formations*, Spring, 69, 144–59.

Docherty, Thomas. 1996. *After Theory*. Edinburgh: Edinburgh University Press.

Dumont, Louis. 1986. *Essays on Individualism: Modern Ideology in Anthropological Perspective*. Chicago: University of Chicago Press.

Dunbar, Robin. 1996. *Grooming, Gossip, and the Evolution of Language*. Cambridge: Harvard University Press.

Dupuy, Jean-Pierre. 2002. *Pour un catastrophisme éclairé*. Paris: Editions du Seuil.

Eagleton, Terry. 2004. *After Theory*. New York. Basic Books.

——2008. *Literary Theory: An Introduction*. Minneapolis: University of Minnesota Press.

——2009. *Trouble with Strangers: A Study of Ethics*. Oxford: Blackwell.

Elliot, Jane and Derek Attridge. 2010. Eds. *Theory After Theory*. London: Routledge.

Else, Liz. 2010. "Biosemiotics: Searching for meanings in a meadow." *New Scientist 2774*. August 18. http://www.newscientist.com/article/mg20727741.200-biosemiotics-searching-for-meanings-in-a-meadow.html?full=true&print=true.

Farrell, Paul B., "Twelve Tips for Profiting on Commodity Demand." *Market Watch*. Dec. 28. 2010. Online. http://www.marketwatch.com/story/twelve-tips-for-profiting-on-commodity-demand-2010-12-28.

Felix Zulauf. 2010. "Any Correction in Gold is a Buying Opportunity." *Business Insider*. October 17. http://www.businessinsider.com/felix-zulauf-any-correction-in-gold-is-a-buying-opportunity-2010-10.

Felman, Shoshana. 1989. "Paul de Man's Silence." *Critical Inquiry* 15.4: 704–44.

Foucault, Michel. 1970. *The Order of Things: An Archaeology of the Human Sciences*. New York: Pantheon Books.

——2009. *History of Madness*. Trans. Jean Khalfa and Jonathan. London: Routledge.

Fraser, Mariam, Sarah Kember and Celia Lury. 2006. Eds. *Inventive Life: Approaches to the New Vitalism*. London: SAGE

Freddoso, David. 2008. *The Case Against Barack Obama: The Unlikely Rise and Unexamined Agenda of the Media's Favorite Candidate*. Regnery Publishing.

Freud, Sigmund. 1991. 'On Narcissism, An Introduction.' Ed. Joseph Sandler, Ethel Spector Person, Peter Fonagy for the International Psychoanalytical Association. New Haven: Yale University Press.

Fry, Eric. 2010. "Goldman's Perfect Quarter." May 12. *Daily Reckoning*. http://dailyreckoning.com/goldmans-perfect-quarter.

Gasché, Rodolphe. 1986. *The Tain and the Mirror*. Cambridge: Harvard University Press.

——1998. *The Wild Card of Reading: on Paul de Man*. Cambridge: Harvard University Press.

Gillis, Justin. 2010."A Scientist, His Work and a Climate Reckoning." *The New York Times*. December 21. http://www.nytimes.com/2010/12/22/science/earth/22carbon.html?nl= todaysheadlines&emc=a2

Gottschall, Jonathan and David Sloan Wilson. 2005. *The Literary Animal: Evolution and the Nature of Narrative*. Evanston: Northwestern University Press.

Grosz, Elizabeth. 2004. *The Nick of Time: Politics, Evolution, and the Untimely*. Durham: Duke University Press.

Hägglund, Martin. 2008. *Radical Atheism—Derrida and the Time of Life*. Stanford: Stanford University Press.

Hanley, Charles J. 2010. "Geo-engineering Debate Surfaces as UN Climate Change Talks in Cancun Falter." *Huffington Post*, December 6. http://www.huffingtonpost.com/2010/12/06/geoengineering-debate-sur_n_792409.html

Hansen, Mark. 2003. 'Affect as Medium, or the 'Digital-Facial-Image,' *Journal of Visual Culture*. 2.2: 205–28.

Hardt, Michael, and Antonio Negri. 2000. *Empire*. Cambridge: Harvard University Press.

Hartham, Geoffrey Galt. 1995. 'Ethics' 387–405. In *Critical Terms for Literary Study*. Eds. Frank Lentricchia and Thomas McLaughlin. Chicago: University of Chicago Press.

Hartman, Geoffrey. 1980. "The Sacred Jungle 2: Walter Benjamin." In *Criticism in the Wilderness: The Study of Literature Today*. New Haven: Yale University Press. 63–85.

Hartmann, Thom. 2002. *Unequal Protection: The Rise of Corporate Dominance and the Theft of Human Rights*. New York: St. Martin's Press.

Hayles, N. Katherine. 1999. *How We Became Posthuman: Virtual Bodies in Cybernetics, Literature, and Informatics*. University of Chicago Press.

Hemmings, Clare. 2005. "Invoking Affect: Cultural Theory and the Ontological Turn." *Cultural Studies* 19.5 (September 2005) 548–67.

Jacobs, Carol. 1993. "The Monstrosity of Translation: Walter Benjamin's 'The Task of the Translator.'" In *Telling Time: Lévi-Strauss, Ford, Lessing, Benjamin, de Man, Wordsworth, Rilke*. Baltimore and London: The Johns Hopkins University Press. 128–41.

Kafka, Franz. 1919. *"Die Sorge des Hausvaters."* http://www.kafka.org/index.php?landarzt. Accessed September 28, 2010.

——2007. "The Worry of the Father of the Family." *Kafka's Selected Stories*. Trans. and ed. Stanley Corngold. Norton Critical Edition. New York: W. W. Norton, 2007. 72–73.

Kull K. 1999. "Biosemiotics in the Twentieth Century: A view from biology." *Semiotica* 127.1/4: 385–414.

Landy, Joshua. 2010. "SUNY Albany, Stanley Fish, and the Enemy Within." *Arcade*. October 14. http://arcade.stanford.edu/suny-albany-stanley-fish-and-enemy-within

Lehman, David. 1991. *Signs of the Times: Deconstruction and the Fall of Paul de Man*. New York: Poseidon Press.

Lentricchia, Frank. 1981. *After the New Criticism*. Chicago: University of Chicago Press.

——1985. *Criticism and Social Change*. University of Chicago Press.

Lewis, David. 1979. "Scorekeeping in a Language Game." *Journal of Philosophical Logic*. 8.1:339–59.

Lovelock, James. 2000. *Gaia: A New Look at Life on Earth*. Oxford: Oxford University Press.

——2009. *The Vanishing Face of Gaia: A Final Warning*. New York: Basic Books.

Macdonell, Diane. 1986. *Theories of Discourse: An Introduction*. Oxford: Blackwell.

Marx, Karl and Engels, Friedrich. 1976. *The German Ideology. Critique of Modern German Philosophy According to Its Representatives Feuerbach, B. Bauer and Stirner, and of German Socialism According to Its Various Prophets*. In *Collected Works*. Vol. 5. New York: International Publishers. 19–539.

McQuillan, Martin and Erin Obodiac. 2011. Eds. *The Political Archive of Paul de Man*. Edinburgh: Edinburgh University Press.

Miller, J. Hillis. 2009. *For Derrida*. New York: Fordham University Press.

Mithen, Steven. 2005. *The Singing Neanderthals: The Origins of Music, Language, Mind and Body*. London: Weidenfeld and Nicolson.

Mohanty, Satya P. 1997. *Literary Theory and the Claims of History: Postmodernism, Objectivity, Multicultural Politics*. Ithaca: Cornell University Press.

Moore, Lisa Jean and Mary Kosut. 2010. *The Body Reader: Essential Social and Cultural Readings*. New York: New York University Press.

Moretti, Franco. 2005. *Graphs, Maps, Trees: Abstract Models for a Literary History*. London: Verso.

Morris, Christopher D. 2006. *The Figure of the Road: Deconstructive Studies in Humanities Disciplines*. Peter Lang Publishing.

Morrison, Paul. 1990. "Paul de Man: Resistance and Collaboration." *Representations*, 32 (Autumn): 50–74.

Morton, Timothy. 2007. *Ecology Without Nature: Rethinking Environmental Aesthetics*. Harvard University Press.

Morton, Timothy. 2010. "Ecology as Text, Text as Ecology." *The Oxford Literary Review* 32.1, 1–17.

Nancy, Jean-Luc. 2005. *La Déclosion: (Déconstruction du christianisme, 1)*. Paris: Galilée.

——2008. *Dis-Enclosure: The Deconstruction of Christianity*. Trans. Bettina Bergo, Gabriel Malenfant, and Michael B. Smith. New York: Fordham University Press.

Nealon, Jeffrey T. 2006. "Post-Deconstructive?" *Symploke* 14. 1–2: 68–80.

Newmark, Kevin. 2009. "Bewildering: Paul de Man, Poetry, Politics." *MLN* 124. 5: 1048–71.

Nussbaum, Martha Craven. 1992. *Love's Knowledge: Essays on Philosophy and Literature*. Oxford: Oxford University Press.

O'Leary, Brad. 2009. *Shut Up, America!: The End of Free Speech*. WND Books.

O'Rourke, James. 1997. "The Fatality of Readings: De Man, Gasché, and the Future of Deconstruction." *Symploke* 5.1–2: 49–62.

Obodiac, Erin. 2011. "DNA: de Man's Nucleic Archive." In *The Political Archive of Paul de Man*.

Pepperell, Robert. 1995. *The Post-Human Condition*. Oxford: Intellect Books.

Redfield, Marc. Ed. 2007. *The Legacies of Paul de Man*. New York: Fordham UP.

Roden, David. 2006. "Naturalising Deconstruction." *Continental Philosophy Review* 38.1–2: 71–88.

Ronell, Avital. 2002. "The Rhetoric of Testing." In *Stupidity*. University of Illinois Press, 95–164.

Rorty, Richard. 1982. *Consequences of Pragmatism: Essays, 1972–1980*. Minneapolis: University of Minnesota Press.

Rorty, Richard. 1989. *Contingency, Irony, and Solidarity*. Cambridge: Cambridge University Press.

Rousseau, Jean-Jacques. 1969. *Oeuvres Complètes*. Vol. 4. Éditions de la Pléiade. Ed. Bernard Gagnebin and Marcel Raymond. Paris: Gallimard.

Salmon, Felix and Jon Stokes. 2010. "Algorithms Take Control of Wall Street." *Wired*, December 27. http://www.wired.com/magazine/2010/12/ff_ai_flashtrading/all/1

Santner, Eric L. 1993. *Stranded Objects: Mourning, Memory, and Film in Postwar Germany*. Ithaca: Cornell University Press.

Schwarz, Daniel. R. 1990. "The Narrative of Paul de Man: Texts, Issues, Significance." *The Journal of Narrative Technique*, 20.2 (Spring, 1990) 179–94.

Smith, Mick. 2009. "Against Ecological Sovereignty: Agamben, politics and globalisation." *Environmental Politics*, 18.1 (February 2009) 99–116.

Spolsky, Ellen. 2002. "Darwin and Derrida: Cognitive literary theory as a species of post-structuralism." *Poetics Today* 23.1: 43–62.

Stanley Fish. 2010. "The Crisis of the Humanities Officially Arrives." *New York Times*. October 11. http://opinionator.blogs.nytimes.com/2010/10/11/the-crisis-of-the-humanities officially-arrives/

Stiegler, Bernard. 2006. "Nanomutations, Hypomnemata and Grammatisation." Trans. Georges Collins. http://arsindustrialis.org/node/2937

Taylor, Mark C. 2009. "End the University as We Know It." *New York Times*. April 26. http://www.nytimes.com/2009/04/27/opinion/27taylor.html

Taylor, Mark C. 2010. *"Academic Bankruptcy."* *New York Times*. August 14. http://www.nytimes.com/2010/08/15/opinion/15taylor.html

Tencer, Daniel. 2010. "German Military Report: Peak oil could lead to collapse of democracy," September 1. http://www.rawstory.com/rs/2010/09/german-report-peak-oil-collapse-democracy/

Teo, Tze-Yin. 2010. "Responsibility, Biodegradability." *The Oxford Literary Review* 32.1, 91–108.

Thiel, Bob. 2009. *2012 and the Rise of the Secret Sect*. Nazarene Books.

Townsend, Mark and Paul Harris. 2004. "Department of Defense 'Report' on Climate Change." February 22. http://www.commondreams.org/headlines04/0222–01.htm

Warminski, Andrzej. 2009. "Machinal Effects: Derrida with and without de Man." *MLN* 124: 1072–90.

Wellek, Rene. 1990. "The New Nihilism in Literary Studies." *Aesthetics and the Literature of Ideas: Essays in Honor of A. Owen Aldridge*. Ed. François Jost and Melvin J. Friedman. University of Delaware Press.

Womack, Kenneth and Todd F. Davis. 2001. Eds. *Mapping the Ethical Turn: A Reader in Ethics, Culture, and Literary Theory*. Charlottesville: University Press of Virginia.

Wood, David. 2006. "On Being Haunted by the Future." *Research in Phenomenology. 36:*1, 274–98.

Wood, David. 2007. "Specters of Derrida – On the Way To Econstruction." *Ecospirit: Religions and Philosophies for the Earth*, eds. Laurel Kearns and Catherine Keller. New York, Fordham University Press. 264–90.

Zizek, Slavoj 2003. *The Puppet and the Dwarf: The Perverse Core of Christianity*. Cambridge: MIT Press.

—— 2008. "Censorship Today: Violence, or ecology as a new opium for the masses: Parts I & II." http://www.lacan.com/zizecology1&2.htm.

—— 2008. "Nature and its Discontents." *SubStance*. 37.3: 37–72.

—— 2009. *First as Tragedy, Then as Farce*. London: Verso.

Zylinska, Johanna. 2011. "Bioethics Otherwise, or, How to Live with Machines, Humans, and Other Animals." *Telemorphosis: Theory in an Era of Climate Change, 1*.

# Index